Hate
Speech

Samuel Walker

Hate Speech

The History
of an American
Controversy

University of Nebraska Press, Lincoln and London

Library of Congress Cataloging-in-Publication Data

Walker, Samuel, 1942–
Hate speech : the history of an American controversy /
Samuel Walker. p. cm.
Includes bibliographical references and index.
ISBN 0-8032-4763-X (alk. paper)
1. Hate speech – United States – History.
2. Hate crimes – United States – History.
3. Freedom of speech – United States – History.
I. Title. KF9345.W35 1994
342.73′0853 – dc20 [347.302853] 93-5389 CIP

To NORMAN DORSEN

*Scholar, teacher, leader in
the fight to preserve free speech*

Contents

Acknowledgments ix

1 Hate Speech in American History 1

2 Origins of the Hate Speech Issue, 1920–1931 17

3 Free Speech for Nazis? Hate Speech as a National Issue, 1933–1940 38

4 The Hateful and the Hated:

The Jehovah's Witnesses and the Emergence of a National Policy 62

5 The Curious Rise and Fall of Group Libel in America, 1942–1952 77

6 Free Speech Triumphant: From *Beauharnais* to Skokie, 1952–1978 101

7 The Campus Speech Codes: Hate Speech in the 1980s and 1990s 127

8 Hate Speech and the American Community 159

Notes 169

Index 207

Acknowledgments

A number of people read early drafts of the book and made extremely helpful comments, both on factual points and on larger questions of interpretation and emphasis. As always, Norman Dorsen took time away from his many responsibilities to give the manuscript a critical reading. Although I was never formally a student in one of his courses, he has been a great teacher in the broadest and best sense of the term. Gara LaMarche of Human Rights Watch, a colleague on the ACLU Board of Directors, also gave me the benefit of his considerable knowledge about this subject. Franklyn Haiman of Northwestern University and David Moshman of the University of Nebraska at Lincoln also read early drafts of many chapters and made helpful comments.

In a much wider way this book has benefited from my ten years of service on the ACLU Board of Directors. The opportunity to participate in the debates on frontier issues, where it is so often a question of responding to competing and compelling civil liberties claims, has been the best education I ever received. To my colleagues on the board and to its current president, Nadine Strossen, my thanks.

Much of the original research for this book was done for a previous work, *In Defense of American Liberties*. Through the process of "total incorporation" advocated by Justice Hugo Black, I should probably thank again everyone I acknowledged for that book. In particular I thank the staff of the Seeley G. Mudd Library at Princeton University, where I spent nearly six months some years ago. It was a magnificent place for research: the staff was always helpful and friendly, responding with dispatch to my constant requests for material.

1 Hate Speech in American History

Hateful Names

The names are all too familiar – "nigger," "kike," "wop," "mick," "spic" – words that carry the baggage of centuries of racism and empty it out in hate. These words are often aimed at people like bullets. They foretell danger and evoke the shame of the past: slavery, riots, massacres, the Holocaust.

If these words are so hateful and hurtful, why not outlaw them? Why not punish anyone who uses them in public to deliberately insult another person? Other forms of harm are punished; why not punish this one? The function of criminal law, after all, is to define the standards of civilized society and prescribe penalties for behavior that violates those standards.

These questions introduce the subject of this book: hate speech. The issue before us is whether offensive words, about or directed toward historically victimized groups, should be subject to criminal penalties. Should it be illegal to call people names based on their race or religion? Should it be illegal to publish defamatory materials – such as the notorious *Protocols of the Elders of Zion* – that incite prejudice against a racial or religious group?

Almost every country prohibits hate speech directed at racial, religious, or ethnic groups.[1] The United States, by contrast, has developed a strong tradition of free speech that protects even the most offensive forms of expression. The First Amendment is one of the glories of American society. It is celebrated as the protector of the most precious liberty of all: the right to express oneself and to participate in the democratic process. Free speech is the cornerstone of democracy; its essential element is the people's right to criticize the government, even during wartime or other national emergencies. Freedom of speech means that any and all ideas may be heard. The people and not the government shall decide what is true and what is false. In the words of Justice Robert Jackson, free speech means that "no official, high or petty, can prescribe what shall be orthodox in politics, nationalism, religion or other matters of opinion."[2] As Justice William Brennan put it, the "central meaning" of the First Amendment is that "debate on public issues should be uninhibited, robust, and wide-open."[3]

This book is a history of the hate speech issue in the United States. It examines the course of events that has led to this country's unique status on a particularly difficult question. Justices Jackson's and Brennan's opinions were important landmarks in that history, but there was nothing inevitable about the outcome. My central argument is that the strong tradition of free speech resulted from a series of choices. These choices have been not only Supreme Court decisions but also choices by advocacy groups that brought the major cases before the Court and choices by American society to affirm a very broad protection of free speech. The central question is why those choices were made.

The choices that have led to current American policy involved rejecting other alternatives, often appealing ones. Uninhibited free speech is not easy: this precious freedom comes at a price, for the First Amendment also protects offensive words. It protects both the words people consider important and those they find offensive. The First Amendment guarantees freedom for both the ideas that people cherish and the thoughts they hate.[4] It means that many deeply offensive and hurtful things can be said without fear of criminal punishment. The drama of the First Amendment is played out every week in front of abortion clinics. Antiabortion protesters scream "murderer" and "baby killer" at pregnant women entering the clinics for a legal medical procedure. The accusations are false (since the procedure is legal), defamatory, and hurtful. Yet these words are protected by the First Amendment as the expression of a political idea: that abortion is a terrible wrong and must be stopped. By the same token, racist remarks such as "nigger" and "kike" are also protected by the First Amendment.

While all forms of offensive speech pose difficult questions, racial and religious hate speech is a special problem. First Amendment authority

Rodney Smolla believes that hate speech poses "the hardest free speech question of all."[5] Many people argue that race introduces special considerations – among them the question of the right to advocate genocide – and also a countervailing constitutional principle of equality.[6]

Equality is enshrined in the Fourteenth Amendment's guarantee of equal protection under law. As one commentator recently reminded us, the Fourteenth Amendment "is no less a part of the Constitution than the First."[7] To advance the principle of equality, some critics argue, it is necessary to prohibit offensive racial speech. The constitutional principle of equal protection extends to many other groups as well. Thus, it is argued, words that offend people because of their religion, ethnic background, gender, age, marital status, sexual preference, or physical capacity should also be restricted.

Difficult though the question might be, the United States has fashioned a clear and coherent answer. As a matter of law and national policy, hate speech is protected by the First Amendment. This policy was recently reaffirmed and even strengthened by the United States Supreme Court in a celebrated cross-burning case. In June 1992 the Court struck down a St. Paul, Minnesota, ordinance prohibiting "any symbol" that "arouses anger, alarm or resentment in others on the basis of race, color, creed, religion or gender." Justice Antonin Scalia wrote that the St. Paul ordinance represented a content-based distinction between different kinds of speech, and "that is precisely what the First Amendment forbids."[8] Earlier, federal courts in Michigan and Wisconsin had declared unconstitutional university codes of student conduct that penalized offensive speech based on race, religion, gender, and other characteristics.[9]

One of the remarkable aspects of the cross-burning decision is that the majority opinion was written by the justice who is generally regarded as the most conservative member of the Court.[10] Scalia was joined by the other more conservative justices, while the Court's moderate justices disagreed with his strong defense of hate speech.[11] These justices have been generally unsympathetic to civil liberties and claims of individual rights. That the most conservative justices would affirm freedom of speech in this extreme case indicates the extent to which the commitment to free speech has become embedded in American law and culture. This case raises the question that is the subject of this book, How did that commitment to protecting hate speech develop?

A History of American Policy on Hate Speech

The hate speech issue first arose in the 1920s and continues to influence American law and policy. Consider the recent controversy over speech codes on college and university campuses and the 1992 St. Paul cross-burning decision.

Here I pursue three questions. First, how and why did American public policy on hate speech develop as it did? This public policy cannot necessarily be attributed to the First Amendment, because First Amendment law could have gone in a very different direction. The real question is, Why has the First Amendment been interpreted this way? One of my main arguments is that there was nothing inevitable about the outcome of the hate speech controversy. At any one of several points, events could have taken a different turn. And as we shall see in chapter 5, in 1952 the Supreme Court gave constitutional sanction to the restriction of offensive speech.[12] Yet surprisingly, that alternative was quickly rejected. This book focuses on why the key individuals and groups who have shaped American policy chose one option over another; why the protection of hate speech triumphed over its restriction.

Second, why have American law and policy developed in a very different direction from the law and policy of virtually every other country in the world? Most countries prohibit the expression of offensive racial, religious, or ethnic propaganda. According to Human Rights Watch, "The United States stands virtually alone in having no valid statutes penalizing expression that is offensive or insulting on such grounds as race, religion or ethnicity."[13] The London-based anticensorship organization called Article 19 argues that on this issue the world could be divided into "the United States and the rest." In the United States "the balance is unequivocally drawn in favour of freedom of speech."[14]

A few examples illustrate the kinds of laws that exist in other countries.[15] The 1986 Public Order Act in the United Kingdom makes it a crime to use "threatening, abusive or insulting words or behavior" with respect to "colour, race, nationality (including citizenship) or ethnic or national origins." In the constitution of Brazil one finds that "propaganda" relating to "religious, race, or class prejudice . . . shall not be tolerated." In Turkey a person faces a prison term of one to three years for publicly inciting "people to hatred and enmity . . . on the basis of class, race, religion, sect, or region." Germany has a specific law allowing any victim of the Holocaust to bring legal action against anyone who denies that the Holocaust occurred.[16] The Canadian Charter of Rights and Freedoms qualifies a guarantee of freedom of expression with the proviso that "reasonable limits" on individual rights may be justified. The Canadian Supreme Court used this rationale to sustain the criminal conviction of a teacher who made anti-Semitic remarks in the classroom.[17]

Several important international human rights declarations also proscribe racial and religious propaganda.[18] In article 19 of the Universal Declaration of Human Rights, one finds that "everyone has the right to freedom of opinion and expression." Its article 29, however, qualifies that right; there one finds that "in the exercise of . . . rights and freedoms" individuals are subject to limitations necessary "for the purpose of securing due recognition and respect for the rights and freedoms of others." Articles 18 and 19 of the 1966 International Covenant on Civil and Political Rights support freedom of speech, but article 20 goes even further in limiting offensive speech: "Any advocacy of national, racial or religious hatred that constitutes incitement to discrimination, hostility or violence shall be prohibited by law."[19] The International Convention on the Elimination of All Forms of Racial Discrimination, also adopted in 1966, calls for outlawing any organization disseminating racial or religious propaganda and for making membership in such organizations a criminal offense.[20]

Students of American history and culture have long wrestled with "American exceptionalism." How different are major features of American society from those of even Western European countries? Suffice it to say that in protecting hate speech, the United States is unique. This book explores how and why that uniqueness developed.

Third, given the strong tradition of free speech that had developed in the United States by the 1970s, why did restrictive speech codes become so popular on college and university campuses? True, the only two codes to reach the federal courts were declared unconstitutional. But how do we explain the support for these codes in the first place? Does this circumstance portend a major change in American attitudes about free speech?

The Present Crisis: A Resurgence of Racism

This inquiry into the history of hate speech is hardly undertaken in a social and political vacuum. Racism has acquired a compelling new urgency. In the 1980s there was an apparent resurgence of racism – or at least its overt expression – across American society. Political scientist Andrew Hacker characterized the state of race relations in 1992 in the title of his book, *Two Nations: Black and White, Separate, Hostile, Unequal.*[21] On college and university campuses in the 1980s there was a disturbing pattern of attacks – verbal and physical – on minority-group students.[22] Race was a major issue in the 1988 presidential election as Republican candidate George Bush used the now famous Willie Horton advertisement to inflame white fear of crimes committed by black Americans. These rising tensions finally exploded in violence on April 29, 1992, following the acquittal of four white Los Angeles police officers accused of beating a black man, Rodney King.

The 1992 riots exposed the country's failure to cope with the fundamental problems of racism and discrimination since the previous wave of violence in the 1960s. Although there has been some progress in racial equality – the end of de jure segregation in the South, the opening of job opportunities, and the growth of the black middle class – the condition of the very poor has worsened.[23]

As the nation grapples with its historic race problem, many solutions have been proposed: more vigorous enforcement of existing civil rights laws, enactment of additional civil rights legislation, and massive public employment projects. Here I discuss one possible response to racism: the restriction of racist speech through criminal law.

Several years before the 1992 riots, a number of colleges and universities decided to restrict hate speech and adopted codes of student conduct penalizing offensive forms of expression based on race, gender, religion, marital status, sexual preference, and physical capacity.[24] Many civil libertarians regarded the campus speech codes as the most serious threat to freedom of expression since the Cold War. This produced a wide-ranging and intellectually rich debate on the meaning of free speech in contemporary society.[25] Long-standing issues surrounding the First Amendment were reexamined from new intellectual and political perspectives. The traditional questions included the scope of the First Amendment: Which words are protected and which are not? Are racial insults "fighting words"? Are fighting words exempt from First Amendment protection? Can we draw a line between words that are offensive and utterly lacking in social value and words that, however offensive, express a political idea? Is it possible to draft a rule proscribing hate speech that would be fairly enforced and not ultimately used against the very people it was designed to protect? Would a rule proscribing hate speech protect members of the majority or some other powerful group from verbal attack by minorities? In short, is it possible to draft any kind of restriction that does not ultimately threaten the expression of controversial but important ideas? First Amendment experts have wrestled with these questions for many decades.[26] Advocates of the campus speech codes added some new elements to this debate. Most important was the recognition that the Fourteenth Amendment's guarantee of equality had as much legitimacy as the guarantee of free speech.[27]

The campus speech codes met a quick and resounding defeat in the federal courts. Not only were the Michigan and Wisconsin codes declared unconstitutional by federal district courts on First Amendment grounds, but the subsequent Supreme Court decision in the cross-burning case provided even stronger protection for offensive forms of expression. These events focus attention on two questions that deserve historical research. First, how did the commitment to protecting hate speech develop? Second, how do we explain the support for restricting hate speech that underpinned the campus speech codes – a degree of support unprecedented in light of the prior history of the hate speech issue?

The Scope of the Book

This book is a social and political history of the hate speech controversy in the United States from the 1920s to the present. It focuses primarily on the social context of intergroup relations, on prejudice and discrimination as a political issue, and on the various proposals that have arisen over the years to control hate speech through law. It is not an exercise in legal history in the narrow sense, and it is not primarily concerned with interpreting case law. Although I give due consideration to important court decisions, I am more concerned with the context in which those cases arose. An approach centered on case law would be far too limiting because the vast majority of controversies over the years never reached a court of law, much less the Supreme Court.

The hate speech issue has followed a somewhat erratic course, erupting at certain times and then disappearing for long periods. This book examines each of those episodes and seeks to understand why they occurred when they did and how each was resolved. One question that will receive considerable attention is why the major civil rights groups, the natural constituency for hate speech laws, historically have put so little emphasis on such legislation as a weapon to combat racism.[28] Another is why many prominent racial minority advocates reversed this historical position in the 1980s and supported the restrictive campus speech codes.

WHAT DO WE MEAN BY HATE SPEECH?

There is no universally agreed-on definition of hate speech. Traditionally it included any form of expression deemed offensive to any racial, religious, ethnic, or national group. In the 1980s some campus speech codes broadened it to include gender, age, sexual preference, marital status, physical capacity, and other categories.[29] Human Rights Watch defines hate speech as "any form of expression regarded as offensive to racial, ethnic and religious groups and other discrete minorities, and to women."[30] Rodney Smolla defines it as a "generic term that has come to embrace the use of speech attacks based on race, ethnicity, religion and sexual orientation or preference."[31] Historically, hate speech has been referred to by several terms. In the late 1920s and early 1930s it was known as "race hate." Beginning in the 1940s it was generally called "group libel,"[32] reflecting the specific legal question whether the law of libel should be expanded to cover groups as well as individuals. In the 1980s "hate speech" and "racist speech" became the most common terms.

The brief definitions of hate speech, however, cover over some important issues that need brief elaboration. The first question is what we mean by "speech." What actions are forms of expression protected by the First Amendment and what are properly punished as criminal acts? "Speech" is generally used as a convenient shorthand for all forms of communication, verbal and nonverbal, and will be so used here. As First Amendment law has developed since the 1930s, many diverse forms of expression have been brought under the meaning of speech. In addition to purely oral statements, the term commonly includes written or visual forms of expression that are specifically covered by the freedom of the press clause of the First Amendment, along with nonverbal forms of communicating such as parades, insignia, armbands, and picket lines.[33] In this book "speech" includes all forms of communication.

A second question involves which groups are covered by any hate speech law. Historically, group libel laws were limited to race, religion, and ethnicity. In the 1980s the list of protected groups expanded to cover many more historically victimized groups, including women, lesbian and gay people, and the physically handicapped.

An important distinction exists between hate speech and a category of criminal offenses commonly called "hate crimes." The latter refers to common-law crimes against persons and property – assault, vandalism, and such – where the perpetrator is motivated by racial or religious hatred for the victim. Thus they involve criminal *acts*, as traditionally defined in the law, rather than communication. The most common hate crimes are physical attacks on African Americans by groups of whites and desecration of synagogues or other religious institutions.[34] Hate crimes do raise difficult First Amendment questions, since they often have a verbal or expressive component (as in an assault begun with the words, "Let's get the Jew!"). As Justice Scalia pointed out in the St. Paul cross-burning case, that act "could have been punished under any of a number of laws" that do not restrict speech.[35]

An even more difficult First Amendment question is posed by state laws that enhance penalties for crimes motivated by bias. These involve a more severe penalty for an assault where the assailant was motivated by racial or religious hatred. In 1993 the Supreme Court ruled that a Wisconsin enhanced-penalty law did not violate the First Amendment.[36] Although extremely important in terms of the First Amendment, recent hate crimes laws like the one in Wisconsin are not my subject here. The most important question is simply what words or other forms of expression fall outside the scope of First Amendment protection. There is a vast body of literature on the First Amendment generally, but my focus is hate speech only.

The Making of an American Tradition

CHRONOLOGICAL OVERVIEW

The history of the hate speech issue begins in the 1920s. Although social and political controversies rarely have clear-cut starting and ending points, that decade marks the first political and legal debates over whether to restrict offensive racial and religious speech. Several circumstances brought the issue to the fore at this time. There can be no controversy without at least two opposing points of view, and the two sides of this issue found their organizational voices in the early 1920s. On one side, the historical victims of racial, religious, and ethnic prejudice and discrimination launched a concerted effort to defend themselves. Some of their effort was directed against hate speech. On the other side, the American Civil Liberties Union (ACLU) was founded in 1920 to defend freedom of speech. The ACLU represented the first organized national effort to fight restrictions on individual liberties.[37] Out of the clash of these two new organizational forces the hate speech issue was born.

The controversies of the 1920s were sporadic and quickly forgotten; none rose to the level of a major national event. These controversies touched on the fundamental underlying issues, but they did not resolve them. That changed in the 1930s. In 1931 the United States Supreme Court issued its first two decisions affirming First Amendment protection for freedom of speech and press and, by incorporating the First Amendment into the Fourteenth, extended those protections to the states.[38] The two 1931 decisions opened a new era in American law in which the Supreme Court emerged as the principal defender of individual rights.[39] Two years later numerous Fascist groups, many of them paramilitary, sprang up in the United States after the Nazis came to power in Germany. The specter of domestic Nazism prompted some concerned Americans to call for legislative restrictions on the speech and assembly of anti-Semitic, paramilitary, and antidemocratic groups. The question of the rights of domestic Nazi groups elevated hate speech to the level of a national debate.[40]

A national policy on hate speech started to emerge in the early 1940s, after the Supreme Court began fashioning a coherent body of First Amendment law protecting various forms of speech and political activity. Some of the most important decisions involved a small religious sect known as the Jehovah's Witnesses, at once a persecuted minority and a venomously hateful group directing particularly vicious attacks at the Catholic church. As I will argue in chapter 4, the Witness cases prompted the Supreme Court to define the scope of the free exercise of religion under the First Amendment. In the context of this crisis that scope came to include the right of a religious group to defame others.

The World War II years were pivotal for another reason as well. Nazi Germany and the Holocaust had a profound effect on international thinking about human rights. In international law the experience spurred numerous declarations on human rights. In response to the Holocaust and the rising movement against Western European colonialism, most of those statements called for criminal penalties for disseminating racial and religious propaganda. But as I will argue in chapter 5, Americans drew a different lesson from the Nazi example, seeing in it the need to strengthen legal protection of powerless and persecuted minority groups. The World War II years gave birth to the modern civil rights movement as a national interracial coalition dedicated to fulfilling the nation's commitment to racial equality.

The protection of hate speech triumphed in national law and policy between the late 1940s and the mid 1970s. This aspect of recent American history is often seen in oversimplified terms as the story of the Warren Court. It is true that from 1953 to 1968 the Supreme Court under Chief Justice Earl Warren vastly extended First Amendment protection of speech and other forms of expression, but chapter 6 argues that there is far more to the story than the Warren Court.

The central influence of the post–World War II years concerning hate speech was the civil rights movement. Many actions by civil rights groups and leaders were deliberately provocative and deemed offensive by their intended audiences. In the words of Justice William O. Douglas, civil rights leaders often resorted to speech that "induces a condition of unrest, creates dissatisfaction with conditions as they are, or even stirs people to anger."[41]

The Court's affording the civil rights movement critical "breathing room" under the protection of the First Amendment had a profound effect on the thinking of civil rights leaders. They came to define their own interests in terms of the broadest protection of constitutional rights – not just under the First Amendment, but under the equal protection and due process clauses of the Fourteenth Amendment as well. The protection of individual rights was seen as the key to advancing *group* interests. Consequently the leading civil rights groups – those representing African Americans and Jewish Americans – chose not to seek laws restricting hate speech, leaving such laws without an advocate. As I will argue in a moment, advocacy is the key to understanding the development of American law and policy. Free speech has had an effective advocate; the restriction of hate speech has not.

THE DYNAMICS OF CHANGE

The history of hate speech raises a number of questions about the role of law in American society. Discussions of the First Amendment routinely refer to an American "tradition" of free speech. The commitment to freedom of expression is cited as the hallmark of the uniquely American approach to individual rights under the Constitution and the Bill of Rights. A closer look at the historical record, however, suggests a more complex picture. Although the formal protection of offensive speech is far stronger in this country than in any other, it is a relatively recent development, which highlights some important points in the history of the hate speech controversy.

The first point is the relatively recent emergence of formal protection of individual rights. Although the First Amendment was adopted in 1791, the reality of American history is that meaningful protection of free speech and other individual rights has emerged only in the past fifty to sixty years.[42] One scholar described American society through the end of the nineteenth century as a set of discrete islands of conformity where the majority freely repressed anyone who dissented from its values.[43] Civil liberties did not become a national political issue until the crisis over the suppression of dissent during World War I.[44] The first Supreme Court decisions protecting freedom of speech and the press were not delivered until 1931, and the Court did not begin to give practical meaning to the equal protection clause of the Fourteenth Amendment for African Americans until the 1940s. Indeed, the entire body of modern civil rights law is encompassed by the career of Thurgood Marshall.[45] The "due process revolution" limiting the power of the police and other government officials did not occur until the 1960s. All the important Court decisions involving the rights of women were products of the Burger Court in the 1970s. In short, what millions of Americans think of as ancient and hallowed rights are of very recent origin.[46]

That meaningful protection of individual rights emerged fairly recently raises some intriguing questions. Why did a body of law protecting civil liberties develop so late? What occurred between the 1920s, when "free speech" was considered a dangerous radical idea, and the 1960s, when it had become fairly well established as a legal principle? Was the process of change simply a matter of court decisions? Did the attitudes and behavior of the American people follow the dictates of the courts, or did the courts respond to changes in public attitudes?[47] Broadly speaking, the choice is between elitist and popular models of social change. The elitist model, often framed in terms of an "imperial judiciary," raises important questions about public compliance with court decisions.[48] The popular model, on the other hand, raises questions about the sources of change in public attitudes.[49]

The role of the Supreme Court in effecting social change is a matter of great controversy. Conservatives such as Robert Bork argue that, on principle, the Court should not have intervened in many of the issues it has ruled on over the past half century. Gerald Rosenberg, meanwhile, argues that as a practical matter Court decisions have failed to achieve their intended goal of changing social policy – on civil rights, abortion, criminal law, and other matters.[50] As will become evident in the chapters that follow, I find persuasive evidence to the contrary: that the Court has exerted a powerful and successful influence on the law, public policy, and public attitudes.

The intriguing questions raised by hate speech, in fact, relate to the complex relationship between law and social change. The argument here is closest to that presented by Lee Epstein and Joseph F. Kobylka in their study of Court decisions on abortion and the death penalty, *The Supreme Court and Legal Change*.[51] They reject traditional interpretations that explain the evolution of the Court's position in terms either of the changing composition of the Court or of public opinion. There is abundant evidence that the posture of individual justices is often unpredictable. At the same time, the Court does not respond to public opinion in any direct way. Epstein and Kobylka make a persuasive case that the posture of the Court has been shaped by the arguments of the advocacy groups that bring cases before it. As we shall see, the course of the hate speech issue has been shaped by the powerful advocacy of free speech groups, notably the ACLU, and the virtual absence of any comparable support for restricting hate speech.

This argument, of course, only raises still more complex questions. Why was there strong advocacy for free speech? Why was it so successful? Why did the idea of restricting hate speech fail to mobilize talented advocates?

We need not resolve these questions at this point. Law and policy evolve through a complex interaction between court mandates and popular will, and the most important idea is that law and policy have changed significantly in recent years. This has important implications because it means that political cultures are not immutable. Sweeping generalizations about "the American people" or "the political culture" are of questionable validity both sociologically and historically, for they do not take into account either the diversity of American society at any given moment or long-term changes. To cite an example unrelated to hate speech, the notion of a right to privacy emerged almost from nowhere in the early 1960s to become one of the central and most volatile issues in national politics. Clearly this reflected some deep-seated changes in the attitudes and behavior of the American people – changes that eventually led to public clashes with existing law.[52]

Recognizing the mutability of political culture also means that the present commitment to protecting offensive speech may not remain as strong as in the past two decades. If law and custom have changed significantly in the past, there is no reason they cannot continue to change. The support for restrictive speech codes on college campuses in the 1980s clearly reflected very different ideas about the scope of the First Amendment. And though the Supreme Court afforded protection for hate speech in the St. Paul cross-burning case, the Court can and does change as time goes on. Its history is filled with surprising twists and turns, the 1991–92 term being one of the best examples. History, in short, clearly shows that the future is fluid and the hate speech issue far from settled.

HATE SPEECH IN AMERICA: A THEORY

As I have already suggested, the central question is why the strong commitment to free speech developed as it did. The corollary is why the idea of restricting offensive speech failed to win any significant support, even from civil rights groups. In response I offer a theory that not only guides us through the chapters ahead but has broader ramifications for legal change in American history. The theory is fairly simple: ideas have no force in the world without advocates. Regardless of the merits of a particular idea, it has little practical effect without a person or organization to persuade others to support it, to bring and argue cases before courts of law, to propose legislation, and eventually to transform the idea into public policy.[53]

Freedom of speech, to take the example at hand, was enshrined in the First Amendment in 1791. Until the middle of the twentieth century, however, it had little practical meaning for most Americans. It certainly had no force in protecting ideas advanced by radical political groups, labor union organizers, dissenting religious sects, or advocates of alternative lifestyles (birth control, plural marriage, whatever): in short, those who needed it most. Freedom of speech for unpopular ideas did not become a living reality until the middle of the twentieth century. Although that protection was ultimately the result of a series of Supreme Court decisions, we must ask what caused the Court to change. The American Civil Liberties Union was a critical advocate for free speech for the unpopular. The ACLU was the lone champion of free speech through the 1920s and early 1930s and filed briefs in all the major cases through which the Court fashioned the body of modern First Amendment law.[54] The perspective here shifts our focus away from the Court, now seen more as a reactive agent, and toward the advocates who brought cases and arguments before it.

Racial equality is another example. The ideal of equality is embodied in the Declaration of Independence and the Fourteenth Amendment. Yet the reality of slavery and racial discrimination has long contradicted this grand ideal. Racial equality did not begin to make any headway as a practical matter until the appearance of the National Association for the Advancement of Colored People (NAACP) in the early part of this century. Even then the NAACP made no real progress until it formulated an effective litigation strategy in the late 1930s and took advantage of the opportunities created by the Roosevelt Court.[55]

My theory helps explain the broad contours of the history of the hate speech issue. The principle of free speech has triumphed in large part because it has had a vigorous and effective advocate. Conversely, there has never been an equally strong and vigorous advocate for laws restricting offensive speech. From an organizational perspective, the battle has been terribly one-sided: a vigorous advocate on one side and weak and disorganized support on the other. But why has support for restrictions on offensive speech been so weak and disorganized? There is no natural reason why this should be so. After all, African Americans have been well served by the vigorous and effective litigation program of the NAACP. The Jewish community has had an even broader array of organizational voices: the American Jewish Congress, the American Jewish Committee, the Anti-Defamation League, and others. Presumably, if these organizations had put their collective minds and resources to work on group libel legislation, the law and public policy of this country might be very different today. The question then becomes, Why didn't these organizations pursue such legislation with much vigor? I examine this question at length in chapters 5 and 6. The basic argument is that the major civil rights groups abandoned group libel legislation because they perceived it as a threat to their larger program of achieving equal rights. Beginning in the 1940s and reaching floodtide under the Warren Court, the principal strategy for advancing *group* rights came to be the expansion of constitutionally protected *individual* rights.[56] Civil rights leaders came to understand that any proposal to limit individual rights, no matter how narrowly defined, threatened the very basis of their larger program. It opened the door to what they perceived as a grave risk and consequently chose not to take.[57] The restriction of offensive speech, in short, became an idea without an effective advocate.

By the same token, laws restricting hate speech are common in most other countries because they do not have the same tradition of individual rights. Not only do many lack a written bill of rights and an amendment protecting free speech, but they lack such an advocacy group vigorously pressing for the protection of free speech.[58] In most countries the organizational balance of power is in favor of those who would restrict offensive speech.

This brings us to the present situation and the spread of restrictive speech codes on college and university campuses in the late 1980s. Campuses represent a special environment where groups that are relatively powerless in the larger society have been able to mobilize considerable power based not only on their own numbers but on the coalitions they have forged with other groups and allies from the "majority" community. Thus African American and Hispanic American groups on campus have been able to forge effective coalitions with women's groups, gay and lesbian student groups, groups of physically disabled students, and so on. In addition, they can count on the active support of organized left-wing white students and the passive support of many other unaffiliated students: white, male, heterosexual, politically moderate, and so on. The resulting coalition has far more power on campus than any of the constituent groups have in the larger society. At the same time, the principal advocate of free speech, the ACLU, has been organizationally weak on campus (although it is strong off campus and has prevailed in the federal courts in the two cases to date). In short, the political context on college and university campuses has been just the reverse of that prevailing in the larger society. Restrictive codes have been adopted because the idea has a well-organized coalition of advocates who have faced poorly organized opposition in defense of an absolutist position on free speech.

2 Origins of the Hate Speech Issue, 1920-1931

A Decade of Intolerance

The 1920s are remembered as a decade of intolerance. Bigotry was as much a symbol of the period as Prohibition, flappers, the stock market boom, and Calvin Coolidge. It was the only time when the Ku Klux Klan paraded en masse through the nation's capital. In 1921 Congress restricted immigration for the first time in American history, drastically reducing the influx of Catholics and Jews from southern and eastern Europe, and the nation's leading universities adopted admission quotas to restrict the number of Jewish students. The Sacco and Vanzetti case, in which two Italian American anarchists were executed for robbery and murder in a highly questionable prosecution, has always been one of the symbols of the anti-immigrant tenor of the period.[1]

Yet the twenties were hardly the most bigoted period in American history – regrettably, there is considerable competition for that dubious honor. The scar of racism runs through the whole course of American history, and religious prejudice has an equally long legacy. The New England Puritans sought religious freedom for themselves and did not hesitate to suppress those who dissented from their version of orthodoxy. The arrival of large numbers of Catholic immigrants in the 1830s and 1840s aroused an ugly anti-Catholic prejudice that still lingers. As recently as 1960, John F. Kennedy found that fear of his Catholicism was the major obstacle to his presidential candidacy. Racial, religious, and ethnic prejudice was probably most intense in the 1890s, when the immigration of southern and eastern Europeans reached its highest level and when institutionalized segregation spread throughout the South.[2]

If anything, the twenties were different simply because prejudice was more openly expressed than ever before and more likely to be written into law. Beneath the surface, however, new currents were stirring: the victims fought back. For the first time in American history African Americans, Jews, and Catholics mounted organized and occasionally successful efforts to combat discrimination.

The fight for acceptance and equality was led by a group of civil rights organizations that began to appear before World War I. The American Jewish Committee was formed in 1906, followed by the National Association for the Advancement of Colored People (NAACP) in 1909, the Anti-Defamation League (ADL) in 1913, and the American Jewish Congress in 1918. Significantly, there was no Catholic civil rights organization equivalent to the NAACP or the ADL. To a certain extent, Catholic Americans did not need one. Through sheer weight of numbers and their consequent control of urban political machines, they had considerable political power. By the early 1930s, moreover, the Catholic church hierarchy was wielding considerable influence over public policy at the national level on such issues as censorship and birth control.[3] Following the vicious anti-Catholic attacks on Democratic presidential candidate Al Smith in 1928, the National Conference of Christians and Jews was formed to promote religious tolerance.[4]

These organizations, often joined by other religious groups and some of the more progressive labor unions, formed the core of what emerged in the 1940s as the national civil rights coalition. The coalition exerted a powerful influence over public policy from that point until the early 1970s, when it split over the issue of affirmative action.

The appearance of another advocacy group set the stage for the hate speech controversy. Following the suppression of dissent during World War I, the American Civil Liberties Union (ACLU) was established in January 1920. The ACLU committed itself to the defense of free speech, including hateful and offensive speech.[5] When Catholics and Jews made their first attempts to suppress expressions of hate – by banning circulation of Henry Ford's anti-Semitic newspaper and prohibiting meetings and parades by the Ku Klux Klan (KKK) – the ACLU stepped in to defend the First Amendment rights of the bigots. In these early clashes, the hate speech controversy in America was born.

It would be a mistake to exaggerate the importance of these initial clashes in the context of the period. Most were relatively minor skirmishes that flared briefly and were quickly forgotten; they are rarely mentioned in standard history textbooks and often do not appear in more specialized accounts of the decade. The exception to this rule was a New York anti-KKK law that resulted in an important Supreme Court decision.[6] These early cases touched on the fundamental problems related to free speech but did not resolve them. By the end of the decade, the situation was still fluid and the outcome by no means certain.

Henry Ford, Anti-Semite

Henry Ford was not the worst anti-Semite in America – only the richest and most famous. Creator of the fabled Model T and the modern automobile assembly line, Ford was a national folk hero in the 1920s, as the inexpensive, mass-produced automobile was already revolutionizing American life. He was also a vicious anti-Semite with the financial resources to disseminate his views widely. His personal newspaper, the *Dearborn Independent*, had a circulation of over 600,000, and he required Ford automobile dealers to sell it as an official company product. Anti-Semitism was one of its main features. The *Independent* published the notorious *Protocols of the Elders of Zion*,[7] with a long series of other articles on the alleged evils of Jewish people. Ford then reprinted the first eighty of these articles as a book, *The International Jew: The World's Foremost Problem*, which sold over 500,000 copies.[8]

Ford embraced the full catalog of traditional anti-Semitism: that a cabal of international Jewish bankers controlled the American economy; that Jews were an alien people destroying the Christian values of America. To these traditional themes he added some slurs related to current events: that Jewish gangsters were behind the "Black Sox" scandal that corrupted the 1919 baseball World Series; that jazz was Jewish music, foisted on America by Jewish-controlled music publishing companies; and so on.[9]

The *Dearborn Independent* encountered relatively little opposition; the twenties were a time of open and unembarrassed anti-Semitism for most Americans. In addition to the admission quotas in colleges and professional schools, many employers refused to hire Jews. The legal profession adopted a number of measures ostensibly designed to raise professional standards that really were blatant attempts to exclude Jews and other recent immigrants from the profession.[10] Restrictive covenants on the sale of real estate were common (as late as 1974 future chief justice of the Supreme Court William H. Rehnquist purchased a vacation home in Vermont with a covenant prohibiting resale "to any member of the Hebrew race").[11] Hotels, country clubs, and resorts openly excluded Jews. Only a few of Ford's dealers objected to carrying the *Independent*.

In some cities, however, distribution of the *Independent* aroused resistance. Street vendors in Toledo, Ohio, were attacked, and a near riot ensued. In New York City threats of violence forced vendors off the street. Officials in several midwestern cities suppressed the paper in an effort to prevent further violence; Cleveland and Toledo banned it altogether. The mayor of Columbus, Ohio, banned it along with an opposition paper, *Facts*, and Cincinnati passed an ordinance prohibiting the distribution of any inflammatory publication.[12]

There was nothing novel about these attacks on the circulation of a newspaper: vigilante attacks on unpopular ideas had long been an American tradition. The majority had assumed a right to suppress whatever it deemed offensive to its values. Direct action, moreover, was far swifter and more certain than the legal process.[13] The suppression of dissent during World War I had continued that tradition and added official proscription of allegedly dangerous publications. The Supreme Court, moreover, had upheld official repression under the "bad tendency" test.[14] The tradition of vigilantism, however, had always been a means of imposing the majority's views on minority groups.

The truly novel aspect of the attacks on the *Dearborn Independent* was that they represented actions by a minority group against views held by the vast majority of Americans. That the Jewish community could command the support of public officials in a few cities reflected an important change in the social and political landscape.

The newly organized ACLU promptly went to Ford's defense.[15] In a 1921 letter to local officials, the ACLU condemned Ford's "ignorant and hateful propaganda against the Jews," but it also criticized the attempts to suppress the *Dearborn Independent*. "Every view, no matter how ignorant or harmful we may regard it," the ACLU argued, "has a legal and moral right to be heard." Banning Ford's paper could easily lead to the "suppression of other ideas now regarded as moderate and legitimate."[16] Defense of Ford's right to freedom of speech and the press seemed a logical extension of the World War I fight against the repression of antiwar activists by government agencies and private vigilantes.

It is especially noteworthy that the ACLU did not agonize over its response to these early events. Even though its policies were still in a formative stage, there is no evidence that any faction felt racist speech was not entitled to First Amendment protection. There was considerable reluctance to oppose censorship of sexually explicit literature and much debate over whether the First Amendment prohibited prayer in the schools. On these other issues, the ACLU had not yet adopted the positions for which it is so well known today. On racist speech, however, there was internal debate. Thus at this early stage the leading defender of First Amendment rights found no exception for racist speech. This position shaped the subsequent course of events on the hate speech issue.

In Cleveland and Toledo, federal courts issued temporary injunctions ending the bans on distribution of Ford's newspaper.[17] None of the cases involving Henry Ford ever ripened into a major test of the First Amendment, and the entire controversy soon passed. In 1927 Ford publicly repudiated his anti-Semitic views. The question of the First Amendment rights of anti-Semites would reappear ten years later, in the very different context of Nazism.

The Ku Klux Klan

A far more important set of controversies arose over the rights of the Ku Klux Klan. The Klan was a major force in American life in the twenties. Revived in 1915, this second version of the KKK was a national organization with a membership estimated at between three and six million. In addition to the Deep South, it was a powerful political force in Indiana, Ohio, Oregon, California, and other states. Nor was it strictly rural. It had 18,000 members in Cincinnati, 38,000 in Indianapolis, 22,000 in Portland, Oregon, and strong appeal in a number of other cities. There were even Klan chapters at Harvard and Princeton, demonstrating that overt racism was respectable even at the best universities.[18]

The Klan's popularity outside the South was due more to its hatred of Catholicism than to racism. In Oregon it successfully sponsored a state law that would have closed Catholic parochial schools (the law was held unconstitutional by the Supreme Court in 1923).[19] In Indiana it dominated state politics. In Ohio it controlled local elections in Akron, Columbus, Toledo, and Youngstown and focused on removing Catholic teachers from the public schools. The 1924 Democratic party convention showed the Klan's power in national politics. The convention was wracked by a long, raucous, and occasionally violent debate over whether to condemn the Klan by name: the Klan's supporters finally defeated the condemnatory resolution by a single vote.[20] The following year KKK members staged a massive march in Washington, D.C., parading in their hoods and robes.

The Klan was also a violent organization. There was one particularly strong outburst of vigilante violence in 1921, much of it concentrated in Texas.[21] Sixteen blacks were reported killed by lynching in 1924 and seventeen in 1925. Although this was a sharp decline from the annual average of more than one hundred a few years earlier, an atmosphere of terror prevailed throughout the South and in many of the border states. The "Report on the Civil Liberty Situation for the Week" that was delivered at each ACLU executive committee meeting included reports of Klan attacks on blacks along with American Legion–led mob actions against socialists and labor unions.[22] Klan violence was an important factor in the question of the organization's right to parade in public; many people regarded supposedly peaceful demonstrations by masked Klan members as a form of intimidation.

The Klan encountered more official resistance than did Henry Ford's anti-Semitic newspaper, probably because of its anti-Catholic views. City governments in many northeastern and midwestern cities were controlled by Catholic-based political machines. The mayor of Cleveland ordered the police chief to "suppress" the Klan, and the Detroit police confiscated copies of the Klan's publication, the *Fiery Cross*. The mayor of Cudahay, Wisconsin, banned all Klan meetings in 1924, and the following year a Kansas court issued a permanent statewide injunction against Klan parades. Texas, Tennessee, Michigan, and other states outlawed parading in masks, and though the ACLU offered to defend the Klan's right to parade or hold public meetings, it refused to defend masked parading. In any event, no test case resulted.[23]

The antimask laws raise an issue that recurs throughout the history of the hate speech issue: the nonuse of laws directed at expressions of bigotry. By 1990 there were seventeen antimask laws in the United States (sixteen states and the District of Columbia).[24] In a test of the Georgia law, the state supreme court found that it did not violate free speech rights under the First Amendment.[25] Similar laws had been declared unconstitutional in three other states (with Florida enacting a revised version). There appears to have been little use of these laws in the nearly seventy years they have been on the books. A 1980 survey found only twelve reported cases.[26] As we shall see, a similar pattern of nonuse afflicted both a 1917 Illinois group libel law (see chapter 5) and a 1935 New Jersey race hate law (see chapter 3). This raises the question whether, quite apart from considerations of constitutionality, hate speech laws have any practical effect. Moreover, in both Illinois and New Jersey, when the laws were used the targets were often persecuted minorities. Thus virtual nonuse was accompanied by arbitrary and selective enforcement.

The NAACP, meanwhile, attacked the Klan from another direction. In 1921 it asked Postmaster General Will Hays to ban KKK literature from the mails. There was ample precedent for doing so. The post office had suppressed virtually all antiwar periodicals during World War I and had been sustained by the Supreme Court.[27] Although closely allied with the NAACP on civil rights issues at the time, the ACLU took issue with it on this question. Declaring that "we are as firmly convinced as you are of the iniquity of the Ku Klux Klan," the ACLU codirector, Albert DeSilver, advised that "we do not think that it is ever good policy for an organization interested in human liberty to invoke repressive measures against any of its antagonists." It would simply create "precedent against itself."[28] The ACLU spoke from experience. During World War I the post office had seized all the publications of its predecessor, the National Civil Liberties Bureau. The post office rejected the NAACP's request and, in fact, Postmaster General Hays had ended most of the wartime restrictions on political literature.

Nor was this the only clash between the ACLU and the NAACP in the twenties over First Amendment issues. The NAACP also attempted, with some success, to have the film *Birth of a Nation* banned in local communities because of its racist content. The ACLU opposed this form of censorship, and the conflict between the two civil rights organizations continued off and on over the years.[29] As with the official bans on Henry Ford's newspaper, the significant aspect of the actions against *Birth of a Nation* was that, in a time when racist views prevailed, the NAACP managed to command some support for its position.

Twenty years later, however, the NAACP opposed a bill to restrict racist propaganda from the mails. This occurred at a time when the NAACP was far stronger and more influential than in the 1920s and involved a bill sponsored by one of the major Jewish civil rights groups. The NAACP reversed itself on post office censorship in the 1940s because it now believed that constitutional litigation to protect individual rights was the most promising avenue for advancing African American rights.[30] This shift by the leading civil rights organization in the country was a key indicator of the trend in American law and policy.

THE KLAN IN BOSTON

One of the most highly publicized confrontations over the Klan occurred in 1923 when Boston mayor James Curley banned all Klan meetings on public property. The Klan enjoyed considerable appeal in the city. One rally, on private property, was attended by more than three hundred supportive Harvard University students.[31] The local ACLU affiliate offered to represent the Klan, and the result was a debate over the scope of the First Amendment. Although relatively brief, the debate touched on the fundamental issues in the hate speech controversy.

Despite his reputation as a corrupt political boss (he was eventually convicted on corruption charges and sent to prison), Curley proved quite articulate on the First Amendment. In a letter to the local ACLU leader, he declared himself a "stout stickler for freedom of meeting." The Klan, however, had placed itself outside the scope of First Amendment protection: it "fosters race and religious hatreds, foments civic dissension, [and] disturbs the peace." Moreover, it was a clandestine criminal conspiracy that made "no secret of its intention to deprive other citizens of their rights and privileges under the Constitution."[32] Because of its violent purposes, public officials had both a right and a duty to prohibit even apparently peaceful activities. The idea that a peaceful meeting could be banned because of violent actions by other members of the organization, or other unlawful purposes, became a standard argument for those who would restrict offensive groups.

Boston ACLU leader John S. Codman replied by accusing Curley of establishing himself as "the sole judge of what organizations have a right" to hold meetings in the city. This arbitrary exercise of power was "not authorized by our Constitution and law." Codman argued the ACLU position on freedom of speech that there was a clear distinction between "word and deed." Overt criminal acts could be punished, but not forms of expression. A public meeting was a form of political expression protected by the First Amendment.[33] Codman also raised the related problems of vagueness and selective enforcement. Citing the widespread suppression of Communists and other alleged radicals under state sedition and criminal conspiracy laws, he argued that there was much disagreement over what constituted "seditious" speech. Curley's vague and arbitrary definition of what was permissible made freedom of speech and assembly entirely dependent on the whims of whoever was in power.

Codman was not speaking hypothetically. Across the country in the twenties, mayors and police chiefs routinely banned meetings by groups they did not like: communists, socialists, labor union organizers, birth control advocates, and the ACLU itself. They either denied permits or arrested people at the meeting. Aside from the question of sedition, the primary free speech issue in the 1920s concerned the right of labor unions and union organizers merely to hold meetings or mount picket lines. The power of local officials to restrict freedom of assembly on public property was not curbed by the Supreme Court until the 1939 decision in *Hague v. CIO*.[34]

Curley himself proved how flexible his definition of a criminal conspiracy could be two years later when he banned meetings by birth control advocate Margaret Sanger. Birth control, he argued, was nothing more than a "euphemism" for the crime of abortion.[35] Curley's actions were no different from those of other local officials during the repressive twenties, though he was probably unique in publicly offering a justification based on an interpretation of the First Amendment – one that made distinctions based on the content of certain ideas and the purposes of different organizations.

Curley's argument that a lawful activity could be banned because of an organization's broader unlawful purposes reappeared during the Cold War. Many anti-Communist measures were based on the rationale that the Communist party was a secret criminal conspiracy rather than a legitimate political party and therefore had forfeited its First Amendment rights. And while Curley was banning Klan meetings in Boston, the New York legislature passed a law requiring the Klan to register and disclose its membership. I now turn to that law and the resulting Supreme Court case.

BRYANT V. ZIMMERMAN: THE FIRST COURT TEST
Efforts to restrict the Klan produced the first important Supreme Court ruling on anti-hate group legislation in 1928. At issue in *Bryant v. Zimmerman* was a 1923 New York anti-Klan law that outlawed parading with

masks and required certain "oath-bound" organizations to register with the state and disclose the names of their members.[36] There were also criminal penalties for any individual who knowingly remained a member of an organization that failed to register. The crucial element of the law was its classification of organizations according to their purposes as determined by legislative finding. It specifically exempted labor unions, the Masonic order, the Knights of Columbus, and others on the grounds that their basic purposes were legitimate. The violence-prone Klan had illegitimate purposes and therefore could be subjected to tighter state regulation.

The Supreme Court upheld the law in 1928, finding no constitutional barrier to its content-based classification of organizations. A legislative finding about the purposes of different organizations, or what the Court referred to as "experience," was a proper exercise of the state's regulatory power. There was no question that the registration and disclosure provision of the law was an attempt to inhibit the Klan through exposure. The point was to intimidate potential members through the obloquy resulting from public knowledge that they belonged to such a disreputable organization. Exposure, however, is simply the polite term for what could also be called harassment. In important respects, the New York law was a more rational approach to the problem of the Klan than Mayor Curley's denial of meeting permits. The law represented a statement of general public policy, directed at more than one organization, based on a legislative finding, and enacted by the majority. Curley's effort was an entirely arbitrary action by one official.

The *Bryant* decision was consistent with existing case law. The Court had not affirmed constitutional protection of any political or civil rights to that point. Exactly thirty years later, however, the Warren Court overturned *Bryant* and established a broad freedom of association under the First Amendment.[37] There was more than mere irony in the conjunction of the 1928 *Bryant* decision and the 1958 NAACP v. *Alabama* decision. The two cases dramatized the underlying problems of vagueness and selective enforcement that seem to be inherent in laws directed at allegedly offensive groups.

NAACP v. *Alabama* yielded the first of several important decisions involving attempts by southern states to suppress the NAACP. In response to the landmark 1954 school desegregation decision, *Brown v. Board of Education*, they sought to restrict the NAACP's activities, often by harassing its members. In this first case, Alabama passed a law forcing the NAACP to register; when the organization refused, the state ordered it to disclose its membership list.[38] On its face, this requirement was no different from the 1923 New York anti-Klan law. It was an attempt to restrict an organization deemed offensive to the local majority, by exposing its members. In the context of the intensifying southern civil rights movement of the late 1950s, there was little doubt that disclosure of NAACP membership would subject individuals to possible loss of employment, physical intimidation, or worse.

We should note that the registration and disclosure requirements of the New York anti-Klan law were similar in form and purpose to many of the anti-Communist measures adopted during the Cold War.[39] The federal government and several states enacted laws requiring the Communist party to register. These laws were based on legislative "findings" that the party was a threat to national security. The attorney general's List of Subversive Organizations was simply a different means of exposing allegedly dangerous groups. Finally, investigations by the House Un-American Activities Committee, and similar committees in the Senate and state legislatures, were a technique for exposing organizations and compelling the disclosure of the names of individual members.

The pairing of the *Bryant* and the NAACP decisions offers an early cautionary tale about content-based restrictions on allegedly offensive groups. In form and purpose the New York and Alabama laws were identical. The only difference was in the political context and the reputation of the organization under attack. Although a majority of Americans might approve harassment of the Klan because of its illegitimate purposes, many of them recoiled in horror at an identical attack on the NAACP by segregationists. This horror was expressed by the unanimous opinion of the Court in the NAACP decision. It is worth noting that this decision came at a time when neither most Americans nor the Supreme Court itself disapproved of similar attempts to harass the Communist party. If a majority of Americans regarded the Communist party as subversive, so the white majority of the southern states saw the NAACP as subversive to its way of life.[40] Allowing a legislative majority to determine which ideas and groups were subversive or offensive opened the door to the problems of vagueness and selective enforcement.

These reflections on the 1928 *Bryant* decision have the benefit of hindsight. The key problems with hate speech legislation were not yet evident or matters of public debate in the 1920s. The most important underlying question, which still lingered below the surface, was the role of the First Amendment. To what extent did the free speech clause protect or not protect offensive forms of expression? The First Amendment – and the Supreme Court – entered the debate with two pivotal rulings in 1931.

New Directions in the Supreme Court

The sporadic clashes over the rights of Henry Ford and the Klan during the twenties occurred in a legal context where there were no enforceable First Amendment protections of freedom of speech, the press, or assembly. The prevailing law of the First Amendment permitted the suppression of offensive forms of expression, either by statute or by executive action, under the "bad tendency" test. Anything that might have the tendency to cause social harm could be restricted. This included criticism of the government during wartime, discussion of birth control, and any literature with a sexual content. The Supreme Court had established this position long before World War I, and the wartime speech cases simply continued it.[41]

The Court's position on the First Amendment gave full license to the Mayor Curleys and other officials across the country, allowing them to routinely ban speakers and groups they did not like. The courts were in accord with the antilabor tenor of the period and regularly issued sweeping injunctions against picket lines, union meetings, and even discussions about strikes and unions.[42] The eloquent opinions of Justices Oliver Wendell Holmes and Louis Brandeis in *Abrams* and in *Whitney* eventually influenced the course of the law in the direction of protecting free speech, but at this point they did not represent the majority view.[43]

The legal climate finally began to change in 1931, when the Supreme Court upheld the First Amendment rights of a Communist and the publisher of an anti-Semitic newspaper. The two decisions were a sharp break from existing legal precedent: in the words of Harvard law professor Zechariah Chafee, the reigning authority on free speech, "something new and astonishing had happened."[44] This was a highly prescient observation, for the 1931 decisions were only the beginning of what would ultimately be called the "rights revolution" in American constitutional law.

The first of the two 1931 cases, *Stromberg v. California,* decided on May 18, involved the "red flag" section of the California criminal syndicalism law, which made it a crime to publicly display a red flag or any "sign, symbol or emblem in opposition to organized government."[45] Yetta Stromberg, nineteen years old at the time of her arrest, was a member of the Young Communist League and a counselor at a left-wing summer camp. Her crime was participating in a daily ceremony where the children saluted and pledged allegiance to a red flag bearing a hammer and sickle. The state of California, it should be noted, continued to be far more aggressive than any other state in prosecuting radicals through the twenties.[46]

The Supreme Court overturned Stromberg's conviction, declaring the red flag section of the law unconstitutional. Chief Justice Charles Evans Hughes argued that "maintenance of the opportunity for free political discussion" was "a fundamental principle of our constitutional system." This section of the California law was "so vague and indefinite" as to be "repugnant to the guaranty of liberty contained in the Fourteenth Amendment."[47] The *Stromberg* decision represented the first meaningful protection of speech deemed dangerous or offensive by the majority.

The *Stromberg* decision was a vindication of Holmes and Brandeis and the view of the First Amendment they had articulated in *Abrams* and *Whitney*.[48] The decision was also a vindication of the ACLU. It was the first Supreme Court victory for free speech after eleven lonely years of advocacy.[49] Two weeks later, on June 1, the Court took another bold step, extending the protection of freedom of the press in *Near v. Minnesota*.[50]

Jay Near was a small-time journalist and political opportunist who harbored all the dominant prejudices of the period. He was anti-Semitic, anti-Catholic, anti–African American and antilabor. His public career involved a series of fly-by-night newspapers devoted primarily to exposing political corruption and other scandals.[51] Minneapolis at the time was known as a "wide open" town, with widespread bootlegging and gambling operations protected by corrupt public officials.[52] As in a number of other cities, the local criminal syndicates were dominated by Jewish Americans. Attacking political corruption therefore afforded Jay Near an opportunity to indulge his anti-Semitism.

The issue of the *Saturday Press* that provoked the Supreme Court case was filled with anti-Semitic outbursts as vile as anything published by Henry Ford. "There have been too many men in this city and especially those in official life who HAVE been taking orders and suggestions from JEW GANGSTERS." "Practically every vendor of vile hooch, every owner of a moonshine still, every snake-faced gangster and embryonic yegg in the Twin Cities is a JEW." "I am launching no attack against the Jewish people," Near insisted; he claimed he only sought to point out the stigma upon all Jews that "THE RODENTS OF THEIR OWN RACE HAVE BROUGHT UPON THEM."[53]

Near accused local officials of being in league with the criminal element. These officials included Minneapolis mayor George Leach, police chief Frank Brunskill, and county attorney Floyd B. Olson. The last was a prominent reformer and future three-term governor. After nine issues of the *Saturday Press* appeared, Olson decided to silence his critic, obtaining a permanent injunction banning any future issues of the paper. The injunction was obtained under a 1925 Minnesota law against public nuisances, originally passed in response to another scandal-mongering paper but never used. The law allowed the prosecution of anyone publishing or circulating "(a) an obscene, lewd and lascivious newspaper, magazine, or other periodical or (b) a malicious, scandalous and defamatory newspaper, magazine or other periodical." The attorney general could "enjoin perpetually the persons committing or maintaining any such nuisance from further committing or maintaining it."

The Supreme Court declared the law unconstitutional, holding that the First Amendment protected the press against prior restraints. *Near* became the cornerstone of modern law on freedom of the press. Commentary on the case by legal scholars has tended to focus on the national security implications, following Justice Holmes's comment that the First Amendment might not protect publication of information about the sailing of troopships during wartime. This was the relevant point, for example, in the famous 1971 Pentagon Papers case.[54]

Near also had important implications for the hate speech issue. The *Saturday Press* was indeed offensive. Its vicious statements about Jews matched anything found in *The Protocols of the Elders of Zion* or Henry Ford's *Dearborn Independent*. From the standpoint of community tolerance and civility, it was certainly a public nuisance under the Minnesota law. Jay Near did not get into trouble with the law because of his anti-Semitism, however. It was his attacks on prominent officials that provoked the suppression of his paper. Had he been merely an anti-Semitic pamphleteer, he probably would have been left alone. After all, there were plenty of other scurrilous anti-Semitic publications around, including Henry Ford's newspaper and book. The Near case, in short, dramatized the problem of selective enforcement. The authorities prosecuted the powerless whose principal crime was offending the powerful.

The two 1931 decisions were harbingers of the revolution in constitutional law that would eventually follow. The protection of individual rights over the next six decades came primarily through Supreme Court decisions interpreting the provisions of the Bill of Rights and, in particular, incorporating those protections into the Fourteenth Amendment and applying them to the states.[55]

Perhaps the most significant aspect of the *Stromberg* and *Near* decisions was what did *not* happen: there was no adverse political reaction. *Stromberg* generated no charges that the Court was protecting Communists, even though the Communist party was enjoying unprecedented growth as a result of the Great Depression. Nor did either decision provoke massive protests that the Court was violating established standards of federalism, intruding into the domain of the fifty states – charges that would be raised in response to many Warren Court decisions. Historian Paul Murphy argues that the absence of a hostile reaction was a sign that the political climate of the country had begun to change in a subtle but powerful way. The fires of the intolerance that raged in the twenties had begun to cool, and Americans were more willing to accept the idea of tolerance for unpopular ideas.[56]

Belonging to America: The Law and American Pluralism

The controversies over anti-Semitism and the Klan in the 1920s raised but did not resolve the basic issues concerning hate speech. One of those issues was the scope of the First Amendment. In the chapters ahead I will trace the development of the law regarding offensive forms of expression. Underlying the First Amendment issues is a larger question regarding the role of the law in resolving intergroup conflict in America. This in turn raises a far broader question about the nature of American society and the place of different racial and religious groups in it. The decade of the twenties made the country think about what it means to be an American – who "belongs" in the sense of full citizenship – and about the role of the law in guaranteeing full membership.[57]

The significant aspect of the twenties, I have already suggested, was not intolerance per se, which had a long history, but that victimized groups began to fight back. In that effort they turned to legal instruments: state laws to ban masked parades by the Klan; the New York anti-Klan law; mayoral and police bans on Klan meetings or on distribution of the *Dearborn Independent*. These actions were possible only because Catholics and Jews had achieved enough political power to help protect their interests. Catholics' power was strongest at the local level, where they frequently controlled city government. But even where they did not command a majority of the votes, as in the New York legislature, they were able to build a coalition by persuading others that their proposed measure was justified. African Americans, meanwhile, were still at least twenty years away from any similar political influence.[58]

Using the law to advance one's interests was in effect a claim to full citizenship in American society. Before the 1920s such claims by Catholics and Jews were unheard of. Two aspects of this process deserve our attention. One involves the overarching vision of American society, the other the use of the law to achieve that vision. In the 1980s, in the controversy over campus speech codes, these two issues would be framed in terms of "inclusion." Hate speech, the argument went, communicated a message of exclusion, in violation of the constitutional promise of equality. Hate speech should be prohibited by law, therefore, as a way of guaranteeing full participation. Although the controversies of the 1920s were not framed in these terms, in retrospect we can view them as early chapters in the long-running struggle over the question of inclusion.

FROM AMERICANISM TO CULTURAL PLURALISM

The dominant vision of American society in the twenties was an aggressive Anglo-Saxon "Americanism." The "true" American either was Anglo-Saxon by heritage or had adopted Anglo-Saxon values and habits – at least as they were understood by most Americans. It was a time of unabashed racist thinking, even among the most educated members of society. Politicians spoke casually about the English "race," while historians and political scientists wrote scholarly pieces demonstrating the virtues of Anglo-Saxon democratic institutions. English parliamentary democracy was viewed as the culmination of centuries of political development. As millions of immigrants from eastern and southern Europe poured into the country (rising to nearly a million a year in the decade before World War I), Anglo-Saxon elitists sounded alarms about "race suicide." Theodore Roosevelt sternly advised Americans of northern European background to have larger families to avoid being outpopulated by the new arrivals. Scientific research on the nature of human intelligence sought to prove that Nordic peoples were more highly evolved than whites of southern and eastern European background, to say nothing of African and Asian peoples.[59] The vicious anti-Semitism of Henry Ford's *Dearborn Independent* or Jay Near's *Saturday Press* and the Klan's hatred of Catholics were simply the crudest versions of ideas that found more elegant expression among the educated elite.[60]

To ensure the preservation of Anglo-Saxon values, civic leaders organized a broad-based Americanization movement. Immigrants were to be assimilated into the cultural norms of Anglo-Saxon America. Old World habits, they argued, could and should be sloughed off. The public school was the primary instrument for this effort, and mastery of the English language the primary goal. The critical role of the schools underpinned two state laws that were eventually struck down by the Supreme Court. A 1919 Nebraska law prohibited teaching in any language but English, and a 1922 Oregon law required all students between the ages of eight and sixteen to attend public schools. Assimilation through public schooling was the product of the best and most progressive thinking in American education. The Gary, Indiana, school system, with an estimated thirty nationalities among its students, modeled its Americanization program on John Dewey's ideas of progressive education.[61]

The Americanization movement was coercive and often repressive. It was a major part of the antilabor, antiradical crusade that reached its peak during World War I. Conservative business interests defined trade unionism, socialism, anarchism, and after 1917, communism as "foreign" imports. This side of Americanization demanded immigration restriction, the deportation of foreign-born radicals, and the outlawing of radical political ideas through criminal syndicalism laws. Right-wing attacks on the ACLU in the 1920s, for example, branded free speech "un-American" because of the organization's defense of labor unions and left-wing groups. Playing the same game, the ACLU replied by asserting that free speech represented "old-fashioned Americanism" and citing speeches by Thomas Jefferson, Abraham Lincoln, and other famous patriots.[62] The attack on political ideas reached its logical culmination in the House Un-American Activities Committee in 1938.[63]

In many respects the Americanization movement resembled the culture wars of the 1980s and 1990s. In both periods a cultural elite felt threatened by the changing demographic profile of the country and the demands for inclusion by the historical victims of prejudice and discrimination. The English Only movement of recent years is a distant echo of the earlier Americanization movement: an attempt to formally define Anglo-Saxon culture as the official version of Americanism and to impose it on everyone. The furious controversy over the "canon" in college and university curricula reflects a similar struggle for control over the official culture.[64]

The moderate or liberal response to the new American demographics was expressed in the concept of the melting pot. Instead of imposing Anglo-Saxon culture on all the new arrivals, the melting pot idea envisioned an entirely new cultural form emerging out of the admixture of different ethnic groups, religions, and cultures. The melting pot idea was more tolerant than the Americanization movement in that it did not completely denigrate the contributions of non-Anglo-Saxon groups. But it did not entirely respect the cultural autonomy of immigrant groups, either. It shared the assumption that Old World cultural traits were inappropriate for America and should pass away.

The radical alternative to both the coercive Americanization and the more benign melting pot idea was a different vision of American society known as cultural pluralism. Its central principle was that the different ethnic and religious cultures in the United States had dignity, were worthy of respect, and made a positive contribution to American life. The idea was introduced by Horace Kallen in 1915. Then a professor of philosophy at the University of Wisconsin and himself of Jewish background, Kallen introduced the idea in an article in *The Nation* and then elaborated it in a 1924 book, *Culture and Democracy in the United States.*[65]

Kallen envisioned a cultural "federal republic" or a "democracy of nationalities." Although English would be the common language, "each nationality would have for its emotional and involuntary life its own peculiar dialect or speech, its own individual and inevitable esthetic and intellectual forms."[66] Kallen's cultural pluralism was based on the assumption that each nationality had dignity, that all nationalities were equal in worth, that all made valuable contributions to American culture, and that the ethnic culture a person was born into provided the nurture that fostered individual development.

By the post–World War II era, and certainly by the 1960s, Kallen's idea had triumphed as the dominant vision of American society. From a purely descriptive standpoint he had accurately foreseen the durability of ethnic group identity even after the doors had been closed to immigration.

PLURALISM AND THE LAW

A philospher and not a legal scholar, Kallen gave little attention to the legal aspects of his cultural pluralism idea in his 1915 and 1924 publications. The body of constitutional law regarding race relations, religious liberty, freedom of association, and freedom of speech, moreover, lay many years in the future. Nonetheless it is important to stress that the body of constitutional and statutory law that subsequently developed eventually embodied, however implicitly, his notion of cultural pluralism.

The central question was – and remains – how to use the law to regulate relations between the various racial and religious groups in American society. Jim Crow, or institutionalized segregation, was simply the most blatant use of the law to establish a particular view of race relations. The civil rights movement was a long-term effort to establish a different view in law. The conflicts of the 1920s illustrate an important aspect of this struggle over the use of the law: "the law" is not a single undifferentiated entity.[67] We can distinguish at least four layers: local police and regulatory measures; state statutes; federal statutes; and constitutional law. There is, of course, a clear hierarchy in which a higher layer preempts a lower level. The struggle over the use of the law to regulate racial and religious group relations involves, to a great extent, a struggle for control over an instrument of the law that would trump a lower authority.

To summarize a very long and complicated story, the conflicts of the twentieth century ended (more or less) with the highest authority – constitutional law – preempting all others. Civil rights forces succeeded in establishing equality as official national policy (as opposed to actual practice) by instituting constitutional law as an active force in American life and controlling the content of that law. Thus, for example, the Fourteenth Amendment preempted state statutes imposing de jure segregation. By the same token, in the realm of religion, the establishment clause of the First Amendment invalidated state and local practices imposing Protestantism as the official religion (as in school prayer and Bible reading).[68]

The hate speech issue was ultimately resolved through a particular interpretation of the First Amendment – one broadly protective of free speech – that invalidated alternative views of offensive speech. The struggle for control over the various instruments of the law are evident in the hate speech controversies of the twenties. When Mayor Curley of Boston banned the Klan he invoked the police regulatory powers that were routinely used by local authorities. With respect to speech, the press, and assembly, enormous power was contained in the regulatory powers over parade permits and licensing of meeting halls.

The 1923 New York anti-Klan law represented a new development: the use of more comprehensive statutory authority to protect minority groups. Ultimately this approach would blossom into the broad range of federal, state, and local civil rights ordinances that we find today. One of the major current controversies concerns which groups should be covered as protected classes, with the bitterest fights occurring over the inclusion of gay and lesbian people. The conflict over gay rights laws dramatizes my point about the role of the law as a statement about inclusion. Advocates on both sides of the gay rights controversy understand that, quite apart from the specific provisions of such laws, the real issue is one of conferring legitimacy upon those in a particular group as full members of the community. By the same token, the controversies of the twenties involved claims to full citizenship by previously outcast groups. Catholic Americans had "arrived" in the sense that they had achieved sufficient political power to use the law against those who believed Catholics were not true Americans.

It is also important to note that the use of the formal instruments of the law was itself a challenge to ingrained American practices. Through the nineteenth century, the majority rarely had to resort to the law to suppress what it regarded as unpopular. Swift and certain results were achieved through direct action. The vigilante committee represented the true flowering of majority rule in nineteenth-century America.[69] Vigilante action, meanwhile, was the crudest and most coercive form of Americanization. "True" Americanism referred to Christian, Protestant, Anglo-Saxon Americans. The Klan was simply the most obvious and most notorious version of this tradition. But it was no less strong in other parts of the country, where vigilante groups had traditionally suppressed religious dissenters, political radicals, and any others who did not conform to the dominant notion of what it meant to be an American.

Beyond the Twenties

In the struggle to define who "belonged" to America, and on what terms, the First Amendment would ultimately play a central role. The outcome was only dimly evident in the twenties. The issue of hate itself had been joined, with the first efforts to control prejudice and discrimination. Among those initial measures were some that restricted freedom of expression. The question whether a tolerant and inclusive society would be best achieved by restricting speech or by guaranteeing its freest exercise would be resolved in the decades ahead.

3 Free Speech for Nazis? Hate Speech as a National Issue, 1933-1940

Nazis at Home and Abroad, 1933–1934

Hate speech emerged as a national – and international – issue in the mid-1930s. After the 1933 Nazi triumph in Germany, domestic Nazi groups proliferated in the United States: the Silver Shirts, the White Shirts, the Khaki Shirts, and others. One journalist counted three hundred paramilitary groups.[1] The head of the Silver Shirts denounced President Franklin D. Roosevelt as a "Dutch Jew" and, in a nonpartisan gesture, claimed that Herbert Hoover had been elected "at the behest of certain great English Jews." Violence accompanied meetings of the Friends of New Germany, and there were rumors that the Silver Shirts received money from the German government. Suddenly a new kind of aggressive, militaristic, antidemocratic political movement was abroad in the land.

The largest and seemingly most respectable group was the Friends of New Germany, organized in 1933 and renamed the German-American Bund in 1938. Its membership was estimated at between 5,000 and 25,000 (and perhaps 60,000 according to an ACLU report). It was particularly strong in New Jersey, where it opened Camp Nordland in 1937. In addition to summer recreation for children and families, Nordland was the scene of military drills; about 18,000 people attended one event. The Bund's membership suggested the potential for mass support of Nazism based simply on ethnic group loyalty.[2]

Three aspects of the domestic Nazi groups were particularly worrisome and potentially altered their legal status as political organizations. First, the paramilitary groups possessed weapons and practiced military drill.

This raised the question whether there was, or should be, a legal distinction between purely political groups and military organizations, allowing stricter government regulation of the latter. In 1933–34 the criminal syndicalism laws that had been used with considerable effectiveness against Communists were still constitutional. Yet the Communists had never engaged in the kind of overt military activity favored by the Fascist groups. Although the Fascists did not call for violent revolution as the Communists did, they were in practical terms a more serious threat.

Second, there were widespread rumors that some Fascist groups were receiving financial assistance from the German government. If true, this would make them foreign agents rather than domestic political organizations and subject to greater regulation. Third, like the Brown Shirts in Germany, they often engaged in deliberately provocative tactics, parading in uniform in or near heavily Jewish neighborhoods.

This last point raised the most difficult First Amendment questions. Did organizations pledged to destroy democracy have a right to use constitutional liberties to do so? This was not an academic question in the early 1930s. In Germany, one Nazi tactic had been to provoke disorder as a way of discrediting both the Weimar government and the principle of democracy. That the brawling Nazi tactics had worked cast the issue of freedom of speech and assembly in an urgent new light. One advocate of restrictive measures argued in *The Nation* that support of free speech for Nazis by the German Socialists and Communists "was in no small degree responsible" for the Nazi triumph.[3] As the Great Depression moved into its fifth year in the winter of 1933–34, with no end in sight and other radical movements flourishing across the country, the threat to democracy seemed especially acute.[4]

In the first year or two it appeared that the Nazi tactic of provoking disorder might succeed. A Nazi rally in Newark, New Jersey, was met by over a thousand counterdemonstrators. In Irvington, New Jersey, an anti-Nazi mob attacked buses carrying people to a Friends of New Germany rally.[5] Members of the Jewish War Veterans threatened to disrupt a pro-Nazi parade in the heavily German Yorkville neighborhood of Manhattan.[6] In all these incidents the actual violence was perpetrated by the anti-Nazi groups. The Nazis themselves could claim that their behavior was entirely lawful. In a curious footnote to history, the mobs attacking the Nazi groups included future organized crime kingpin Meyer Lansky and Jack Ruby, who later assassinated Lee Harvey Oswald.[7]

CIVIL LIBERTIES AND THE NAZI CRISIS

The conflict between pro- and anti-Nazi groups produced numerous restrictions on civil liberties across the country. In some communities Fascists' activities were suppressed; in others, anti-Fascists were censored. The
mayor of Milwaukee revoked the licenses of taverns that hosted meetings
of the Fascist Silver Shirts. The police, meanwhile, helped an anti-Nazi
mob break up a 1938 meeting of the German-American Bund.[8] Authorities in Chicago and New York City granted the Bund meeting permits, but
only in the face of strong pressure to deny them. Anti-Nazi films and
literature were heavily censored. An anti-Fascist film on the Spanish Civil
War (*Blockade*), and one on Nazi Germany (*Professor Mamlock*) were
banned in Providence, Rhode Island, Somerville, Massachusetts, and other
cities. The city of Chicago and the state of Virginia banned all anti-Nazi
films. Ernest Hemingway's novels were banned in Detroit and other cities
because of his well-known sympathy for the Republican side in the Spanish
Civil War. The Catholic church was particularly aggressive in seeking to
suppress anti-Franco voices in this country. It pressured New York mayor
Fiorello La Guardia to bar anti-Franco groups from picketing Saint Pa-
trick's Cathedral. Always ambivalent about First Amendment rights, La
Guardia defended himself by saying, "You can't picket God."[9]

Events in New Jersey, where the Bund was strongest, brought the First
Amendment issues to a head. Several New Jersey communities responded
to Nazi-provoked violence by banning all future Nazi parades or demonstrations. The Newark riot prompted the police chief of nearby Elizabeth, New Jersey, to prohibit a rally by the Friends of New Germany;
Newark authorities later denied permits for all further Nazi meetings.
These actions brought the ACLU into the picture. ACLU general counsel
Arthur Garfield Hays represented the Friends of New Germany in challenging a ban in Union City.[10]

The ACLU immediately found itself under attack from some of its own
members and allies.[11] Since its founding, the ACLU had faced strong
criticism from right-wing groups over its defense of the rights of Communists. ACLU leaders could easily dismiss these criticisms because the
right-wing groups had no evident interest in freedom of speech or human
rights of any sort.[12] Criticism from members and friends over the defense
of First Amendment rights, however, was a different matter. Here were
people committed to the general proposition of free speech arguing that
an exception should be made in the case of the Nazis. Roger Baldwin
confessed that the ACLU Board of Directors was "considerably exercised"

over what to do.[13] As I have already noted, the defense of the First Amendment rights of Henry Ford and the Ku Klux Klan in the 1920s had not provoked any similar internal dissent.

The pressures on the ACLU were both personal and organizational. The top ACLU leaders were far more aware of the Nazi threat than most Americans. All were highly internationalist in outlook and very well informed about events in Europe. Roger Baldwin had seen Austrian Nazis firsthand on his 1927 trip through Europe.[14] Arthur Garfield Hays served as one of the defense counsels in the Reichstag fire trial in 1933.[15] Many ACLU members and top leaders were Jewish, notably the co–general counsels Hays and Morris L. Ernst. ACLU leaders moved in a social and political milieu that included far more Jews and Jewish organizations than most Americans were exposed to. Finally, the ACLU was a small and struggling organization that could ill afford any major loss of support.

It was by no means certain that the still-young ACLU would defend the rights of Nazis. Its policies on many issues were still in flux. It shied away from fighting censorship of sexually explicit literature, was ambivalent about religious exercises in schools, and did nothing to oppose due process violations accompanying enforcement of Prohibition. On the specific question of the defense of Nazis, it did not have the weight of its own tradition behind it as it would in the 1977–78 Skokie controversy.[16] Some people in the small civil liberties–human rights community were arguing that the Nazis represented a very different and very dangerous threat to democracy. Margaret DeSilver, widow of ACLU cofounder Albert DeSilver, a major financial contributor and an influential voice in the organization, argued forcefully that Nazis should not be granted "the liberty to organize to destroy liberty. It is time now to take the offensive instead of remaining on the defensive." DeSilver did not explain how she would reconcile this with her staunch defense of the rights of Communists, who were being repressed across the country on similar grounds. Nonetheless, she was not the only person with close ties to the ACLU leadership demanding restrictions on the Nazis. One of the few defenses of the Nazis' freedom of speech came from the *New York Post*. Editorial writer I. F. Stone counseled that guaranteeing the rights of such groups as the Nazis and the Ku Klux Klan was "part of the price we pay for democracy."[17]

The ACLU's first response was to commission journalist Travis Hoke to prepare an investigative report on the domestic Fascist groups. Baldwin and the other ACLU leaders believed that exposure was the best antidote to hate groups, which was consistent with the general ACLU response to civil liberties problems in those years. With the courts almost universally hostile to civil liberties claims, the ACLU relied primarily on public education. Its instinctive response to a problem was not to file a suit but to publish a pamphlet.

Hoke's report, *Shirts!* – which the ACLU published in pamphlet form – provided detailed information on the leading domestic Fascist groups.[18] After describing their leaders and tactics and estimating their memberships, Hoke concluded that the domestic Fascist groups posed no serious threat to public order. They were all very small, with little support outside their immediate membership, and led by cranks and crackpots who had no evident ability to organize an effective political movement. Even William Dudley Pelley's Silver Shirts, which the pamphlet characterized as the "most vocal, most wild-eyed, and in some ways most dangerous" of them all, did not appear to be a serious threat. In early 1934 its publishing arm went into bankruptcy over a $110 printing bill.[19] Armed with Hoke's report, the ACLU concluded there was no clear and present danger to the survival of democracy.

Shall We Defend Free Speech for Nazis in America?

To say there was no clear and present danger at the moment, however, did not convince everyone that some restrictions on Nazis were not warranted. The Nazi party in Germany, after all, had been a weak, disorganized, ragtag band of apparent crackpots not too many years earlier. Some people were already arguing that the "lesson" of recent German history was the importance of nipping Fascist movements in the bud. Roger Baldwin finally concluded that the issue was important enough to warrant an ACLU statement. He appointed a special committee to consider the question and draft a formal statement. The result was a document titled *Shall We Defend Free Speech for Nazis in America?* published in October 1934.[20]

Shall We Defend? answered the question affirmatively, declaring that the First Amendment protected freedom of speech, the press, and assembly for Nazis and all other antidemocratic groups. This 1934 statement contained the essentials of what eventually became American public policy. The numerous policy statements, law review articles, court decisions, and other published items affirming the rights of hate groups that have appeared in the intervening sixty years are largely elaborations of this 1934 ACLU statement.

Shall We Defend? began by confronting the argument that the Nazis represented a special case and should be exempt from First Amendment protection. It noted that some ACLU members had "sharply criticized" the organization for defending the Nazis. Nazism, these critics argued, was "a regime so brutal that it forfeits all tolerance." The Nazis had already suppressed civil liberties in Germany "and would do so here if they had a chance."

In the long battle concerning hate speech over the next six decades, two arguments for restricting speech would continually reappear. The first is that a particular group represents a special case and a limited exception to free speech protection should be made for it.[21] The second argument is that free societies have a right and possibly even an obligation to restrict the activities of antidemocratic groups pledged to destroy free speech and other democratic principles if they come to power. Supreme Court justice Robert Jackson stated this position most succinctly in 1949 when he declared that the Bill of Rights was not a "suicide pact."[22]

The ACLU's reply to the special-case argument was a mixture of principle and pragmatism. "Is it not clear," it asked rhetorically, "that free speech as a practical tactic, not only as an abstract principle, demands defense of the rights of all who are attacked in order to obtain the rights of any?" This comment was really addressed to the ACLU's critics on the left, principally the Communists. The ACLU sought to answer opposition from the Left by arguing that their rights were inextricably bound up with the rights of Nazis. A broad-principled affirmation of free speech offered the most practical protection for the Communists.

The ACLU sought to deflect criticism from Jews by pointing out that one of its own general counsels, Arthur Garfield Hays, had represented a Nazi group in New Jersey. If this Jewish lawyer could defend Nazis, the ACLU suggested, then other Jews could also defend their rights. The ACLU used the argument frequently during this period, pointing out that both of its general counsels, Hays and Morris L. Ernst, were Jewish.[23] By the 1940s this special and somewhat cheap appeal had disappeared.

Shall We Defend? then introduced the vagueness problem and the consequent threat to the rights of other political groups. "To those who advocate suppressing propaganda they hate," the ACLU asked, "where do you draw the line?" "Experience shows," it continued, that the term "political enemies" is extremely elastic. It did not elaborate on the repression of American Communists, apparently assuming that most of its readers were familiar with these events. The ACLU also did not cite the most obvious "lessons" of experience – its own. The attacks on the National Civil Liberties Bureau during World War I – banishment of its pamphlets from the mails, massive government spying, a raid by Justice Department officials, seizure of all its office files, and the near prosecution of the top leaders – were based on the government's argument that the NCLB was aiding the country's "political enemies."[24]

The pamphlet addressed the clear and present danger test somewhat briefly. "To those who urge suppression of meetings that may incite riot or violence," it argued, "the complete answer is that nobody can tell in advance what meetings may do so." Prohibiting a meeting or parade because some people thought it might result in violence was a convenient excuse for arbitrary suppression of unpopular groups. The pamphlet did not, however, elaborate on the crucial distinction between advocating radical ideas and inciting to criminal action. Three years earlier the ACLU had gone to great lengths to explain this point and defend its position of defending the free speech rights of Communists.[25]

A particularly serious omission was the pamphlet's failure to address squarely the question of deliberately provocative demonstrations. This tactic, after all, was the most threatening aspect of Nazi groups both here and in Europe. After World War II, moreover, the question of how far the First Amendment protected the provocative speaker in the face of a hostile audience prompted a series of extremely important Supreme Court decisions. Yet for some reason the question was bypassed.

Shall We Defend? then returned to the vagueness problem, arguing that there was "no general agreement on what constitutes race or religious prejudice." "Once the bars are let down," it argued, "the field is open to all comers." It warned that even Jews attacking Nazis could be punished under a general prohibition on offensive racial and religious speech. This was a telling point, given that some of the overt violence of the past year and a half had been committed by members of anti-Nazi groups. Events would soon prove the ACLU prescient on this point. A year later New Jersey would pass a hate speech law, and the first person prosecuted would be a Jehovah's Witness for circulating anti-Catholic literature.[26]

The pamphlet also discussed some practical considerations. Prosecuting Nazis would only make martyrs of them, "attract[ing] to them hundreds of sympathizers with the persecuted who would otherwise be indifferent." The best way to fight Nazi propaganda was "in the open," with counter-propaganda, demonstrations, and the like. In later years the argument that the best response to bad speech was more speech would become a more important part of the ACLU's position on defending the rights of hate groups.

The ACLU concluded by describing possible restrictions that did not infringe First Amendment rights. It endorsed limits on gun ownership, arguing that paramilitary exercises were not a form of political expression. It also reiterated its long-standing support for laws prohibiting the Ku Klux Klan from parading in masks.[27]

Published in October 1934, *Shall We Defend Free Speech for Nazis in America?* proved to be an enduring statement. The basic points it raised remained essentially unchanged over the next half century. The same basic arguments reappeared, with only slight revision, in 1939,[28] again in a 1946 ACLU statement opposing group libel legislation,[29] in a 1978 statement on the right of Nazis to march in Skokie, Illinois,[30] and in a 1992 Briefing Paper titled "Hate Speech on Campus."[31] The ACLU never wavered from the position it formulated in 1934: while conceding that there were risks in granting the full measure of rights to Nazis and other totalitarian groups, it insisted that the risks of suppression were far greater. As John Haynes Holmes, ACLU cofounder, put it in a 1938 debate over anti-Nazi laws, "I think we have to take the risks of free speech."[32]

Even more significant, the arguments set forth in *Shall We Defend?* formed the basis of the 1978 decision of the Seventh Circuit Court of Appeals affirming the right of a Nazi group to demonstrate in Skokie, Illinois,[33] and the Supreme Court's 1992 cross-burning decision.[34] There is, in short, a direct line of development between the 1934 ACLU statement and American public policy on the First Amendment rights of hate groups.

The Example of European Anti-Fascist Laws

As the thirties progressed, the situation in Europe steadily worsened. In addition to the growing attacks on German Jews, Hitler was increasingly belligerent about his designs on more territory. Many people were convinced that another world war was inevitable and saw the Spanish Civil

War as a testing ground for German military tactics. These developments heightened calls for restrictions on American Nazi groups: the European experience seemed to illustrate the importance of stopping Fascist movements before they could gain a foothold. Nearly every European country passed laws restricting antidemocratic groups, and Americans groping for the proper response to Fascism examined these laws with great interest.

It is important to note, however, that the debate over how to respond to domestic fascism involved a very small circle of people. The vast majority of Americans were, in varying degrees, isolationist, indifferent to the fate of European Jewry, or sympathetic to certain aspects of German and Italian Fascism. A 1938 public opinion poll, for example, found that 58 percent of Americans believed the European Jews were wholly or partly responsible for their own persecution.[35] As a matter of national policy, the United States was extremely indifferent to the fate of European Jews and even to refugees from Nazism seeking entry to this country.[36] Alarm over the Nazi threat was limited to some but by no means all liberals, most of the organized political Left, and the American Jewish community.

"MILITANT DEMOCRACY":
THE LEFT-LIBERAL CASE FOR REPRESSION

The most articulate case for restricting antidemocratic movements was made by Karl Loewenstein, a political scientist at Amherst College,[37] who studied the European anti-Fascist laws in detail. His work has lasting significance because he elaborated on the basic argument that democratic societies have a self-preservationist right and obligation to suppress antidemocratic political movements. David Riesman developed this argument at greater length a few years later in a series of widely cited law review articles.[38] Loewenstein's writings merit attention because they appeared first, at a critical early juncture, and without the benefit of the five years of hindsight that Riesman enjoyed.

Loewenstein went directly to the heart of the matter. The fundamental weakness of democracy was the very nature of democratic principles. Its most cherished values left it vulnerable to aggressive tactics of Fascists and other antidemocratic groups. He argued that European Fascist movements had been extremely successful in exploiting "the extraordinary condition offered by democratic institutions." The problem was tolerance: "Democracy and democratic tolerance have been used for their own destruction."[39] A decade later, Supreme Court justice Robert Jackson put the issue even more bluntly. In a vigorous dissent in the *Terminiello* case, which involved a violent clash between anti-Semitic and anti-Nazi forces, he argued that the Bill of Rights was not "a suicide pact" and that the preservation of liberty required some restrictions to maintain order.[40]

Loewenstein chastised civil libertarians for their rigid absolutism, which he derided as "democratic fundamentalism." Adherence to absolute legalistic standards was too abstract, too rigid, and fatally unrealistic.[41] An "exaggerated formalism of the rule of law," which failed to take into account the content of particular forms of speech and assembly, created the opportunity for Fascists to destroy democracy. In this respect Loewenstein challenged the core principle of what was still developing as the American approach to civil liberties. He did not mince words: the free speech absolutists were blind and impractical, unwilling or unable to face the practical consequences of their own ideas.[42]

Loewenstein would not be the last to criticize civil libertarian absolutism. As the protection of individual rights expanded over the next half century, particularly under the Warren Court, conservatives and moderate civil libertarians alike would argue that pushing individual rights too far had very undesirable consequences for the health of society. Unlimited freedom of speech and the press, many would argue, unleashed a flood of pornography on an unwilling public. Pressing separation of church and state too far, others would argue, resulted in the exclusion of religion from public life. Excessive concern for the rights of criminal suspects, meanwhile, endangered the law-abiding public.[43] Loewenstein, in short, had raised one of the fundamental issues about the scope of individual rights in contemporary society.

As an alternative to the "exaggerated formalism of the rule of law," Loewenstein proposed something he called "militant democracy."[44] This represented a combination of the special-case exception and the contextualized approach to First Amendment questions. A militant democracy was one willing to make strategic compromises on its own principles as part of an anti-Fascist strategy. Repression of antidemocratic movements was simply a necessary self-defense measure. On this point as well, Loewenstein was completely candid about what he was advocating. Democracies had to adopt some of the same tactics as Fascists: "A political technique can be defeated only on its own plane and by its own devices."[45] In plain English, you had to fight fire with fire.

The concept of "militant democracy," or *wehrhafte Demokratie,* became one of the fundamental concepts underlying the constitution of post–World War II West Germany, particularly its anti-Nazi provisions.

The principal measure permitted the government to outlaw and disband political groups deemed a threat to constitutional government.[46]

Loewenstein justified the use of antidemocratic measures on the grounds that established democracies, such as those in Western Europe, could survive a little compromise of principle. The damage would be slight and temporary: "Where fundamental rights are institutionalized, their temporary suspension is justified."[47] In support of this crucial point, he cited the experience of World War I. The Western democracies survived the Great War because they had been willing to temporarily suspend individual liberties: "Democracies withstood the ordeal of the World War much better than did autocratic states – by adopting autocratic methods."[48]

This interpretation of the World War I experience was certainly the weakest part of Loewenstein's argument. His view that "few seriously objected to the temporary suspension of constitutional principles for the sake of national defense"[49] is hardly supported by the history of the war years. In fact, there was a very strong reaction to the massive suppression of civil liberties in the United States. The wartime free speech cases provoked Justices Oliver Wendell Holmes and Louis Brandeis to rethink the meaning of the First Amendment. Holmes's dissent in the 1919 *Abrams* case, which Brandeis joined, eventually became the cornerstone of modern First Amendment law.[50] The wartime crisis also provoked the creation of the first organization dedicated to the defense of individual rights, the ACLU.[51] Insofar as there was a coherent body of thought defending free speech by the mid- to late thirties, it was a reaction to the wartime suppression of liberties.

The wartime suppression of civil liberties also did lasting damage. The Socialist party[52] and the more radical Industrial Workers of the World were both crushed.[53] The furies of repression continued through the 1920s and into the 1930s, crippling both the labor movement and the political Left.[54] It also established the principle of guilt by association, such that anyone who defended the rights of dissidents was immediately branded "un-American." For someone with obvious left-wing sympathies, Loewenstein's refusal to acknowledge the destruction of the political Left in America during World War I is hard to explain. His dismissal of the wartime suppression of liberties as mild and temporary was far too glib, and his neglect of the continuing repression of the Left, under the very rationale he was offering, was a serious omission. Although attacking the free speech "fundamentalists" for being impractical, he refused to explore fully the consequences of the very measures he advocated – about which there was substantial historical evidence.

EUROPEAN ANTI-FASCIST LAWS

Lowenstein supported his case for "militant democracy" by reviewing the experience of European anti-Fascist legislation.[55] A fair reading of his evidence, however, readily points to a very different and more pessimistic conclusion. In many cases the suspension of democratic freedoms led to the complete end of democracy. His analysis is even more chilling when viewed from the perspective of post–Cold War America. The anti-Fascist measures he recommended for the United States were in fact adopted in both letter and spirit as anti-Communist measures during the Cold War.

Reviewing developments in Europe, Loewenstein concluded that, even after allowing for the variations in political traditions and the relative gravity of the Fascist threat in different countries, there was "considerable uniformity" to European anti-Fascist legislation.[56] Moreover, the European experience clearly proved to him that action should be taken as early as possible. Countries that waited until after Fascism had "taken root" had much greater difficulty controlling it later.

European anti-Fascist laws were generally framed in broad terms, directed at "subversive movements or groups other than Fascist or National Socialist if they are considered detrimental to the democratic state."[57] Loewenstein divided the various restrictive measures into several categories. The first and least significant group included laws to strengthen the power to impose martial law. This power had long existed in most countries, and the new measures were not directed specifically at Fascist movements.

The "most comprehensive and effective measures" were those proscribing "subversive movements altogether."[58] These laws allowed the government to restrict the speech, press, and assembly rights of party members, exclude party candidates from elections, or even declare the party illegal, dissolve it, and confiscate its property. Some countries named specific parties: Switzerland, Luxembourg, and the province of Quebec outlawed the Communist party. Most anti-Nazi laws, however, applied "indiscriminantly to all political groupings which fall under the general category of a subversive party, an unlawful association, or an organization inimical to the state."[59]

With respect to enforcement, Loewenstein approvingly noted that in virtually every country the decision by which political parties would be outlawed or otherwise restricted "lies with the discretionary power of the government." Nor did he object that "guilt by association is generally deemed sufficient" to apply restrictions to individual party members. Loewenstein was not troubled by the vagueness problem: quite the contrary, he argued that legislation needed to be framed in very broad language because banned parties often resurfaced under different names. He cited the example of the Iron Guard in Romania reappearing as the "All-for-the Country Party."

A third group of laws applied specifically to paramilitary groups. Sweden, Norway, Denmark, Switzerland, and Czechoslovakia banned the public wearing of uniforms in 1933; they were joined by Finland, Belgium, and the Netherlands in 1934 and by England in 1936. He stressed that the German government had taken no strong action against paramilitary groups before 1933, suggesting that this might have stopped the Nazi movement. Seven countries, meanwhile, banned the formation of private armies; four, including England and France in 1936, outlawed military training by "unauthorized" persons.[60] Many countries strengthened their already strong laws on the possession and use of firearms.

Another set of laws limited participation in the electoral process. The basic purpose was to prevent the "abuse of parliamentary institutions by political extremism." A 1937 Dutch law let the parliament refuse to seat alleged subversives even though they had been duly elected. Belgium banned "frivolous" by-elections.

A final set of laws restricted freedom of speech, the press, and assembly. Although conceding that this represented the "thorniest problem" of all, Loewenstein dismissed the absolutist approach to freedom of expression as "more or less a sham."[61] Fascist groups had deliberately used the right of freedom of assembly to provoke violent disturbances that undermined social stability. The most provocative tactic was to march into neighborhoods where anti-Fascists were known to be organized. Czechoslovakia restricted freedom of assembly as early as 1923. The 1936 Public Order Act in the United Kingdom empowered the police to ban demonstrations or control their routes.[62]

As an example of successful anti-Fascist measures, Loewenstein cited the case of Finland. The government adopted a series of anti-Fascist measures between 1932 and 1934, banning private armies and the "ostentatious" wearing of political uniforms or other insignia. Writing in mid-1937, Loewenstein concluded that Finland appeared to have survived the nascent Fascist threat and was developing in the direction of Scandinavian democracy rather than "Baltic authoritarianism."[63]

Loewenstein also pointed to Czechoslovakia, calling it "the most conspicuous example of a democratic country maintaining its fundamental structure against overwhelming odds."[64] His own description of events there, however, suggested that democratic freedoms had been destroyed by 1937. The trend toward authoritarianism began early. In 1923 the government passed a vaguely worded law designed to ensure the "protection of the Republic." In October 1933, following the Nazi triumph in Germany, a new law allowed the government to dissolve any political party or social group that was "apt to endanger the constitutional unity, the integrity, the republican-democratic form of the state or the safety of the Czechoslovakian Republic."[65] The sweeping law authorized restriction of the speech, press, and assembly rights of allegedly subversive parties. Public display of party banners and symbols was specifically prohibited, and the government could confiscate the property of any organization it deemed a threat. The law was directed not only at political parties as organizational entities, but at individual members as well. Mere membership in any subversive group was sufficient evidence of guilt, and such persons were barred from holding public office. The 1933 law authorized the abrogation of virtually every aspect of political freedom as defined by Western democracies. The descent into authoritarianism in Czechoslovakia did not stop there. In 1936 an even more sweeping law effectively suspended the constitution and placed the entire country under martial law. In light of these events, it is not clear how Loewenstein managed to conclude that the "fundamental structure" of democracy had survived. It appears that all vestiges of political freedom had been eliminated.

Loewenstein's analysis raised a general question about the impact of the European anti-Fascist laws: To what extent did they help preserve public order and democracy? Did they play some role in curbing Fascism in England and the Netherlands, for example? This question has direct relevance for the hate speech issue. Do restrictions on racial and religious propaganda help to curb racist thinking and discriminatory practices?

The 1936 Public Order Act in the United Kingdom offers a possible case study. The law was prompted by a series of violent clashes between

Fascist and anti-Fascist groups that reached their peak in 1935. As in other countries, the Fascists staged deliberately provocative demonstrations, on some occasions parading through Jewish neighborhoods chanting "We want Jewry's blood." The Public Order Act allowed the police to control the location of demonstrations, confining them to certain areas, or to ban them altogether. The National Council for Civil Liberties (NCCL), established in 1934 as an equivalent to the ACLU, opposed the law on the grounds that it restricted basic political rights and would be enforced in a discriminatory fashion.[66]

Enforcement of the law confirmed the NCCL's worst fears. There were slightly more arrests of anti-Fascists than of Fascists, although the disparity had been far greater before the law went into effect in January 1937. The NCCL's greatest complaint was that in several instances the police refused to arrest Fascists chanting anti-Semitic slogans even when they were asked to.[67]

A historian who studied these events found that disorder was already declining before the law went into effect and continued to do so afterward. Democracy was never really in danger in England: "Britain was not, at the time, fertile ground for planting fascism or communism; in all likelihood, neither movement would have threatened the state."[68] Democracy survived in England and the Netherlands probably because of deeply rooted commitment to democracy, not because of the anti-Fascist laws that were enacted.

The American Response to Nazism and Communism

The most important aspect of the American response to domestic Fascism is that very few measures of any sort were adopted. New Jersey passed a "race hate" law in 1934 and supplemented it four years later with a law against wearing military-style uniforms.[69] The New York state legislature debated but rejected a similar law. Even the American Jewish Committee opposed the bill, arguing that "intolerance thrives on suppression." The state did, however, successfully prosecute the German-American Bund in 1939 for failing to comply with the law requiring oath-bound organizations to register, the law originally directed at the KKK and upheld by the United States Supreme Court in 1928.[70] The most important anti-Nazi measure adopted in the United States was the House Un-American

Activities Committee, which, as we shall see, concentrated on alleged Communist subversion and gave little attention to Fascist groups.

The paucity of anti-Fascist measures was hardly due to any strong commitment to First Amendment principles. The real reason was the indifference of most Americans to Nazism or any potential Nazi threat. German Americans were the largest single ethnic group in the country after English Americans, and anti-Nazi sentiment was still confined to a small circle of liberals and leftists. With respect to threats from antidemocratic movements, Americans were obsessed with Communism rather than Fascism.

The debate over the Fascist threat remained confined to the political Left, which had little influence over national events. Even the major Jewish groups did not at this time organize a major effort for anti-Fascist legislation. The debate on the left again focused attention on the ACLU and its defense of the First Amendment rights of Nazis. In response to "numerous complaints" about its position, the ACLU took another look at the question in 1938. Another special committee examined the European laws and considered proposals circulating in the United States.[71]

Not surprisingly, the ACLU reiterated its opposition to restraints on political expression, adamantly objecting to the kind of laws adopted in Europe. The public display of flags, insignia, and uniforms was protected by the First Amendment. ACLU executive director Roger Baldwin argued that "the Swastika has as much right to fly as the Stars and Stripes or any other flag."[72] The vagueness problem could not be wished away. "What is a uniform?" the ACLU asked rhetorically, quickly answering that it is "impossible to define them in law." Any prohibition on uniforms might be applied to parades by the Masons and Knights Templar, or even the Republican and Democratic parties.[73] Lucille Milner, ACLU secretary, published an article in *The Nation* noting that the Public Order Act in England had been used more often against organized labor and the Left than against Fascists.[74]

The ACLU did approve of two restrictions on freedom of assembly, however. The first was a prohibition on parading in masks. Several states had adopted such laws in the 1920s in response to the Ku Klux Klan, and the ACLU had argued that they did not violate the First Amendment. Given the Klan's record of violence, masked parading was regarded as a form of intimidation.[75]

The ACLU toyed with the idea that provocative demonstrations could be regulated. The special committee's report concluded that the Nazi tactic of parading "provocatively" into "districts inhabited by Nazi opponents" was not protected by the First Amendment: the police could require that such demonstrations be confined to "safe" neighborhoods.[76] The English Public Order Act granted such power to the police.[77] The ACLU did not adopt this idea as official policy, however. It always supported provocative forms of expression, from the Nazi demonstrations of the 1930s through the civil rights marches of the 1960s, to the 1977–78 controversy over a proposed Nazi march in the heavily Jewish community of Skokie, Illinois. This brief flirtation with possible restriction of provocative demonstrations, in short, represented an important turning point. The principal defender of First Amendment rights in the United States considered a major limitation on freedom of assembly but rejected it.

The question of paramilitary groups posed another set of problems. The ACLU argued that for the most part existing federal and state laws were adequate. Federal law restricted the sale and shipment of firearms, and some states had laws prohibiting the formation of unauthorized military groups. A new 1937 federal law, meanwhile, required the registration of agents of foreign governments.

In a somewhat surprising exception to its general defense of First Amendment rights, the ACLU endorsed federal legislation "prohibiting the formation of private military forces and the prohibition of private military training." Curiously, it did not find the same vagueness problem as in other kinds of restrictions of political activity. It did not attempt to define "military" groups or explain how one could distinguish between military training and a weekend hunting club. The ACLU glossed over these problems, arguing that all military activities were properly the province of the War Department. A bill was introduced in the House by Representative Hamilton Fish, certainly a strange bedfellow for the ACLU. A prominent conservative, Fish had chaired a 1931 legislative investigation into alleged Communist subversion where he personally baited Roger Baldwin about the ACLU's supposed ties to Communism.[78]

Klapprott: The New Jersey Race Hate Law

In the end, only one hate speech law was enacted in the 1930s, a 1934 New Jersey law outlawing racial and religious "propaganda."[79] The battle over the law illustrates three important points about the hate speech issue:

the relative weakness of support for such laws; the dangers of selective enforcement; and ultimately, the growing commitment to First Amendment values.

The New Jersey law was a direct outgrowth of violent clashes between Nazi sympathizers and anti-Nazi groups. A Friends of New Germany meeting on October 16, 1933, was greeted by a thousand anti-Nazi demonstrators; the confrontation ended in a full-scale riot. In response, officials in several New Jersey cities banned meetings by the Friends of New Germany. Meanwhile, a race hate bill was introduced in the state legislature. It passed the house but died in the senate, in part but not entirely because of vigorous opposition by the ACLU. After several more violent clashes, the legislature passed the race hate law on April 9, 1934.[80]

The New Jersey race hate law embodied the basic principle that has guided nearly all such proposals over the years: that enhancing the freedom of most Americans requires certain limited restrictions on the rights of some other groups. The law's preamble declared that "freedom of conscience in the matter of religious worship" and "equality in the protection of life, liberty and property" were protected by both the federal and state constitutions. Criminal penalties for disseminating hate propaganda were therefore necessary to protect "said constitutional assurances and guarantees."

The specific provisions of the law imposed potentially sweeping restrictions on freedom of expression. The law established criminal penalties for anyone disseminating "propaganda or statements creating or tending to create prejudice, hostility, hatred, ridicule, disgrace or contempt of people . . . by reason of their race, color or creed or manner of worship." It was also illegal to exhibit such propaganda "at any meeting of two or more persons or in any parade, public or private," including the use of "any flag, banner, emblem, picture, photography." Possession of propaganda literature with intent to distribute was also illegal. Finally, it was illegal for a property owner to rent out a place where hate propaganda was disseminated. These provisions appeared to cover even a situation where two people met in private while in possession of any material that might be deemed propaganda.

Enforcement of the New Jersey race hate law dramatized the hazards of such legislation. The most important point was that it was hardly enforced at all. For six years there was not a single recorded prosecution of any anti-Semitic individual or group. The first and only recorded case involved a member of the Jehovah's Witnesses who was charged with distributing anti-Catholic literature. The Witnesses were indeed virulently anti-Catholic at that time, and this was the source of some of the most important court cases emerging from the national controversy over them.[81] The ACLU, opposed to the New Jersey law all along, came to the defense of the Jehovah's Witness, and the charges were quickly dismissed. As a result, there was no immediate constitutional test of the law.[82]

Events in Illinois paralleled those in New Jersey. In the wake of the 1917 race riot in East St. Louis,[83] Illinois enacted a group libel law prohibiting publication of material that portrayed "depravity, criminality, unchastity, or lack of virtue of a class of citizens, of any race, color, creed or religion." The law remained a virtual dead letter for two decades, however, and was not used against either antiblack agitators or local Nazi groups. Local authorities finally discovered it in the 1940s as a weapon against the Jehovah's Witnesses. Offended by the Witnesses' anti-Catholic propaganda, citizens in Belleville and Harrisburg, Illinois, pressured the local sheriffs to arrest them. A test case reached the federal courts as the Witnesses sought to enjoin these officials from interfering with their rights of free speech, freedom of the press, and free exercise of religion. The district court rejected their claims and upheld the constitutionality of the Illinois group libel law in June 1941.[84] No Supreme Court test of the Illinois law resulted from this case, but the Court did sustain its constitutionality in 1952 in *Beauharnais v. Illinois,* which I shall examine in detail in chapter 5.[85]

A constitutional test of the New Jersey race hate law was finally set in motion in 1940, with Europe now at war and the United States headed toward intervention. Fears of German sabotage seemed to be realized in September 1940 when an explosion at the Hercules Powder Plant in New Jersey killed forty-two people. New Jersey authorities raided the German-American Bund's Camp Nordland, seized anti-Semitic literature, and eventually indicted ten Bund leaders under the race hate law. Significantly, August Klapprott and his codefendants were not charged with any crimes directly related to the explosion and the forty-two deaths.[86]

Klapprott and his associates were eventually convicted both of possessing race hate propaganda and, as Bund officials, of leasing Camp Nordland to people who disseminated such literature. On appeal, the New Jersey supreme court overturned the convictions on the grounds that the law violated both the New Jersey constitution and the First

Amendment to the United States Constitution. The decision in *State v. Klapprott* remained the most important decision on the hate speech issue for many years.[87]

The New Jersey court began by affirming the importance of freedom of expression as guaranteed by the state and federal constitutions. It then attacked the New Jersey law on grounds of vagueness. The definition of the prohibited forms of expression, it argued, "could scarcely be more general or indefinite." The words "hatred," "abuse," and "hostility" had no precise meaning. "Nothing in our criminal law can be invoked to justify so wide a discretion" as would be required to apply these terms, the court held. It went on to list a number of potential abuses. The law could cover statements made to one other person in a private home; or parents whose attempt to explain religious practices to their children aroused the children's hostility toward neighbors; or high-school and college teachers whose explications of religious philosophy offended someone.

The New Jersey court cited as precedent several United States Supreme Court decisions on the First Amendment. It cited the *Near* decision declaring prior restraint on the press as unconstitutional. Even more to the point, it quoted three long paragraphs from the 1940 *Cantwell* decision where the Court overturned the conviction of a Jehovah's Witness for disturbing the peace. In matters of religion and politics it is inevitable that "sharp differences arise," often including "exaggeration," "vilification," and even "false statement."[88] I will consider *Cantwell* in the context of the Jehovah's Witness cases in the next chapter. For the moment, however, it is important to note that in this opinion the Court gave constitutional protection to offensive speech, including even "vilification" and "false statement." The remedy for this kind of speech was more speech. The Court invoked Justice Holmes's concept of the marketplace of ideas: protecting freedom of expression, even of offensive views, was "in the long view, essential to enlightened opinion and right conduct on the part of the citizens of a democracy."

The New Jersey court did find two permissible limitations on freedom of expression. Citing the leading United States Supreme Court decisions beginning with the World War I sedition cases, it held that only speech that "menace[s] the state itself" could be punished. Even then there needed to be a clear and present danger "to a substantial interest of the State." The *Klapprott* case, however, involved speech that offended private citizens rather than the state. Offensive attacks on individuals, the court argued, could be remedied through libel and slander actions.

One of the crucial elements in the case was the amicus brief filed by the ACLU, coauthored by ACLU general counsel Arthur Garfield Hays. Hays was perhaps the earliest advocate of an absolutist interpretation of the First Amendment, holding that it protected the right to say anything, about any subject, at any time or place.[89] In the *Klapprott* opinion the New Jersey supreme court explicitly referred to the ACLU's "excellent brief" and adopted its reasoning virtually in toto.[90]

Klapprott was a resounding affirmation of free speech and a great victory for the ACLU. As the United States entered World War II, it was the most important court test of legislation on race hate, or what would soon be known as group libel. To this point, however, there had been no Supreme Court test of such legislation.

Investigating Hate Groups: The Tragedy of Samuel Dickstein

Of all the proposals offered in response to the threat of domestic Fascist groups in the United States, the most lasting was the technique of exposure through legislative investigation. The creation of the House Un-American Activities Committee (HUAC) in 1938 was a tragedy of enormous dimensions and a cautionary tale on the question of hate speech and hate groups. Originally promoted by Representative Samuel Dickstein to expose domestic Fascist groups, HUAC gave them only passing attention and instead became the vehicle for attacks on leftists and liberals. The cruelest irony was that HUAC also became a platform for the grossest anti-Semitism and for attacks on civil rights groups.

Legislative investigation of political groups became a common feature of American political life during World War I. Congress investigated alleged German influence during the war. In the postwar Red Scare, the New York legislature's Lusk Committee smeared a broad array of liberal and left-wing groups, accusing them of serving German and then Bolshevik interests. The 1923 New York anti-Klan law, which the Supreme Court upheld in the *Bryant* decision, was based on a legislative finding about Klan violence. The House investigated alleged Communist activity in 1930–31 (the Fish Committee) and again in 1934–35 before creating a permanent Committee on Un-American Activities.[91] The special characteristic of legislative investigations of political groups in this country was the underlying assumption of "un-Americanism," that certain ideas and groups were not merely bad but unpatriotic.

Congressional investigations were also a very popular technique for advancing liberal programs in the 1930s. The Nye Committee exposed the role of munitions makers in World War I; the La Follette Committee exposed the violation of workers' rights by industrialists;[92] House and Senate committees investigated the role of the leading banking firms in causing the Great Depression. A committee chaired by senator and future Supreme Court justice Hugo Black exposed lobbying by private utility companies.[93]

The use of legislative investigations to expose social problems was consistent with basic principles of American democracy. As of the mid-1930s many civil libertarians saw no great danger in the technique, and some even considered it a positive measure.[94] The right and the power of Congress to investigate had always been considered a legitimate if not necessary part of its lawmaking role.[95] Facts, after all, were essential if the people were to make informed decisions.

Given the popularity of legislative investigation, it was hardly surprising that someone proposed it as a method of exposing domestic Fascists. The most vigorous advocate was Representative Samuel Dickstein of New York, who was Jewish and represented a heavily Jewish district in Brooklyn. His demand for an investigation of Fascist groups initially found little support in the House. This was partly a result of indifference to the idea of a Fascist threat and partly a reaction to Dickstein's abrasive personal style. As chairman of the Committee on Immigration and Naturalization, he conducted his own investigation in 1933. The following year the House overwhelmingly adopted his resolution creating a Special Committee on Un-American Activities. Popularly known as the McCormack-Dickstein Committee, it conducted hearings for several months in the summer and fall of 1934. The hearings were relatively orderly when Representative John W. McCormack served as chairman, but they degenerated into unruly confrontations when Dickstein presided. The committee's 1935 report cited examples of German financing of pro-German propaganda and concluded that some German American summer camps promoted Nazi propaganda. The committee's work yielded one tangible piece of legislation: the 1938 Foreign Agents Registration Act.[96]

After the committee disbanded, Dickstein continued his personal crusade, holding stormy hearings in New York City and publishing his own list of suspected Nazis.[97] Again he found little support for a permanent committee or anti-Fascist legislation. The situation changed only after conservatives in the House decided to revive investigations of left-wing groups. This was a result of several factors: the increasingly conservative mood of the Congress, the consequent desire to attack the New Deal, a desire to offset the success of the La Follette Committee's exposure of antilabor activities, and a response to the growing size and prominence of the American Communist party. The liberal Dickstein joined forces with conservative Texas Democrat Martin Dies, and together they pushed through a resolution creating a Special Committee on Un-American Activities in May 1938.[98]

Dickstein lost more than he won. In a personal rebuke, the House did not appoint him to the new committee. Public hearings began in the late summer of 1938 under committee chairman Martin Dies. Giving only the briefest attention to Fascist groups, HUAC directed virtually all its fire at Communists, alleged Communists, the labor movement, liberals, and the New Deal. Moreover, HUAC became a prominent vehicle for some of the worst anti-Semitism. Over the years committee members went out of their way to emphasize prominent Jews in the Communist party, the labor movement, the New Deal, and among alleged leftists in Hollywood. In fairness to Dickstein, it should be said that, given the anti-Communist temper of the country, some form of legislative investigation of alleged leftist subversion would probably have occurred in any event. Nonetheless, his role in promoting the creation of HUAC stands as a sobering lesson on how measures designed to attack ethnic and religious intolerance can readily be used to promote intolerance itself.

Nazis and the Beginnings of an American Tradition

The 1930s ended with little meaningful action taken against domestic Nazis in the United States. In retrospect, it is doubtful that the German-American Bund, the Silver Shirts, or any of the other paramilitary groups posed any real threat to American democracy. The political system ultimately proved to have considerable resilience. The economic reforms of the New Deal and the acceptance of government economic regulation by the Supreme Court persuaded the vast majority of Americans that the established political system was capable of responding to a major crisis, thereby undercutting the appeal of radical groups.[99]

The problem of the domestic Nazi groups did have a significant and lasting effect on American thinking about hate speech. Most important, it brought the question of free speech for antidemocratic groups to the forefront of national attention. The ACLU's response, the 1934 statement *Shall We Defend Free Speech for Nazis?* framed the debate in terms of protecting First Amendment rights and eventually shaped the course of constitutional law.

The 1934 New Jersey race hate law was eventually struck down by the New Jersey Supreme Court on First Amendment grounds. The decision was an important milestone in the growth of American policy. Equally important, the almost complete nonuse of the law dramatized one of the enduring problems with hate speech legislation: along with the few other measures that appeared over the years, it was rarely if ever used. For all practical purposes such laws were hortatory statements that had no effect on expressions of racial prejudice. Finally, the case of the House Un-American Activities Committee dramatized how a measure designed to attack one hate group could easily be used against other groups, with devastating and lasting damage to individual liberties.

4   The Hateful and the Hated: The Jehovah's Witnesses and the Emergence of a National Policy

Toward a National Policy

In the early 1940s a national policy on hate speech began to emerge, its central thrust being a broad commitment to the protection of offensive speech. Grounded in the First Amendment as interpreted by the Supreme Court, it was truly national, overriding the patchwork of state and local laws and practices. This new policy was still only partially formed by the end of World War II; several important ambiguities and unanswered questions remained. Nonetheless, the general outlines were clear and would set the direction for the development of American law in the future.

At this critical juncture, moreover, American policy diverged radically from international trends. Laws prohibiting hate speech, or what was generally referred to as racial and religious propaganda, were enacted by most other countries.[1] These laws followed the mandate of the various international statements on human rights issued after the war. Article 7 of the Universal Declaration of Human Rights, adopted by the United Nations in 1948, stated that "All [people] are equal before the law" and "are entitled to equal protection against any discrimination in violation of this Declaration and against any incitement to such discrimination." Subsequent human rights agreements included more specific prohibitions on offensive racial and religious expression,[2] codifying the similar provisions of pre–World War II European anti-Fascist laws. World War II was a turning point because of the Holocaust. Reaction to the destruction of six million Jews fueled an international movement to ensure that it would never happen again.

The American response to the war and the Holocaust differed in response to unique domestic circumstances. The most important result was the birth of the modern civil rights movement as a broad-based interracial coalition. Persecution of the European Jews heightened American awareness of racism at home. On the one hand, African American leaders adopted a more militant posture: asked to fight for justice abroad, they demanded freedom at home under the slogan of the "Double V." A. Philip Randolph threatened a march on Washington to demand a federal fair employment practices law – a show of militancy that was unthinkable just a few years earlier.[3] A series of racial riots in 1943 jolted many white Americans into realizing that racial discrimination not only contradicted the ideal of equality but could threaten the war effort. A number of predominantly white organizations joined the NAACP's stepped-up litigation program. These included the ACLU, the major Jewish civil rights groups, many Protestant and Catholic organizations, and the more progressive labor unions. The United States also joined the United Nations and became its principal supporter. This support for international cooperation was a complete reversal of the opposition to membership in the League of Nations following World War I.

On the question of hate speech, however, Americans drew a different lesson from the Nazi experience. Primarily, it heightened their consciousness about the importance of constitutional protection for persecuted minorities. The Supreme Court's new concern for protection began in 1937. To a great extent American thinking about constitutional rights was stimulated by the example of totalitarianism abroad, in Germany and the Soviet Union.[4]

The single most important influence on American attitudes, law, and policy on the hate speech question was a unique domestic event: a national crisis over the Jehovah's Witnesses. A small but aggressive and highly offensive group, the Witnesses posed the hate speech question in a way that had special relevance for American constitutional law: How should society respond to offensive religious propaganda when the source of that vilification was itself a persecuted religious minority? This invoked the free exercise clause of the First Amendment and stimulated the development of a separate body of First Amendment law.

The National Crisis over the Witnesses

It probably surprises most Americans today to learn that the Jehovah's Witnesses were the cause of a national crisis during the late 1930s and 1940s. The Witnesses today are a gentle and passive lot, noticed mainly for their Kingdom Hall places of worship and their occasional door-to-door canvassing. They are among the least assertive of all the evangelical religious groups in the country. For more than a decade, however, they were the most hated group in America, the target of legal restrictions and mob violence.[5] Rising public hostility finally exploded in an orgy of vigilante violence in 1940. In Maine a mob of 2,500 burned down a Kingdom Hall and went on to attack the homes of individual Witnesses. Reportedly the entire adult population of Litchfield, Illinois, mobilized to attack a group of Witnesses. And in Nebraska one member of the sect was kidnapped and castrated.[6] Long before this outburst of violence, the Witnesses were the target of innumerable state and local laws designed to restrict their proselytizing.

Challenges to the persecution of the Witnesses produced a long series of Supreme Court cases: one scholar counted fifty from the 1930s to the 1980s, almost all of which the Witnesses won.[7] With the possible exception of African Americans, no other group in American history has made as great a contribution to constitutional law as the Jehovah's Witnesses, expanding the protection of individual rights in a number of important areas.[8] Their attorney, Hayden Covington, rivals the NAACP's Thurgood Marshall for the number of landmark cases argued and won in the Supreme Court. The most celebrated case was the 1943 Supreme Court decision upholding the right of their children to refuse to salute the flag. Justice Robert Jackson's opinion in the *Barnette* case is one of the most eloquent statements on behalf of freedom of individual conscience.[9]

The Jehovah's Witness cases, involving a group that was simultaneously an object of hate and a source of hateful propaganda, forced the United States to come to grips with the question of hate speech. The general thrust of the cases was a strong affirmation of the rights of unpopular minority groups.

Before examining those cases in detail, we should note one seeming paradox. One of the Witness cases gave constitutional sanction to the restriction of offensive speech. The 1942 *Chaplinsky* decision held that certain "fighting words" were not protected by the First Amendment.

This included words "which by their very utterance inflict injury or tend to incite an immediate breach of the peace." Curiously, however, *Chaplinsky* did not lead to the enactment of state and federal laws restricting hate speech. If anything, the trend was in the opposite direction. Few laws were enacted, and the Supreme Court steadily narrowed the application of the fighting words doctrine.[10] One of the keys to understanding the development of the hate speech issue is unraveling the paradox of *Chaplinsky*: Why did American law and policy reject the alternative offered by the "fighting words" decision and, instead, move in the direction of greater protection of offensive speech?

ORIGINS OF CRISIS: THE WITNESSES AS A HATE GROUP

The Jehovah's Witnesses were a religious sect, sincere in their beliefs. But they also constituted a hate group, mounting vicious attacks on other religions, particularly the Roman Catholic church. In their wildly paranoid vision of the world, Satan was everywhere: in business, politics, and religion. Most of all, he manifested himself in organized religious groups. Since the Witnesses believed they were the true people of God, it logically followed that other religions were "imposters" or "racketeers" – their favorite epithets for these alleged agents of Satan. Since the Catholic church was the largest and oldest Christian denomination, it was necessarily the biggest "racket" of all. Witness leader Joseph Rutherford devoted an entire book titled *Enemies* to the purported evils of the Catholic church, denouncing it as an old "harlot," with a "long and bloody record as [an] inquisitionist" and a "filthy record."[11]

To a lesser extent the Witnesses also targeted Jews for attack. Before 1931 they believed that Jews had a special relationship with Jehovah, but in their newly aggressive posture they asserted their own claim as the chosen people of God and denied any similar claims by Jews.[12] The Witnesses' animosity toward Jews differed from conventional anti-Semitism, however, and was never as dominant a theme as their hatred for Catholics.

The crisis over the Witnesses was the result of a fortuitous conjunction of events: changes in the sect's doctrine and tactics; a revolution on the Supreme Court; and the rise of totalitarianism abroad. In the early 1930s the Witnesses underwent a profound organizational transformation. Until then they had been a relatively passive religious sect, little different from the many others that dot the American religious landscape. Several leaders had been prosecuted and imprisoned during World War I for their opposition to the war, but in this respect they were no different from other religious and political dissenters.[13] In the 1920s there were a few isolated controversies over their childrens' refusal to salute the flag in public schools, but none of these incidents rose to the level of a major controversy, and all passed quickly.[14]

In the 1930s, however, Rutherford reorganized the group, establishing a theocracy under his centralized authority.[15] In terms of doctrine, he refashioned the group's self-image, emphasizing its status as the chosen people of God. Each member was considered a minister with a responsibility to spread the faith. (Their belief that each member was a minister, and thus eligible for conscientious objector status, led to a major confrontation with the government over selective service during wartime.) Tactically, Rutherford launched an aggressive proselytizing campaign to carry their message to the world and to recruit new members. This effort was extraordinarily successful, with membership rising from about 400,000 in the late 1920s to almost two million by the late 1930s and over four million by the early 1940s.[16] Clearly, the Witnesses' promise of salvation in a world overwhelmed by evil struck a responsive chord in a certain segment of American society.

RELIGIOUS TACTICS AND LEGAL CONFRONTATION
The Witnesses' tactics were irritating even when they were not blatantly offensive. Seeking to confront the heathen face-to-face, groups would descend on a community en masse in what they called their "locust" strategy. They would go door-to-door or confront individuals on the street in what they called "street-corner witnessing." Even had their message been inoffensive, many people would have found their actions a nuisance. The hateful attacks on Catholics and other religions triggered a bitterly hostile response. These tactics, it should be noted, were as willfully provocative as those of the domestic Nazi groups: deliberately going into neighborhoods they knew were predominantly Catholic; confronting people face-to-face with a message they knew insulted the hearers' religion. The Witnesses aroused a more hostile response than the Nazi groups because they impinged on the consciousness of Americans to a much greater degree. Their membership eventually reached into the millions and was spread across the entire country.

The result was a massive confrontation with authorities throughout the United States. In addition to vigilante violence, local communities sought to restrain the Witnesses through the law. One set of confrontations arose from laws designed to restrict their proselytizing, some enacted in direct response to their actions. A second set arose from the arrest and conviction of Witnesses for breach of the peace or related offenses. Both raised questions about the scope of free speech, the press, and assembly and resulted in landmark Supreme Court decisions. A third set of cases involved the refusal of Witness schoolchildren to participate in compulsory flag salute exercises. Although not directly related to the hate speech issue, the *Barnette* decision affirming the rights of the Witnesses was an extremely important benchmark in the protection of minority rights.

The Witnesses before the Supreme Court

In the first important Jehovah's Witness case, *Lovell v. Griffin* (1938), the Supreme Court struck down a Griffin, Georgia, ordinance requiring a permit for the distribution of "any literature." The Court ruled the ordinance an unconstitutional violation of freedom of the press.[17] The following year, in *Schneider v. Irvington*, the Court struck down ordinances in four states forbidding the distribution of leaflets in public places.[18] The Court held that the nominally legitimate purpose of keeping the streets clean was not a sufficient justification for such a broad restriction on freedom of communication.

Neither of these two early cases dealt with the content of the Witnesses' message, even though distaste for that message was the real reason for the original arrests and convictions. They were, however, important milestones in the development of First Amendment law. The Court began to establish the principle that in a free society freedom of expression has a higher priority than public order. Content-neutral laws designed to promote such seemingly worthy goals as maintaining public order were invalid if they restricted freedom of expression. That these cases involved an unpopular group dramatized for the Court the extent to which the majority could use seemingly innocuous laws to suppress ideas or groups it did not like. This principle was a radical departure from the law and practice of just a few years earlier, and it marked the ascendancy of First Amendment values in American life.

The Court had addressed content-based restrictions in cases involving Communists. In two important 1937 cases, *De Jonge v. Oregon*[19] and *Herndon v. Lowry*,[20] the Court struck down those restrictions and expanded First Amendment protection of an unpopular political group. In a 1939 decision involving labor union organizers (*Hague v. CIO*), the Court established a broadly protective freedom of assembly on public property, ending the historical suppression of the assembly rights of unpopular groups by local authorities.[21] Another Witness case established a First Amendment right to engage in door-to-door solicitation.[22] In one of the few major cases the Witnesses lost, the Court held that local authorities could establish reasonable restrictions on the "time, place, and manner" of public assemblies.[23] This was less of a defeat for the Witnesses than it might appear, however, because the Court ruled that such restrictions had to be applied "without unfair discrimination."

The series of decisions affirming freedom of speech and assembly on a content-neutral basis was a major breakthrough in establishing the principle of tolerance. In narrow legalistic terms, the decisions said that authorities could no longer suppress groups and ideas they did not like: local regulatory power had been preempted by a higher constitutional authority. In a broader sense, however, the decisions declared that even the most unpopular groups belonged to America. They too had a right to express their views and even to use public property for that purpose.

Belonging to America: The Free Exercise of Religion

The first important case directly involving the content of the Witnesses' message, with direct implications for the hate speech issue, was *Cantwell v. Connecticut* in 1940.[24] Newton Cantwell and his two sons had deliberately gone into a predominantly Catholic neighborhood in New Haven, Connecticut, and broadcast recorded excerpts from Rutherford's anti-Catholic *Enemies* on a portable record player. Inevitably some neighborhood residents were offended and a confrontation ensued. One person later said he had felt like hitting Cantwell, but no actual violence resulted; in fact the Cantwells moved on when asked to. Nonetheless, the police arrested them. They were eventually convicted of disturbing the peace even though there was no evidence that any member of the family had committed any violent act. The charge, in short, was based entirely on the allegedly provocative nature of their message.[25]

The Court overturned Jesse Cantwell's conviction, holding that his activities were protected by the free exercise of religion clause of the First

Amendment. That some of the audience might find the content of his message offensive was not sufficient to restrict Cantwell's religious freedom. The Court tried to define as narrowly as possible exactly what kind of activity was constitutionally protected. It found that although the content of *Enemies* "not unnaturally aroused animosity," the Cantwells' behavior did not constitute a clear and present danger to any state interest. They had committed no assault, threatened no bodily harm, and committed "no intentional discourtesy [and] no personal abuse." Instead, they were simply trying to get their listeners – whom the Court characterized as "willing" – to buy a book or contribute money to support what they believed to be the "true religion."

The Court walked a very fine line. To say that the Witnesses engaged in "no intentional discourtesy" was true only in a very narrow sense. Although it was indeed true that they had sought permission to play *Enemies* and had left when asked to, they had deliberately chosen to enter a predominantly Catholic neighborhood to spread a message they knew to be virulently anti-Catholic. To attack someone's religion as the Witnesses did was discourteous to say the least, and at worst deliberately abusive. Nonetheless, in a passage with the greatest relevance to the hate speech issue, the Court held that "in the realm of religious faith, and in that of political belief, sharp differences arise." In many instances members of one faith resort "to exaggeration [and] to vilification" of other faiths. The right to express one's views, however offensive, was "essential" to the development of enlightened public opinion. A few months later the New Jersey supreme court would quote this passage in striking down that state's race hate law.[26]

With *Cantwell*, the Court incorporated the free exercise of religion clause of the First Amendment into the Fourteenth Amendment, extending its protection to the states. This continued the Court's process of selectively incorporating the various provisions of the Bill of Rights into the Fourteenth Amendment.[27] In terms of constitutional law doctrine, *Cantwell* was a major breakthrough, creating a new protection for the free exercise of religion.

This new constitutional right had broad ramifications for the meaning of American society. The message of *Cantwell* was unequivocally one of inclusion. Religious minorities were entitled to full participation in American society, no matter how strange or offensive they might be to the majority. This principle preempted the centuries-old American tradition of suppressing religious dissenters. In place of a coercive, conformist vision of American society, the Court substituted a tolerant, pluralist vision. In terms of the long-range development of American society, it happened that it was the Supreme Court that gave practical meaning to the principle of tolerance. Thus the protection of group rights, in the sense of inclusion in the larger community, was achieved through litigation over individual rights.

By the same token, the later Court decisions regarding the establishment clause of the First Amendment contained a similar message of inclusion. The decisions outlawing prayer and Bible reading in school had the effect of disestablishing Protestantism as the quasi-official religion of the United States.[28] Since the founding of the Republic, local schools had been dominated by the Protestant majority, which assumed that religious instruction was an integral part of education. Being the majority, Protestants further assumed they that had a right to control the curriculum, which meant incorporating their religious views into it. The imposition of Protestantism was, in fact, one of the main reasons the American Catholic Church hierarchy decided to create a network of parochial schools. The establishment clause decisions that removed formal religious practices from the schools conveyed a message of inclusion in the sense that public education was neutral and non-Protestants could not be subjected to religious practices that were not their own. As with other constitutional rights, the protection of group interests was achieved through litigation based on individual rights.

The "Fighting Words" Exception

The major exception to the expansion of freedom of expression under the Roosevelt Court was the 1942 *Chaplinsky* decision that produced the famous "fighting words" doctrine.[29] Also a Witness case, *Chaplinsky* marked another appearance by Newton Cantwell before the Supreme Court. He and other Witnesses had descended on a New Hampshire town in their standard fashion to proselytize among the heathen. As happened so often, a confrontation with local authorities ensued. At one point Chaplinsky called a police officer "a God-damned racketeer" and "a damned Fascist." For this he was arrested and convicted under a state law making it a crime to "address any offensive, derisive or annoying word to any other person who is lawfully in any street or other public place, nor call him by any offensive or derisive name." "Racketeer" was a standard Witness epithet for leaders of other religions. The Witnesses also frequently called their opponents "Fascists" because, like Jews, they were being persecuted by the Nazis in Germany. In the context of World War II, moreover, the term "Fascist" was highly offensive to most Americans.

In a unanimous opinion, the Court sustained the conviction. Justice Murphy, normally one of the strongest libertarians on the Court, offered a two-tiered analysis of the First Amendment. Although most speech was protected, he wrote, "There are certain well-defined and narrowly limited classes of speech, the prevention and punishment of which have never been thought to raise any Constitutional problem. These include the lewd and obscene, the profane, the libelous, and the insulting or 'fighting' words." Murphy went on to define two kinds of fighting words: words that "by their very utterance inflict injury," and words that "tend to incite an immediate breach of the peace."[30]

Both parts of Murphy's definition of fighting words had implications for offensive racial or religious speech. The first swept very broadly. The category of words that "by their very utterance inflict injury" potentially included virtually any epithet that gave offense, if not many statements of fact or opinion that were merely embarrassing. Murphy did not define injury, but it could be interpreted to include psychological harm and injury to one's reputation or to the reputation of a group. The second class of fighting words, those tending to incite an immediate breach of the peace, was narrower but still had important implications for the hate speech issue. Many of the actions of controversial groups were and are deliberately provocative. Pre–World War II domestic Nazi groups paraded in or near predominantly Jewish neighborhoods, knowing full well that this might provoke a hostile reaction. The Jehovah's Witnesses had deliberately entered Catholic neighborhoods to broadcast their anti-Catholic message. The underlying question was whether one person's right to speak could be restricted because of threatened (or actual) violence by the audience. Often referred to as the "heckler's veto," this issue became the subject of an important series of Court cases from the late 1940s through the 1960s.

As I indicated at the beginning of this chapter, the real long-term significance of *Chaplinsky* was that it did not shape the direction of the law. Subsequent decisions, which I shall examine in the next chapter, greatly limited both prongs of the fighting words definition. When we pair the *Cantwell* and *Chaplinsky* decisions, then, it is evident that in 1940–42 American law and policy were still very fluid. Although the Court had clearly embarked on a libertarian course, it was still uncertain about the scope of First Amendment protection of offensive speech. At this point there was no necessary reason the law would develop as it eventually did. The central question, then, is why it chose one path and not the other.

Belonging to America: The Flag Salute Controversy

The most famous controversy over the Jehovah's Witnesses, and the one best remembered today, involved their objections to compulsory flag salutes.[31] It eventually resulted in one of the most eloquent defenses of constitutional protection of freedom of individual conscience. Justice Robert Jackson's justly famous opinion in *Barnette* has been quoted many times: "If there is any fixed star in our constitutional constellation, it is that no official, high or petty, can prescribe what shall be orthodox in politics, nationalism, religion, or other matters of opinion or force citizens to confess by word or act their faith therein."[32]

Although the *Barnette* case did not involve hate speech per se, it had (and continues to have) direct relevance to the question of unpopular groups and offensive behavior. Perhaps more than any other decision, it committed the Court, and ultimately the country, to the principle of constitutional protection for even the most hated minority group.

ORIGINS OF THE CONTROVERSY

The facts of the flag salute controversy and the background of the *Barnette* decision may be summarized briefly. The issue originated in the Jehovah's Witnesses' interpretation of Exodus 20:3–5, "You shall have no other gods before me" and "You shall not make yourself a graven image, or any likeness of anything. . . . You shall not bow down to them or serve them." The Witnesses came to believe that this injunction prohibited saluting the national flag.

There were a few scattered conflicts over compulsory flag salutes in the 1920s. One scholar identified ten cases in eight states between 1918 and 1929.[33] Not all of them involved the Witnesses; Mennonites and a few other small sects held a similar interpretation of the relevant biblical passages. For two reasons, none of these conflicts developed into a major confrontation or court test. First, the Witnesses did not attach great importance to the passage from Exodus. It was an issue, but not a fighting issue. Second, the point was not that important to most school administrators either. The rules on flag salutes in school existed only in some jurisdictions; many were vague and did not compel participation; and many school officials were willing to accommodate students and parents who objected.

All that changed in the 1930s. The new assertiveness of the Witnesses after 1931 included a deep sense of alienation from mainstream society and a felt need to resist any compulsion by civil authority. As the decade progressed, a vicious circle of alienation, conflict, paranoia, and greater resistance developed. Their offensive tactics bred hostility and legal sanctions, which only strengthened their commitment to resisting civil authority. By the late 1930s the persecution of Witnesses in Nazi Germany heightened the sense of persecution among adherents in this country. The escalating militancy of the Witnesses stiffened the resolve of local authorities to compel obedience from this small and obnoxious group. The anti-Catholic propaganda won the Witnesses no friends in communities with significant Catholic populations, nor did their mass proselytizing endear them to non-Catholics.

International events influenced the attitudes of local officials. With the world apparently headed for another global conflict, many Americans felt a need to reinforce patriotism and moral strength in the population. A convenient method was to require all schoolchildren to salute the flag, recite the Pledge of Allegience, and say a prayer each morning. Thus there was a spread of both compulsory flag salutes and religious practices in the late thirties. A similar desire to instill patriotism gave rise to compulsory loyalty oaths for teachers, which spread rapidly in the late 1930s. And in the same vein, Congress institutionalized the idea of "Americanism" by creating the House Un-American Activities Committee in 1938. In the minds of self-styled patriots, the promotion of Americanism logically required the exposure and extirpation of "un-Americanism."

GOBITIS: THE FIRST FLAG SALUTE CASE

The escalating militancy of both sides in the controversy was evident in the background of *Gobitis,* the first flag salute case decided by the Supreme Court. The parents of William and Lillian Gobitis had joined the Witnesses in 1931, as part of the initial surge in membership. A morning flag salute had been customary, but not necessarily compulsory, in the Minersville, Pennsylvania, schools since at least 1914. The Gobitises, however, did not decide that their faith required them to challenge it until 1935 when they heard sect leader Rutherford discuss the issue in a radio broadcast. After another Minersville child refused to participate, school officials obtained opinions from both the state department of public instruction and the attorney general permitting them to punish students who refused on grounds of insubordination. Armed with these opinions, the school board adopted a new policy requiring, for the first time, a flag salute by both teachers and students. At the same meeting, the Gobitis children were expelled. The Gobitises attributed these actions to persecution by the two members of the school board who were Catholic.[34]

Challenging the expulsions in federal district court, the Gobitises won a stunning victory. The judge ruled that the compulsory flag salute was "not a reasonable method of teaching civics" and that the children's refusal did not threaten public safety. More significantly, compelling them to "render a lip service of loyalty in a manner which conflicts with their sincere religious convictions" was a "totalitarian idea."[35]

The reference to totalitarianism was particularly significant. In a number of important civil liberties cases in the late 1930s and early 1940s, judges explained their defense of individual rights with pointed references to foreign totalitarianism. In the landmark *Hague v. CIO* case, which established a broad protection for freedom of assembly, district court judge William Clark ended his 1938 opinion with disparaging references to both Nazi Germany and the Soviet Union. He observed, "Ultimately, Soviet Russia will not be judged by how much bread it has given its people . . . but by how much freedom, self-respect, equality, truth, and human kindness it has brought into the world."[36] As so much of the rest of the world descended into authoritarian regimes of both the Right and the Left, Americans gained a clearer sense of the special capacity of American constitutionalism to protect the rights of individuals, and particularly of powerless individuals.

The Supreme Court, however, reversed the lower courts in *Gobitis* and upheld the power of school authorities in an eight to one decision. Writing for the majority, Justice Felix Frankfurter rejected the religious freedom argument and held that "conscientious scruples" did not "relieve the individual from obedience to a general law not aimed at the promotion or restriction of religious beliefs." Only Justice Harlan Fiske Stone dissented, arguing that the law in question "does more than suppress freedom of speech and . . . religion"; it "seeks to coerce these children to express a sentiment which . . . violates their deepest religious convictions."[37]

The reaction to the *Gobitis* decision was immediate, national in scope, and violent. A wave of vigilante violence swept the country. Groups of Witnesses were attacked and beaten in Maine, Texas, Arkansas, and elsewhere. In Litchfield, Illinois, the entire adult population attacked a group of sixty Witnesses. In Maine a mob of 2,500 attempted to seize six Witnesses in the local jail and, failing, attacked and burned the local Kingdom Hall. In Nebraska a Witness was beaten and castrated. A mob of one thousand attacked the Kingdom Hall in Klamath Falls, Oregon.[38] It would not be fair to blame the Supreme Court for this outburst of savagery; considerable violence had been directed at the Witnesses for some years. Nonetheless, the *Gobitis* decision did seem to trigger a dramatic escalation. If there is any truth to Justice Louis Brandeis's argument that the law is a great teacher – a point he made in his famous dissent in the 1928 *Olmstead* case – it seems that in the *Gobitis* decision the Supreme Court sent the country the message that this particular group did not deserve the protection of the law.[39]

The decision also encouraged state and local authorities to impose more stringent flag salute requirements. Mississippi passed a new law in 1942; the Oklahoma superintendent of schools issued a new interpretation of the existing requirement, authorizing expulsion of those who refused to participate; the attorney general in the state of Washington reversed an earlier opinion that had advised school officials to avoid expelling noncomplying students. Congress, meanwhile, passed a law in 1942 imposing a code of conduct for all citizens during the Pledge of Allegiance. It required that citizens "will always show full respect to the flag when the pledge is being given by merely standing at attention, men removing the headdress."[40]

REVERSAL: *BARNETTE*

The *Gobitis* decision settled nothing, and the flag salute controversy continued to rage in the streets and in the courts. Then one of the most remarkable events in the entire history of the Supreme Court occurred. In an unrelated Jehovah's Witness case, three justices – Hugo Black,

William O. Douglas, and Frank Murphy – publicly confessed error, announcing that they had been wrong in *Gobitis*.[41] This set the stage for another Supreme Court test of the flag salute requirement. The second thoughts of Black, Douglas, and Murphy did not occur in a vacuum. Reaction to *Gobitis* in the press and the legal community had been very negative. Also, three state supreme courts ruled in favor of the Witnesses under their state constitutions.[42]

Out of many post-*Gobitis* cases, a case from West Virginia finally reached the Supreme Court in the spring of 1943. In a dramatic reversal, the Court overruled *Gobitis* eight to one with only Justice Frankfurter dissenting. Writing for the majority, the normally conservative Justice Robert Jackson upheld constitutional protection for individual conscience.[43]

The decision was remarkable not just for its substance but for the context in which it was delivered. The justices of the Court surely understood what they were doing when they chose June 14, Flag Day, to rule that a hated and persecuted minority group had a right to conscientiously refuse to salute the flag. It was additionally significant that the United States was then in the midst of a two-front world war. And as of June 1943 the outcome of that war was not yet certain, either in Europe or in Asia. The Court said, in effect, that there was no wartime exception to the right of freedom of conscience. Even in the midst of war, there was a constitutional right not to be compelled to salute the national symbol.

More than any other single decision in the entire history of the Court, *Barnette* affirmed the principle of inclusiveness. The meaning of American democracy was tolerance for even the most obnoxious groups. More clearly here than in any other decision, the Court rejected the historical tradition of a coercive conformity where everyone could be compelled to publicly affirm respect for the national symbol. Most of the Witness cases beginning in 1937 had been tending in that direction: *Barnette* was a fitting and logical culmination. The special contribution of the Witnesses to the hate speech issue was that the principle of inclusiveness, of toleration of small and offensive minorities, also meant tolerance of hate speech. The Witness cases marked the birth of a national policy on hate speech.

5 The Curious Rise and Fall of Group Libel in America, 1942-1952

Paradox: Failure out of Success

In the years between 1942 and 1952 the idea of restricting hate speech enjoyed a brief moment of favor. Until the flurry of support for campus speech codes in the 1980s, this was the only period in American history when such restrictions received serious consideration. The specific proposal called for group libel legislation extending the traditional law of criminal libel to statements about racial and religious groups.[1] Group libel legislation received intellectual backing from some influential voices; it was advocated by a few civil rights groups, debated in Congress, and enacted into law by several states and cities.

Most important, in 1952 the Supreme Court upheld the constitutionality of a 1917 Illinois group libel law.[2] For the advocates of restrictions on hate speech, the Court's decision in *Beauharnais* was a great victory. Justice Felix Frankfurter's majority opinion granted virtually everything they could have hoped for. Yet something curious happened. Instead of spurring a wave of group libel laws across the country as might have been expected, the *Beauharnais* decision produced nothing. It received an extremely lukewarm reception, and the concept of group libel was soon repudiated even by its strongest supporters. The American Jewish Congress, which had been its principal advocate, repudiated it eight years after *Beauharnais*,[3] and in 1961 the state of Illinois repealed the 1917 law itself.

The repudiation of group libel laws following the Supreme Court victory is a paradox that raises a number of questions. The first is why success at the highest level of the law should produce a contrary result. Why did group libel disappear just as it won its greatest victory? This chapter and the next argue that several factors account for this result. First, support for group libel legislation, although stronger than at any other period in American history, was actually rather weak. Second, and far more important, virtually all civil rights groups chose not to make it a priority. As I argued in chapter 1, it is the lack of an effective advocate that accounts for the failure of hate speech restrictions to gain any ground in the United States.

The important question is why the major civil rights groups not only were uninterested in group libel legislation but actively opposed it. The principal advances in civil rights were achieved through Supreme Court decisions expanding the scope of individual rights. The major civil rights groups came to understand that any exception to the seamless fabric of individual rights, which group libel represented, threatened the entire structure. One critical element of the civil rights movement, which had direct ramifications for the hate speech issue, was that activity on behalf of racial equality often involved provocative and offensive tactics by civil rights groups themselves.[4] The need to protect such activity became a major concern of civil rights leaders.

A second question involves the uniqueness of American law and policy in an international context. After World War II the United States diverged radically from the rest of the world on the hate speech question. Just as group libel laws disappeared in this country, other countries were adopting such restrictions, in accord with the letter and spirit of the various international human rights statements that emerged after the war.[5] How and why did the United States diverge from the standards of the rest of the world on this issue? The question is all the more intriguing because the various international statements were modeled on the American Bill of Rights. As I argue later in this chapter, they are written bills of human rights, defined in terms of individual rights, with particular emphasis on the American-style rights of freedom of speech, the press, and assembly, equality, and due process of law. It appears, then, that the rest of the world adopted the general American approach to protecting individual rights but took a very different path on the specific issue of hate speech.

The Impact of World War II: Group Libel's Brief Moment

For a few years after World War II the idea of restricting offensive racial and religious speech received serious consideration in the United States. Proposals included state group libel laws criminalizing the defamation of groups and a federal law barring hate propaganda from the United States mails. In the end very little legislation was enacted, but the debate provides some revealing insight into why these proposals received so little support. There is no question that the war and the Holocaust spurred interest in group libel legislation. Anti-Semitism stood exposed not merely as a hateful idea but as the mainspring of the most horrific event in modern history. For some people it seemed obvious that restricting hateful ideas was the proper thing to do in a civilized society. The interesting question is why so few people in the United States accepted this argument.

"DEMOCRACY AND DEFAMATION":
DAVID RIESMAN AND GROUP LIBEL

The most important statement in support of restricting offensive racial and religious speech was a three-part series of articles by David Riesman in the *Columbia Law Review,* published in 1942.[6] Fifty years later these articles are still regularly cited as the principal authority on the subject. Riesman is known today as one of the most prominent American sociologists and author of the best-selling book *The Lonely Crowd* (1950). Sociology, however, was Riesman's second career: his first was as a very successful legal scholar. He clerked for Supreme Court justice Louis Brandeis and taught at the University of Buffalo Law School. The group libel articles expressed his growing discontent with traditional precedent-based jurisprudence and represented a search for a sociologically based alternative.[7]

Riesman pursued the line of thinking charted by Karl Loewenstein five years earlier.[8] Both argued that the primary threat to freedom in the world was Fascism; that Fascist movements sought to undermine democracy by exploiting its commitment to tolerance and free speech; and that democracies had both a right and a duty to curb this threat. The five years that passed between Loewenstein's and Riesman's articles, however, made an enormous difference. By 1942 the world was engulfed in war, Germany stood astride virtually all of continental Europe and much of the Soviet

Union, and the threat to European Jewry was far clearer than before, to the extent that some people now recognized the Nazi plan for genocide. What Loewenstein had described as a serious threat to freedom could now be seen as a clear and present calamity. Riesman was blunt and unequivocal about his basic position. He concluded with the declaration that recent "German and French experience shows how [the law] can be a weapon for Fascism. There is no inherent reason why it cannot be a weapon for democracy."[9] In the midst of World War II and the struggle against totalitarianism, this was a powerful argument.

Riesman's argument consisted of several parts. The first installment was a traditional law review discussion of the law of libel and defamation, with reference to English and European as well as American law. The second was a historical survey of Fascist movements in Germany and France and how they had taken advantage of democratic freedoms to both disrupt democracy and incite group hatred through defamation of Jews and other groups. This section followed Loewenstein's earlier analysis, but with the advantage of hindsight.

The innovative aspect of Riesman's argument was his sociologically based analysis of the role of public opinion in modern society, which appeared in the third installment. Drawing on the work of other prominent social scientists (many of whom were also responding to European Fascism), Riesman argued that in mass society public opinion could easily be manipulated. The mass media played a far more important role in influencing public opinion than in older societies, while the influence of intermediate institutions such as the family, kinship circles, religious institutions, and inherited ideas and values was greatly weakened. Riesman argued that mass society rendered inappropriate the traditional legalistic approach to resolving conflicts over libel and defamation through abstract, universalist standards. Society was both heterogeneous and rapidly changing, so that "no single normative standard governs the community."[10]

As an alternative, Riesman proposed a contextualized standard for judicial decision making that would be informed by social science research. A contextualized approach holds that a word has different meanings and effects depending on the time, place, speaker, and audience. "The identical words, in the mouths of different persons," Riesman wrote, "can carry a radically different weight."[11] He illustrated his point by arguing that calling a political candidate in New York City anti-Semitic would be "clearly devastating" and therefore defamatory under the law.[12] The same charge in another city where the Jewish vote was not so crucial would be less damaging and therefore not defamatory.

To determine whether a particular charge was defamatory, Riesman continued, courts should engage social scientists to examine the social context. They could assess, for example, the reputation of the group in question, the power of a particular news medium, and so on. Thus if Fascists were found to be held in universal contempt in a particular community, calling someone a Fascist would be defamatory. If a newspaper had a high circulation and if one of its columnists was very influential, then published statements by him could be defamatory in that context.[13] Riesman cited a recent New York City case where a local labor union had referred to an employer as a Fascist and a "Hitlerite." He argued that the statement was indeed defamatory (although the New York supreme court ruled that it was not) and that the labor union, a strong craft union in a "strong union town," did not need judicial protection against costly damage suits.[14]

We should reject the temptation to cynically dismiss Riesman's proposal as a form of make-work for social scientists (even though, taken at face value, it would indeed provide abundant employment for sociologists and psychologists). Instead, we should regard it as a serious attempt to think about the impact of speech on society and the role of the law in promoting both democracy and human values. Riesman's contextualized approach to defamation was a more elaborate and sophisticated statement of the idea Loewenstein put forth in 1937. Following Loewenstein, Riesman criticized the absolutist approach to First Amendment issues for disregarding the practical consequences of words. He offered a fact-finding process for determining the nature and degree of harm in particular contexts.

Riesman's contextualized approach to defamation did not take hold in American law. In fact the law developed in just the opposite direction, toward a universal, content-neutral standard rather than a particularistic, fact-based one.[15]

Arguments for a contextualized approach reappeared in the 1980s. Some advocates of hate speech laws argued, for example, that an African American's calling a white person a "honkie" was less harmful than a white person's calling an African American a "nigger" – and consequently that the latter but not the former should be subject to criminal penalties. Another advocate of hate speech laws argued that the offensiveness of the term "Zionist" depended on whether it was uttered by an oppressed person such as a Palestinian or by a member of a powerful group.[16]

STATE GROUP LIBEL LEGISLATION

At the time Riesman wrote in 1942, there were only a handful of state group libel laws. The 1934 New Jersey race hate law had been declared unconstitutional by the state supreme court only the year before. The New York legislature had considered but rejected a similar law. A West Virginia law applied only to offensive movies or theatrical productions, and a Connecticut law applied only to commercial advertisements.[17] The oldest law in existence was a 1917 Illinois statute prohibiting the manufacture, sale, or distribution of material that "portrays depravity, criminality, unchastity, or lack of virtue of a class of citizens, of any race, color, creed or religion." I will discuss the 1952 Supreme Court decision holding the law constitutional later in this chapter.[18]

The most notable product of the war years was a Massachusetts group libel law passed in 1943, which imposed a fine of up to one thousand dollars, imprisonment of up to one year, or both for publishing "any false, written or printed material with the intent to maliciously promote hatred of any group of persons in the commonwealth because of race, color or religion." The law originated with a petition from Rabbi Joseph S. Shubow, head of the New England Division of the American Jewish Congress. Through the 1940s the American Jewish Congress was the leading advocate of group libel legislation.[19] In this respect it parted company with its allies in the emerging civil rights coalition. The other major Jewish groups, notably the American Jewish Committee, opposed such legislation, but at the hearings on the Massachusetts law no one spoke in opposition, and it passed without dissent in both houses.[20]

The Civil Liberties Union of Massachusetts (CLUM) privately confessed to being very ambivalent. It did not oppose the bill publicly, fearing that this would put it in "an extremely anomalous position." Apparently this meant it was afraid of alienating its normal civil rights allies. Instead, the CLUM planned to challenge the law in a test case at some point in the future.[21]

A test case never developed, however, apparently because there were no prosecutions.[22] Like the New Jersey race hate law and the 1917 Illinois group libel law, the Massachusetts hate speech law was a nullity – on the books but essentially unenforced. This appears to be the general fate of such legislation. A survey of European hate speech laws published in 1992, meanwhile, found a similar pattern of sporadic prosecutions, with many of them directed against unpopular political dissidents rather than against racists who were members of powerful majority groups.[23] Quite apart from the constitutional questions raised by such laws – the subject of virtually all the published commentary – this nonuse raises serious questions about their practical effect.

Group libel legislation made very little headway elsewhere in the country. The Rhode Island legislature passed a bill in 1944, only to have it vetoed by the governor.[24] Indiana passed a law in 1947 resembling the Illinois statute, making it an offense to "advocate . . . or disseminate hatred for or against a person, persons, or group of persons, . . . by reason of race, color, or religion which threatens to, tends to, or causes riot."[25] Similar bills were introduced in Ohio and other states, but virtually all failed to pass. Chicago, Cincinnati, Denver, and Houston had local group libel ordinances, while a few other cities had laws limited to offensive material in advertisements or entertainment productions.[26] A widely cited *Columbia Law Review* article offered a model statute authorizing courts to enjoin defamatory expression and to order the offending speaker or writer to issue a public retraction. This proposal found little if any support, however.[27]

PROPOSED FEDERAL GROUP LIBEL LEGISLATION

At the federal level a few bills were introduced in Congress to ban hate literature from the mails. Several aspects of this effort are notable. First, the proposals were extremely narrow in scope, limited to material sent through the mail. Second, support for them was very weak, and none ever came close to passage. Finally, the debate over the bills revealed the deep divisions among civil rights groups over the group libel issue.

The most serious effort in Congress to restrict hate speech arose in 1943–44. A bill (H.R. 2328) sponsored by the American Jewish Congress would have allowed the postmaster general to bar from the mails any material containing "defamatory and false statements" based on "race or religion" that would expose persons "to hatred, contempt, ridicule, or obloquy, or tend to cause such persons to be shunned or avoided, or to be injured in their business or occupation." The law would carry a penalty of up to five years in prison, a fine of up to five thousand dollars, or both.[28] An alternative, drafted by Louis Boudin for the National Lawyers

Guild, would have barred only anti-Semitic literature. Even the Jewish groups advocating group libel laws quickly rejected this as an embarrassing piece of special interest legislation.[29]

In support of H.R. 2328, Nathan Perlman, vice president of the American Jewish Congress and chairman of its Commission on Law and Social Action, cited the use of the mails by Nazi groups and pointed to a recent upsurge in anti-Semitic violence: attacks on individuals and the desecration of synagogues and Jewish cemeteries. Gerald L. K. Smith's emergence as a prominent public figure was another manifestation of an apparent rise in anti-Semitism. Perlman also argued that existing criminal libel laws were inadequate. He dismissed the objection that the law would violate the First Amendment and create a system of censorship, arguing that the post office had a basic right to control the mails. Nor would the law restrict discussion of racial and religious issues, he claimed, since it was limited to false and defamatory statements.[30]

The ACLU led the opposition to H.R. 2328, arguing that it authorized a dangerous form of government censorship of the mails.[31] Post office censorship was one of the ACLU's major battles at that time. Under existing law the postmaster general had virtually unlimited power to exclude from the mails anything he regarded as objectionable. During World War I the post office had used this authority to ban virtually all publications by critics of the government, including the National Civil Liberties Bureau, which it ruthlessly suppressed. The censorship of political material eased somewhat during the 1920s and 1930s, with the post office focusing more on sexually oriented materials. The ACLU had won a major victory in the government's attempt to censor a sex education pamphlet in 1929, and a twenty-year battle over nudist material began in 1934.[32] The ACLU saw H.R. 2328 as a serious step backward in its twenty-three year campaign against post office censorship, because it would give clearer statutory authority for administrative decisions to ban publications.

As the hearings were being held, the ACLU was representing *Esquire* magazine, which Postmaster General Frank Walker had banned on the grounds that it was not "of a public character." The *Esquire* case had roused considerable support from the literary community, which saw in it a very broad threat to freedom of expression. The Supreme Court's 1946 decision in the *Esquire* case (*Hannegan v. Esquire*) curbed the post office's arbitrary power and was regarded as a major breakthrough for freedom of expression.[33]

The ACLU organized an impressive group of experts to oppose H.R. 2328, including philosopher John Dewey, writer Franklin P. Adams, playwright Elmer Rice, NAACP leader Arthur Spingarn, and poet and literary critic Mark Van Doren.[34] It also coordinated testimony from the major civil rights organizations, including the NAACP, the American Jewish Committee, the National Council of Jewish Women, and the American Council of Christian Churches. Opposition from the NAACP and the American Jewish Committee was particularly important. This meant that the principal African American group and one of the three major Jewish civil rights groups, representing the natural constituents of the bill, actively opposed it.[35] The American Jewish Congress was virtually alone among the national civil rights organizations in supporting the bill. Other groups testifying on its behalf included the National Lawyers Guild and a number of local Jewish organizations and small leftist labor unions.[36]

The opposition of the NAACP was significant because twenty years earlier it had advocated banning Ku Klux Klan materials from the mail and had sought to ban showing of the film *Birth of a Nation* because of its racist content. Its changed attitude suggests that its leaders had been persuaded that the interests of African Americans were best advanced through a more absolutist protection of individual rights, including offensive speech.

Hearings on the bill introduced an alternative approach to controlling the use of the mail by hate groups. After presenting the ACLU position, attorney Morris L. Ernst offered his personal proposal to require all organizations using the mails to disclose the names of their officers and the sources of their finances.[37] Ernst's was a voice to be reckoned with. He was the most prominent anticensorship attorney in the country and had won the famous *Ulysses* case in 1933. He was the author of several popular books on censorship, was the first attorney to litigate issues of reproductive freedom, and served as an influential member of President Truman's 1947 Civil Rights Committee.[38] He had championed the idea of compulsory disclosure for several years, arguing that it would enhance the democratic process by making more information available to citizens.[39] With respect to hate literature, he believed that disclosure would expose the true political nature of a book or pamphlet. Someone receiving anti–civil rights literature in the mail, for example, could determine that it was generated by a right-wing or anti-Semitic organization. Ernst managed to persuade President Truman's Civil Rights Committee to recommend a federal disclosure law, but the idea never won any other significant backing.[40]

Ernst, of course, was not the first to advocate disclosure as a remedy for hate speech. The 1923 New York anti-Klan law went even further, requiring disclosure of the names of all members of certain organizations. In important respects, Ernst's proposal was far more limited and less threatening to individual rights. The purpose of disclosing the names of individual Klan members was to subject them to embarrassment, if not outright harassment. Ernst's proposal was limited to the names of officers and sources of finances.

Also with respect to the technique of exposure, there was one aspect of the support for H.R. 2328 that received no comment at the time but appears particularly significant in retrospect. Nathan Perlman of the American Jewish Congress based much of his argument about the domestic Nazi menace on reports by the House Un-American Activities Committee (HUAC). The inherent danger of using legislative investigations to expose unpopular groups was dramatized with cruel irony by the fact that Perlman's article on behalf of the proposed federal law was published in the *Lawyers Guild Review*.[41] Within just a few years, the Lawyers Guild itself would become a target of HUAC investigations and, branded as the "legal bulwark of the Communist Party," would be nearly destroyed.[42] Exposure of "unpopular" groups was a double-edged and deadly sword.

The 1944 hearings marked the high point of the effort to secure federal legislation on hate speech. Although occasional bills were introduced over the years, neither the restriction of mailing privileges nor Ernst's proposal for compulsory disclosure received any significant support. This did not represent a triumph of civil libertarian thinking in the Congress. Both houses of Congress were dominated by southern Democrats committed to segregation who, by virtue of seniority, controlled the key committees. It is worth remembering that the southern bloc had prevented the passage of a federal antilynching law since the 1930s and stopped the enactment of any meaningful federal civil rights legislation until 1964. They understood that any restriction on hate literature threatened segregationist thought. After the brief flurry of activity in the mid-1940s, proposals for federal restrictions on hate speech steadily declined and virtually disappeared by the early 1950s.[43]

International Developments on the Hate Speech Issue

THE INTERNATIONAL HUMAN RIGHTS MOVEMENT

Just as the idea of group libel legislation began to vanish from the American political scene, developments around the world were moving in a completely opposite direction. The Holocaust, together with an attack on colonialism, spurred an international commitment to promote human rights and, in particular, to combat racism. This commitment took the form of a series of declarations, covenants, and treaties on human rights. Between the end of World War II and the 1980s, more than forty such statements were promulgated: twenty-one United Nations documents, ten statements by the International Labor Organization, four European conventions, three relating to Latin America, and four relating to Africa and Asia. Not all of them addressed the question of free speech, but among those that did, the trend was in the direction of more explicit calls for restricting offensive racial and religious forms of expression.

These restrictions are intended to protect the rights of persecuted minorities. As Mary Ann Glendon argues, the distinctive feature of the post–World War II human rights movement is that "rights discourse has spread throughout the world."[44]

The movement toward the international protection of human rights was truly remarkable, with one commentator calling it a "revolution" in international law.[45] Traditionally, international law dealt with relations *between* nations, leaving *internal* issues as matters of national sovereignty. The post–World War II human rights movement, however, enunciated standards that should prevail within each country. Even more significant than the actual content of the various declarations – which I shall examine in a moment – is that they exist at all. Even though they may be honored more in the breach than in the observance, their mere existence represents a commitment to protecting human rights unprecedented in human history.

THE CONTROL OF OFFENSIVE RACIAL AND RELIGIOUS SPEECH

With respect to hate speech, the various international human rights statements embraced the concept of group libel. All affirmed freedom of speech for individuals but subjected it to certain limitations necessary for the general welfare. Most of the statements contained a specific prohibition on offensive racial and religious propaganda.

The original mandate for the protection of human rights was set forth in article 55 of the United Nations charter, declaring that the United Nations would promote "universal respect for, and observance of, human rights and fundamental freedoms for all without distinction as to race, sex, language, or religion." This general mandate has been elaborated in a series of subsequent documents. It is not necessary to examine them all here: for our purposes the three most relevant are the Universal Declaration of Human Rights, adopted on December 10, 1948, the 1966 International Covenant on Civil and Political Rights, and the International Convention on the Elimination of All Forms of Racial Discrimination, also adopted in 1966.

The Universal Declaration of Human Rights is the single most important document in the international human rights area. It includes a broad affirmation of freedom of expression and belief. Article 18 states, "Everyone has the right to freedom of thought, conscience and religion; this right includes freedom to change his religion or belief, and freedom, either alone or in community with others and in public or private, to manifest his religion or belief in teaching, practice, worship and observance." Article 19, meanwhile, declares, "Everyone has the right to freedom of opinion and expression; this right includes freedom to hold opinions without interference and to seek, receive and impart information and ideas through any media and regardless of frontiers."

The Universal Declaration goes on to state that none of the rights therein are absolute.[46] Article 29, paragraph 2, defines the scope of permissible limitations: "In the exercise of his rights and freedoms, everyone shall be subject only to such limitations as are determined by law solely for the purpose of securing due recognition and respect for the rights and freedoms of others and of meeting the just requirements of morality, public order and the general welfare in a democratic society." Article 30, meanwhile, says that no "state, group or person" has a right to "engage in any activity or to perform any act aimed at the destruction of any of the rights and freedoms set forth herein."

The Universal Declaration contains no specific limitations on hate speech, but the exceptions defined in articles 29 and 30 clearly imply that such restrictions are permissible, if not required. Subsequent human rights statements have clarified this intent by defining in more detail the kind of limits on individual rights that are permissible. These include specific prohibitions on offensive racial and religious speech.

The International Covenant on Civil and Political Rights defines in specific terms the permissible limitations on freedom of speech. Article 18 reaffirms freedom of speech and conscience, declaring that "everyone shall have the right to freedom of thought, conscience and religion." Article 19, paragraph 2, meanwhile, declares that "Everyone shall have the right to freedom of expression." Paragraph 3, however, states that the right to freedom of expression "carries with it special duties and responsibilities." It can be restricted, if necessary, "(a) For respect of the rights or reputations of others; (b) For the protection of national security or of public order [*ordre publique*], or of public health or morals." Article 20, paragraph 2, is even more specific: "Any advocacy of national, racial or religious hatred that constitutes incitement to discrimination, hostility or violence shall be prohibited by law."[47]

The United Nations Human Rights Committee subsequently interpreted article 20, paragraph 2, to mean that signatory states were obligated to enact legislation prohibiting hate speech, although such laws did not necessarily have to include criminal penalties. Other "appropriate" sanctions were acceptable.[48]

The provisions of the International Covenant and other human rights declarations are not binding upon signatories, however. Individual countries may ratify this and other agreements but attach certain reservations, understandings, or declarations (sometimes referred to as "RUDs"). By spring 1992, six of the 105 countries ratifying the International Covenant on Civil and Political Rights had attached a reservation regarding article 20, paragraph 2 (another eight included a reservation regarding paragraph 1, prohibiting propaganda for war). The six were Australia, Belgium, Luxembourg, Malta, New Zealand, and the United Kingdom.

The United States Senate finally ratified the covenant in April 1992 and attached its own set of reservations, including the statement that the United States was not bound by any provision that violated the First Amendment to the United States Constitution.[49]

The 1966 International Convention on the Elimination of All Forms of Racial Discrimination defines its basic purpose as the adoption of "all necessary measures for speedily eliminating racial discrimination in all its forms and manifestations, and to prevent and combat racist doctrines and practices." To that end, article 4 declares that signatory countries shall "condemn all propaganda and all organizations which are based on ideas or theories of superiority of one race or group of persons of one colour or ethnic origin, or which attempt to justify or promote racial hatred and discrimination in any form." Signatories are also directed "to adopt immediate and positive measures designed to eradicate all incitement to, or acts of, such discrimination." Article 4 then specifies restrictions on both expression and political activity. Paragraph 4a states that signatories "shall declare an offence punishable by law all dissemination of ideas based on racial superiority, or hatred, incitement to racial discrimination." Paragraph 4b goes even further, proscribing racist organizations. Signatories are obliged to "declare illegal and prohibit organizations . . . which promote and incite racial discrimination, and shall recognize participation in such organizations or activities as an offence punishable by law."[50]

During the drafting of the International Covenant, article 4 proved to be "one of the most difficult and controversial" parts of the entire document.[51] Debate focused on how the proposed language might infringe on freedom of speech. By spring 1992, twelve of the 129 countries ratifying the convention had attached a reservation regarding article 4, including the United States.[52]

Restrictions of offensive racial and religious speech are also contained in other international human rights statements. The Genocide Convention (1948) prohibits "direct and public incitement to commit genocide." The 1967 Draft Convention on the Elimination of All Forms of Religious Intolerance calls for "equal protection of the law against promotion of or incitement to religious intolerance or discrimination" (article 9). The American Convention on Human Rights (1969) proscribes "any advocacy of national, racial, or religious hatred" (article 13, paragraph 5).[53]

REFLECTIONS ON THE
INTERNATIONAL HUMAN RIGHTS MOVEMENT

The international statements on human rights are significant in several respects. As I have already noted, they represent a revolution in international law, establishing for the first time standards for the internal affairs of sovereign nations. There is another aspect that has direct relevance for the hate speech issue. Although the relevant international human rights statements depart from American law and practice on the specific question of hate speech, they generally follow the American model of protecting individual rights. This matter deserves extended comment.

One of the most notable features of the many international human rights statements is that, taken as a group, they have a distinctly "American" flavor. A quick survey gives one the feeling of reading a primer on American constitutional law or civil liberties. The American influence in this area has been greater than is generally recognized by most Americans. Mary Ann Glendon argues that today, "where rights are concerned, lawyers and judges the world over frequently consult American sources." Anthony Lester characterizes this influence in terms of "the overseas trade in the American Bill of Rights." Glendon emphasizes the point that the United States has given far more to the world than it has received in terms of defining the scope of human rights.[54]

The specifically American features comprise three elements. The first is that they adopt the American approach of codifying human rights in a *written* bill of rights. In fact, the international declarations are sometimes referred to collectively as an "international bill of rights." The point is that the international human rights movement rejected the English model of an unwritten bill of rights, to say nothing of the more common practice around the world of relying on informal custom. It may well be that, in some objective sense, the only realistic way to codify human rights is through a written enumeration of specific rights. That question goes beyond the scope of this book. Suffice it to say, however, that if the proposition is true, it highlights the profound wisdom of those American citizens who framed the first ten amendments to the United States Constitution.

The second American feature of the international human rights statements is their emphasis on *individual* rights. The habit of thinking in terms of individual rights is so deeply ingrained in our culture that most Americans are unaware of how unusual it is. And by all accounts, the emphasis on formal individual rights has become steadily more intense since the 1960s. Most of the rest of the world has traditionally preferred communal or collective rights.[55]

Perhaps the most significant indicators of this American approach are the various provisions protecting the right of religious dissent – a peculiarly Anglo-American tradition, now rooted in several hundred years of historical experience. Much of the rest of the world defines the good society in terms of a merger of church and state and equates religious dissent with heresy. The death threat issued against author Salman Rushdie is, by the standards of world history, not all that unusual. The American policy of separation of church and state, and particularly of keeping religious practices out of state-supported schools, is very unusual.

Given these first two features – codification in a written bill of rights and an emphasis on individual rights – it is hardly surprising to find a third American element: incorporation of most of the specific rights enumerated in the United States Bill of Rights. These rights fall into three main categories: (1) freedom of speech, the press, and assembly and the free exercise of religion; (2) equality or, in its American constitutional formulation, equal protection of the law; and (3) due process of law, particularly with respect to the rights of suspects in criminal proceedings.

There are, of course, a number of important differences between the American Bill of Rights and the international statements. The most notable is that many recognize economic rights. In addition to statements on economic issues per se, many of the declarations on *political* rights affirm specific economic rights such as the right to employment, social security, and so on. The United States Constitution, in contrast, contains no specific references to economic rights. Insofar as economic rights ever received constitutional protection in this country, it was in the pre–1937 era when the Fourteenth Amendment was interpreted to protect property rights, not the economic welfare of individuals. Nor has the ACLU argued that the Constitution guarantees the right to employment, sustenance, or shelter[56] – although the issue has been hotly debated within the organization for twenty-five years and several of the state affiliates have affirmed certain economic rights.[57] At the same time, the international human rights statements do not affirm a right to privacy – a new and contentious area of American rights.

These reflections raise a number of intriguing questions. The central point is how much the American approach to protecting human rights has influenced international trends. It is not going too far to say that the American approach to civil liberties – a written bill of rights, emphasis on individual rights, and so forth – has become the model for the rest of the world. There are a number of questions that go beyond the scope of this book: What was the exact nature of the American influence on the international human rights movement? How conscious was the imitation? Were other models considered and explicitly rejected? How direct was the influence of particular Americans in the drafting of particular documents?[58]

With respect to hate speech, perhaps the most interesting questions surrounding the international human rights statements are the various limitations on individual rights they permit. An American reads those provisions with either alarm or amusement. One hardly need be an expert on First Amendment law to realize that the terms "national security," "public order," and "public health or morals" are extraordinarily vague and elastic.[59] In fact they have been the traditional rationales for restricting individual rights in the United States with respect to political speech and association, public demonstrations, the censorship of sexually related literature, and access to contraceptives and abortion services, to name only a few of the more prominent areas. The trend in American constitutional law has been toward narrowing the permissible application of each of these rationales.

In the end, the international human rights statements introduce the problem of hate speech but hardly settle it. The crucial questions – such as when an inflammatory speech is a protected form of political activity and when it threatens "public order" – remain to be answered. The United States has wrestled with these First Amendment problems since 1919, and the result is a vast body of case law. One leaves the subject thinking that the rest of the world has much to learn from the American experience in grappling with the thorny questions of offensive speech.

The Paradox of *Beauharnais*

The question of group libel finally reached the Supreme Court in 1952 in a challenge to a 1917 Illinois law. The law made it unlawful for anyone "to manufacture, sell, or offer for sale, advertise or publish, present or exhibit in any public place . . . [anything that] portrays depravity, criminality, unchastity, or lack of virtue of a class of citizens, of any race, color, creed or religion," when such publication would expose "the citizen of any race, color, creed, or religion to contempt, derision, or obloquy or which is productive of breach of the peace or riots."[60] The law had been enacted on June 29, 1917, in response to a race riot in East St. Louis, Illinois, a few weeks earlier. Three days later a second riot broke out in that city and proved to be one of the worst race riots in the early twentieth century.[61] Two years later an even more serious riot occurred in Chicago.[62]

The *Beauharnais* case posed the group libel issue in particularly urgent terms. The prosecution of Joseph Beauharnais grew out of a bitter and often violent racial conflict over housing in the city of Chicago. The issue was particularly acute after World War II. The city's black population had doubled between 1940 and 1950, from 249,000 to over 500,000, largely as a result of wartime employment opportunities, and housing construction did not keep pace with demand. The battle for housing was literally fought neighborhood by neighborhood. White residents resisted with every method available, from discrimination by realtors and financial institutions to outright violence. Black families moving into previously all-white neighborhoods encountered threats and vandalism. A race riot erupted in the suburb of Cicero in 1951, and the National Guard was called out to restore order. The Cicero riot occurred between the time of Beauharnais's arrest and the Supreme Court's decision in his appeal, and the Court cited this record of racial conflict as a justification for upholding the group libel law.[63]

The seriousness of interracial violence in Chicago remained hidden from much of the public. Civic leaders agreed on a strategy of giving the disorder as little publicity as possible. These leaders included influential figures in the local Democratic party, the business community, the news media, and even many civil rights leaders, who believed the news would harm the city's reputation and discourage business development as well as encourage additional violence. It was better, they all agreed, to manage the crisis as quietly as possible.[64]

However well intentioned, the policy of news management had the effect of insulating most Chicagoans – and the rest of the country – from the spectacle of northern white racist violence. This allowed even liberal white northerners to define the "race problem" in terms of southern segregation. It meant that when the urban riots of the 1960s erupted, most Americans believed that race relations had suddenly "deteriorated" and that violence was strictly a black-initiated affair. A 1969 government report titled *The History of Violence in America,* with contributions from prominent scholars, for example, contained no references to the Chicago violence or to similar events in other cities in the post–World War II years.[65]

Joseph Beauharnais was the president of the White Circle League of America, which he organized in January 1950 to fight racial integration. His literature was viciously racist, calling on the mayor and city council of Chicago to "halt the further encroachment, harassment and invasion of white people, their property, neighborhoods and persons by the Negro." Whites, it continued, were in danger of being "mongrelized by the negro" and were in imminent danger from the "rapes, robberies, knives, guns and marijuana of the negro." This literature did not call for or even hint at violent resistance. On its face, it asked people to petition government officials to change public policy – actions that were clearly protected by the First Amendment. The material did fit some of the terms of the Illinois law, however. It portrayed "criminality" in a way that held African Americans up to contempt or derision. More difficult to determine, although clearly uppermost in everyone's mind, was the other section of the law: whether the material might cause a breach of the peace. Given the immediate context of racial violence in Chicago at that time, a case could be made that any inflammatory material might trigger violence.

The Supreme Court upheld Beauharnais's conviction and sustained the constitutionality of the law in a sharply divided five to four decision. The majority opinion, written by Felix Frankfurter, gave advocates of group libel legislation everything they could have asked for. Justice Frankfurter held that group libel fell outside the scope of First Amendment protection and that the legislature had full authority to take reasonable measures to mitigate a serious social evil – namely, racial conflict.

Frankfurter disposed of the free speech issue by drawing on the two-tiered analysis of the First Amendment set forth in *Chaplinsky*. Justice Murphy had included libel among those "certain well-defined and narrowly limited classes of speech" that fell outside the protection of the First Amendment. Frankfurter held that the Illinois law extended the traditional law of criminal libel from individuals to "designated collectivities" in a logical and reasonable manner.[66]

By placing the Illinois law outside the scope of the First Amendment, Frankfurter sidestepped difficult questions related to the clear and present danger test, then the prevailing standard for free speech issues. Given the context of racial violence in Chicago at the time and the inflammatory nature of Beauharnais's literature, it is conceivable that the Court could have upheld his conviction on much narrower grounds: that these particular words posed a clear and present danger to the community. Under this approach, other offensive kinds of literature could be constitutionally protected in the absence of an immediately volatile social setting. Having dismissed First Amendment considerations, Frankfurter found it "unnecessary" to wrestle with this issue.[67]

Frankfurter also brushed aside the New Jersey supreme court decision striking down that state's race hate law, which was probably the most relevant precedent at that time. He dismissed *Klapprott* in a footnote, finding the New Jersey law "quite different" from the Illinois law under review.[68] Although the New Jersey law had included far more sweeping restrictions, its basic thrust was essentially the same as that of the Illinois law. Frankfurter's cavalier dismissal of the New Jersey decision allowed him to avoid confronting the vagueness problem and dealing with precisely which kinds of offensive statements were protected and which were not.

Considering the law from the standpoint of social policy, Frankfurter eagerly gave much attention to the history of racial conflict in Illinois. The "tragic experience of the last three decades" sustained the conclusion "the willful purveyors of falsehood concerning racial and religious groups promote strife and tend powerfully to obstruct the manifold adjustments required for free, ordered life in a metropolitan, polyglot community."[69] The requirements of civic harmony fully justified criminal penalties for offensive racial propaganda that was likely to disturb the peace. The need to preserve social order, I might note, is the basis for the restrictions on hate speech in the various international human rights declarations.

Justice Frankfurter's deference to legislative judgment was identical to the rationale the Court used in sustaining virtually all of the anti-Communist measures that came before it in the 1940s and 1950s. Society, acting through its freely elected representatives, had a right to prevent those substantive evils it identified. By the late 1950s this issue would be defined in terms of the "balancing test." In deciding First Amendment issues, the Court should balance the interests of free speech against the needs of society, as defined by legislative majorities.[70]

The *Beauharnais* decision included four vigorous dissents. Justice Stanley Reed emphasized the vagueness of the law, arguing that "the language of the statute did not limit the meaning of words like 'virtue,' 'derision,' or 'obloquy.'"[71] Justice Hugo Black argued that Frankfurter's opinion "degrades First Amendment freedoms to the 'rational basis' level."[72] This was one more salvo in Black's continuing battle against Frankfurter's deference to legislative judgment on civil liberties. Black found the decision a far broader threat to free speech than *Chaplinsky*, which was limited to face-to-face encounters.

Justice William O. Douglas delivered what proved to be a prophetic opinion. He warned that allowing legislative majorities to determine which kinds of speech might be harmful to the public welfare opened the door to arbitrary enforcement: "Today a white man stands convicted for protesting in unseemly language against our decisions invalidating restrictive [housing] covenants." The danger was that "tomorrow a Negro will be haled before a court for denouncing lynch law in heated terms." The decision was "a warning to every minority."[73] As we shall see in chapter 6, it was precisely the felt need to protect civil rights and other forms of protest that led the Supreme Court to expand the protection of provocative speech.

Justice Robert Jackson made the same point and, significantly, concluded with an oblique but nonetheless obvious reference to Nazi Germany. Jackson was acutely conscious of Nazi tactics, having served as the chief American prosecutor at the Nuremberg trials of former Nazi leaders. "I have had occasion to learn," he commented, how "sinister abuses of our freedoms of expression . . . can tear apart a society, brutalize its dominant elements, and persecute, even to extermination, its minorities." But though organized hate groups posed a serious threat to democracy, it was important not to fight hate by suppressing fundamental liberties. The majority opinion upholding the Illinois group libel statute, he concluded, had "lost sight of" this point.[74]

Justice Jackson seems to have had some difficulty making up his mind about the meaning of the Nazi experience. Three years earlier, in the *Terminiello* case, he had forcefully argued a contrary point with his famous statement that the Constitution was not a "suicide pact."[75] Better than anything else, Jackson's ambivalence reflected the different interpretations of the lessons of Nazism. The idea that democracies had a legitimate right to restrict antidemocratic movements and organizations underpinned the restrictions on hate speech in the international human rights movement. Americans, after some ambivalence, opted for the position argued by Jackson and the other dissenters in *Beauharnais*, that offensive speech was the price one paid for a free society.

In the long run the point made by Justice Douglas proved to have the greatest influence over the development of First Amendment law. As we shall see in the next chapter, many of the most important advances in the protection of unpopular expression involved not just African Americans but civil rights activists.

AFTERMATH: DEFEAT OUT OF VICTORY

In the long run, the minority position in *Beauharnais* became the Court's majority view on First Amendment issues. That development, which I shall examine in the next chapter, took many years. Even more significant is that even the leading supporters of group libel legislation were losing interest in it by the time of the *Beauharnais* decision. They did not seize the opportunity offered by the Supreme Court and press for group libel laws across the country. Paradoxically, they rejected the concept at precisely this moment of seeming triumph. Explaining this paradox is the key to understanding the development of American law and policy after World War II.

A number of statements by advocates of group libel legislation provide some insight into the change in their thinking. Immediately following the *Beauharnais* decision, Joseph Tanenhaus, one of the leading advocates of group libel statutes, offered a comment on the opportunity it created.[76] Writing in *Phylon,* a leading African American journal, he proposed a surprisingly cautious and tentative plan of action. He recommended enacting group libel laws in a few states as experiments to see whether they "can be effective" and whether the "fears" of opponents were "justified." Tanenhaus cautioned that "until such an experiment has been conducted . . . the presumption must run against group libel legislation as an efficacious method of combatting group defamation."[77] In the space of only two years, the former advocate of group libel laws had become a skeptic. Even though the Supreme Court had given the concept constitutional sanction, Tanenhaus now argued that the burden of proof was on its supporters.

To a certain extent Tanenhaus reflected the dominant current of thought about prejudice among social scientists. Harvard psychologist Gordon W. Allport, in his classic work *The Nature of Prejudice,* published in 1954, surveyed the efficacy of legislation in combating racial and religious prejudice. Reflecting the consensus among psychologists and social scientists who studied intolerance, Allport concluded that though civil rights and fair employment laws were effective, "the weight of opinion seems against" group libel legislation.[78] Prejudice was best fought through restrictions on discriminatory behavior, education on group differences, and a free flow of ideas, not through the restriction of expression.

One person's change of heart on the group libel issue was particularly significant. David Riesman, author of the highly influential group libel articles in 1942, had changed his mind by 1951. A year before the *Beauharnais* decision, in *Commentary,* a magazine sponsored by the American Jewish Committee, Riesman delivered a sharp criticism of self-styled "militant" tactics against anti-Semitism by some Jewish activists. Specifically, Riesman cited attempts by Jewish leaders to have Shakespeare's *Merchant of Venice* banned from public schools because of the anti-Semitic aspects of the character of Shylock. Not only were such tactics futile, Riesman advised, but they represented a serious threat to freedom of expression. "In the present context of American society," he continued, "freedom of expression is one of the great safeguards for Jews and all other minorities subject to prejudice."[79]

Riesman had done a complete about-face since his "Democracy and Defamation" articles. He now believed that the self-interest of Jews and other persecuted groups lay in protecting freedom of expression. In a pointed critique of the American Jewish Congress, the leading advocate of group libel laws, Riesman warned that threats to freedom of expression were equally serious whether they came from the American Legion, the Legion of Decency, "or the Commission on Law and Social Action" (the civil rights unit of the American Jewish Congress). Riesman did not acknowledge his intellectual reversal, much less explain it, and we can only infer the causes. His reference to the fiercely anti-Communist American Legion and the Catholic Legion of Decency, then the most vigorous advocate of censorship in the arts, was especially revealing. Restricting hate speech, no matter how worthy a goal it might seem, played into the hands of other groups that posed serious threats to freedom of expression. Riesman had done some serious thinking since writing "Democracy and Defamation" and had reached a very different conclusion about the role of the First Amendment and group conflict.

There would be a postscript to Riesman's intellectual odyssey on the hate speech question. Thirty-six years after the *Columbia Law Review* articles appeared, he rejoined the ACLU in the midst of the Skokie controversy as a way of affirming his commitment to defending even the most odious speech.[80]

Other people followed Riesman's lead. In 1960 the American Jewish Congress adopted a resolution at its biennial conference officially repudiating group libel legislation as a remedy for prejudice and discrimination.[81] It had lost interest in the issue shortly after the *Beauharnais* decision; the issue vanished from the agenda of the Congress's Commission on Law and Social Action in the early 1950s. The formal reversal in 1960 represented an open acknowledgment of its commitment to the idea that human rights were best advanced through an absolutist protection of individual rights.

The other major Jewish groups followed suit. In 1962 the National Jewish Community Relations Advisory Council (NJCRAC), an umbrella organization representing all the major groups, adopted an official Policy on Censorship opposing all prior restraints.[82] Although Nazis were not specifically mentioned, opposition to restraints on their activities was implied. (The dissenting votes by two member groups, the Jewish Labor Council and the Philadelphia Jewish Community Relations Council, indicated that they at least understood the implied protection of Nazi activities.) The following year the NJCRAC officially rejected group libel legislation as "ill-advised, self-defeating and in conflict with our firm adherence to the principle of protection of even abhorrent speech." In part this policy was motivated by a growing self-confidence within the Jewish community. The NJCRAC dismissed the American Nazi groups as "a nuisance and an irritant rather than a threat."[83]

Finally, in the most directly relevant switch of all, in 1961 the state of Illinois repealed the 1917 law.[84] This move, part of a general recodification of its criminal code, and influenced by the work on the Model Penal Code,[85] reflected the prevailing consensus among the leaders of the legal profession. Group libel had vanished as a recommended remedy for racial and religious hatred. Thus in 1977, when a small Nazi organization wanted to march in the predominantly Jewish village of Skokie, Illinois, the state's group libel law was no longer on the books.[86]

6 Free Speech Triumphant: From *Beauharnais* to Skokie, 1952-1978

Toward a National Policy

Between the late 1940s and the mid-1970s the United States developed a national policy on hate speech. That policy, protecting offensive forms of expression, was part of a much broader development of First Amendment law reflecting "a profound national commitment to the principle that debate on public issues should be uninhibited, robust, and wide-open."[1]

The period begins, roughly, in the years following World War II and ends with the Skokie controversy in 1978. In that case the federal courts upheld the right of a Nazi group to demonstrate in the predominantly Jewish community of Skokie, Illinois, and declared unconstitutional three municipal ordinances, including one that prohibited the dissemination of materials inciting hatred based on race, national origin, or religion.[2] The Supreme Court did not hear an appeal of the Skokie case, letting the Seventh Circuit Court of Appeals decision stand. The lower court rejected the village of Skokie's arguments that the Nazi slogans constituted "fighting words" as defined by *Chaplinsky* and group libel under the *Beauharnais* decision.

The Skokie decision affirmed a national policy that had evolved over the previous decades. This chapter examines how and why that policy developed as it did. One specific question is why the courts in the Skokie case rejected the opportunities to restrict hate speech that presumably were available under *Chaplinsky* and *Beauharnais*.

PERSPECTIVES ON THE PERIOD

Several general features characterize the developments during this period. First, the protection of offensive speech was a genuinely *national* policy in the sense that it was based on Supreme Court rulings on First Amendment rights. As in so many other areas of American life – church-state relations, due process of law, civil rights – the Court subjected social and political issues to constitutional scrutiny, established general principles rooted in the Bill of Rights, and erased the historical patchwork of state and local laws and practices. As Archibald Cox put it, "Hardly a political issue arose . . . that was not converted into a legal question and taken to the courts for decision."[3] The result was a set of national standards on religion in the schools, police interrogations, obscenity – and offensive speech. With respect to free speech, the trend was steadily in the direction of disallowing any content-based restrictions.

The emergence of the Supreme Court as a maker of national policy stands as one of the most important changes in modern American history. The policies and practices of public institutions were radically transformed. The Court's activist role generated a powerful reaction, however. Issues such as whether public schools could conduct daily prayers and how police officers interrogated suspects were catapulted into national politics, with presidential candidates pledging to reverse Court rulings on the rights of suspects, school prayer, and pornography. From 1968 on, conservative presidential candidates promised to appoint justices committed to judicial restraint. Most of the "social agenda" of the New Right in the 1980s was a reaction to the libertarian decisions of the Supreme Court. Instead of episodic events, crises surrounding the Supreme Court became a permanent feature of American political life.[4] The nominations of several people to be justices of the Court, notably Robert Bork (1987) and Clarence Thomas (1991), precipitated bitter debates over the role of the Court and the issues of privacy and civil rights.

Second, as protection of offensive expression became broader and more clearly defined, the contrast sharpened between American law and policy and those of the rest of the world. International developments moved steadily in the direction of a more explicit condemnation of racial and religious propaganda. The milestones in this movement were the International Covenant on Civil and Political Rights and the International Convention on the Elimination of All Forms of Racial Discrimination, both drafted in 1966 and both proscribing racial and religious propaganda.[5] England, responding to its own growing racial problems, enacted the 1965 Race Relations Act, prohibiting words or publications "likely to stir up hatred . . . on grounds of colour, race, or ethnic or national origins."[6] It strengthened the prohibitions on racist speech and activity with the 1986 Public Order Act. Other countries followed the mandate of the international human rights declarations. France enacted a hate speech law in 1972; India followed suit in 1973; Brazil in 1985; Argentina in 1988. The prohibition of hate speech was a worldwide movement that reached its peak in the 1970s and 1980s.[7]

The third and perhaps most significant aspect of the period was the issue of civil rights. The mid-1960s marked the high point of the American civil rights movement, defined as a broad-based interracial coalition committed to racial equality and to ending all forms of discrimination. Arguably, civil rights became the central issue in American politics in the mid-1950s, eclipsing the national hysteria over domestic Communism. One historian has labeled the period "the civil rights era."[8] The movement's achievements were truly monumental: the end of de jure segregation in public schools and public accommodations; the end of systematic racial discrimination in voting; and commitment to equal opportunity as a matter of national policy, embodied in a host of laws and regulations. These were events of truly historic dimensions, even if by the 1980s some African Americans were inclined to emphasize the lack of progress.

The national civil rights movement was not confined to equality for African Americans. There was a parallel attack on anti-Semitism and discrimination against Jews in housing, employment, education, and other areas of American life.[9] The major Jewish civil rights groups – principally the Anti-Defamation League, the American Jewish Congress, and the American Jewish Committee – were full partners in the national civil rights coalition.[10] They not only joined the NAACP on issues concerning African Americans, but frequently joined the ACLU in a concerted attack on official censorship and religion in the schools.[11] In the early years after its founding in 1945, the Commission on Law and Social Action of the American Jewish Congress had more attorneys working full time on civil rights issues than the United States Department of Justice.[12]

The agenda of the civil rights movement holds the key to understanding the course of the hate speech issue. At first glance there is an apparent paradox: civil rights groups, as part of their broad-based attack on discrimination, chose *not* to make the restriction of hate speech one of their goals. Moreover, they rejected this potential remedy even as their counterparts in other countries opted for it. They made this choice because their greatest successes came through constitutional litigation on behalf of individual rights. Thus the advancement of minority *group* rights was pursued through litigation based on claims of *individual* rights to equal protection, freedom of speech and assembly, and due process of law.[13] Any restriction on individual rights was seen as a threat to the entire fabric of constitutional rights. Thus group libel laws, which restricted freedom of expression, came to be seen as a danger rather than as a remedy for racial injustice.

The Expanding Boundaries of Freedom of Expression

To many observers, the Seventh Circuit's decision in the Skokie case was entirely predictable, given the trend of First Amendment law to that point. Lee Bollinger argues that the court's opinion was cast in terms of being "compelled" to reach the decision it did – that it was forced into a distasteful result by established case law.[14] For the same reasons, the leaders of the ACLU initially saw it as a routine First Amendment case involving long-settled issues.[15] They were stunned by the hostile reaction to their defense of the Nazis' right to demonstrate. The organization had faced protests over its previous defense of Nazis – in the 1930s, as we saw in chapter 3, and on several occasions in the 1960s over Nazi leader George Lincoln Rockwell – but these had always involved little more than a few angry letters and perhaps a handful of resignations.[16] By the 1970s the defense of unpopular groups, including Nazis, was a settled issue.

The developments in First Amendment law that led to the Skokie decision fall into three general areas: speech before hostile audiences in situations that involved potential breach of the peace; the law of libel, including questions of possible defamation of public figures and groups; and the relatively new concept of freedom of association, specifically as related to unpopular political groups. Many of these cases arose from the civil rights movement, and the courts were clearly motivated by a desire to protect civil rights advocacy – to give it breathing room, as one important decision put it.[17]

THE HOSTILE AUDIENCE AND THE THREAT OF DISORDER

The two-pronged definition of "fighting words" enunciated in the 1942 *Chaplinsky* decision seemed to offer two avenues for restricting offensive speech.[18] The first involved words that might cause "an immediate breach of the peace"; the second included words that "by their very utterance inflict injury." The former opened the door for the "heckler's veto," whereby a hostile audience, by threatening to become unruly, could force the arrest of the speaker and effectively prevent that person from speaking. The latter related even more directly to hate speech, since any offensive statement about a person's race or religion could be defined as inflicting injury. Over the next thirty years, with a few notable exceptions, the Court steadily closed off these avenues, creating ever greater protection for the offensive speaker.

The Court addressed the hostile audience problem in the 1949 *Terminiello* case.[19] Arthur Terminiello was a defrocked Catholic priest who had become an active anti-Semitic, quasi-Fascist organizer. On one appearance in Chicago he was greeted by a crowd of about a thousand angry demonstrators. When he denounced them as "slimy scum," the crowd became unruly; some rocks were thrown through the windows. Instead of the rock throwers, the police arrested Terminiello and charged him with disturbing the peace. He was then convicted on the grounds that his speech was the kind that "stirs the public to anger, invites disputes, brings about a condition of unrest, or creates a disturbance."

The confrontation that led to Terminiello's arrest was not an isolated incident. The protesters outside the building represented the self-styled "militant" wing of a national campaign against anti-Semitism. The major Jewish civil rights groups chose to combat anti-Semitism through a two-fold campaign of legal challenges to restrictive practices and education about race and religion. They adopted a strategy of "quarantining" anti-Semitic rabble-rousers – ignoring them as much as possible in order to deny them the publicity they sought.[20] The "militant" groups, on the other hand, opted for a confrontational approach.[21] They frequently demanded that local officials deny speaking permits to anti-Semites, and if that failed they would organize noisy demonstrations protesting the speech itself. The militants included primarily left-wing organizations, with the Communist party playing a very prominent role.

The major target of militant protest in the 1940s was Gerald L. K. Smith, a former associate of Huey Long of Louisiana, who had emerged as the most prominent American anti-Semite. Attempts to prevent him from speaking arose in St. Louis, Pasadena, and other cities. On a number of occasions the ACLU defended his right to a speaking permit.[22] Arnold Forster and Benjamin Epstein of the Anti-Defamation League argued that militant protests only gave Smith's 1947 Boston speech more publicity than it would ever have received: "No circus ballyhoo artist could have done a better advance promotion job for Smith." They accused the Communist party of exploiting the crusade against anti-Semitism for its own purposes: "The Party, in the name of combating anti-Semitism . . . succeeded only in promoting the very cause it pretended to oppose."[23] As I argued in the previous chapter, these militant tactics spurred David Riesman to rethink the entire issue of group libel in 1951 and to become an advocate of unrestricted speech.[24]

The question of how best to respond to anti-Semitic groups and speakers runs through a forty-year span of history. In the 1930s militant Jewish groups organized counterdemonstrations to protest Nazi activities. As we saw in chapter 3, this played into Nazi hands, since the resulting violence was often perpetrated by Jewish counterdemonstrators rather than by the Nazis. And as we shall see, the established Jewish leaders during the Skokie affair initially tried to defuse the controversy by permitting the demonstration and persuading everyone to ignore it. They were quickly upstaged by a new generation of militants, some who wanted the demonstration banned and others who threatened counterdemonstrations – and some who issued thinly veiled threats of violence.

When the Supreme Court considered the *Terminiello* case it reversed his conviction in an opinion that set the direction for developments in free speech law over the next several decades. For the majority, Justice William O. Douglas held that the very "function of free speech under our system of government is to invite dispute." Provocative speech, he argued, should be not just grudgingly tolerated but welcomed or even encouraged: "It may indeed best serve its high purpose when it induces a condition of unrest, creates dissatisfaction with conditions as they are, or even stirs people to anger."[25]

The *Terminiello* decision had important implications for the political controversies in the years ahead, when provocative speech, the deliberate creation of "dissatisfaction with conditions as they are," would become an important ingredient in the civil rights, anti–Vietnam War, and anti-abortion movements, to name only three of the more turbulent political controversies from the 1960s to the 1990s. The Court's interpretation of the First Amendment opted for social change rather than the maintenance of public order and civility or respect for people's sensibilities.

The Court retreated a bit from *Terminiello* in the *Feiner* decision two years later. In a militant political speech, Irving Feiner "gave the impression that he was endeavoring to arouse the Negro people against the whites, urging them to rise up in arms and fight for equal rights."[26] He, rather than the unruly audience, was arrested for disorderly conduct, and the Court sustained the conviction. *Feiner,* however, did not set the direction for future decisions. When the Court returned to the problem of the hostile audience in the 1960s, a libertarian majority dominated the Warren Court, and decisions consistently favored provocative speech at the risk of disorder. In the most important decision, *Edwards v. South Carolina* (1963), the Court reversed the convictions of 187 African American students arrested on March 2, 1961, for demonstrating in front of the South Carolina capitol.[27] They had been ordered to disperse within fifteen minutes and were arrested when they failed to do so. The Court held that the students were exercising their constitutionally protected rights of freedom of speech and assembly and that there was no evidence of violence by either the students or onlookers; nor were any fighting words uttered. In yet another civil rights demonstration case (*Cox v. Louisiana*), the Court curtailed the "uncontrolled discretion" of local authorities "to determine which expressions of view will be permitted and which will not."[28]

The context of these decisions was extremely important. Following the first sit-ins on February 1, 1960, protests erupted across the South as African American students challenged institutionalized segregation. Massive demonstrations were clearly provocative, inherently racial, and fraught with potential for disorder. As Harry Kalven put it, southern communities regarded the civil rights movement as a subversive force, no less dangerous than Communism.[29] Civil rights demonstrations represented an action by a minority group that challenged the most cherished values of the majority and the established legal institutions in that particular context. Quite apart from whatever words were uttered, mere assertiveness by African Americans was profoundly offensive to the white majority, and so large demonstrations were routinely met with arrests by southern officials. Such demonstrations inevitably carried with them the danger of disorder, and southern officials were only too ready to define even a peaceful demonstration as a disorderly event. In these civil rights cases the Court raised a broad umbrella of protection over political speech in the face of a hostile audience and hostile authorities.

The problem of the hostile audience for civil rights marches was not confined to the Deep South. As the civil rights movement moved north, similar confrontations occurred involving demonstrators, hostile and potentially unruly bystanders, and often unsympathetic police. The most important case reaching the Supreme Court (*Gregory v. Chicago*) involved a march on the home of Chicago mayor Richard Daley, led by black comedian Dick Gregory.[30] When the demonstrators reached Daley's home in an all-white neighborhood, a number of the bystanders became unruly. To prevent what they believed to be likely disorder, the police ordered the demonstrators to disperse and, when they refused, arrested them for disorderly conduct. The Court overturned the convictions, finding no evidence that the demonstrators themselves were disorderly.

Chicago had previously been the scene of a 1966 march by Martin Luther King, Jr., into the suburb of Cicero, a center of organized white supremacist activity (and the scene of a violent anti-integration riot in 1951). King's march, in the face of bitter community hostility and potential violence, would be cited ten years later as a justification for permitting the Nazis to march in Skokie.[31] Allowing community sensibilities to veto political expression would block Nazis in one context but also stifle civil rights groups in others, both North and South.

NEW BOUNDARIES FOR OFFENSIVE SPEECH: THE "F WORD"

A different First Amendment issue arose in situations where there was no threat of public disorder but the speech in question offended public sensibilities. Public sensibilities were sorely tested during the 1960s: one of the many contributions that tumultuous decade made to American life was a new set of standards for public discourse. The intense emotions aroused by the civil rights movement, the Vietnam War, and later the abortion controversy resulted in the most extreme forms of vilification. In retrospect, there was a direct line from the anti–Vietnam War chant, "Hey, Hey, LBJ, how many kids did you kill today?" to the antiabortion protesters' shouts of "murderer" and "baby killer." Emotionally loaded words were a crucial part of a strategy of arousing an audience by dramatizing the profound moral issues at stake. The word "fuck" entered political discourse, particularly in its "motherfucker" variation, and in one extremely important case as "fuck the draft."

The change of standards in the political arena spilled over into general discourse, bringing into public words that had previously been confined to the barracks or the men's locker room. By the 1980s teenage girls routinely used the words "fuck," "suck," and "dick." Two popular slogans for T-shirts and bumper stickers were "Shit Happens," and "Life Sucks." A number of comedians, most notably Richard Pryor and then Eddie Murphy, made the "F word" a central element of their routines. In earlier years the casual public display or utterance of such words had been unthinkable and would probably have resulted in immediate arrest.

In the late 1950s and early 1960s, one professional comedian's willful offensiveness had direct political implications. Lenny Bruce has been virtually canonized by many of his fans.[32] Bruce became a celebrity through his routines attacking the hypocrisy of contemporary society. His targets included puritanism about sex, racism, anti-Communism, organized religion, and the follies of self-styled liberals, among others. Offending nearly every established group, he inevitably ran afoul of the law; he estimated that he had been arrested nineteen times. His later legal troubles involved drugs, but the initial arrests were prompted by his sexual material (one of his more famous routines was a meditation on the phrase "to come") and his attacks on organized religion (Cardinal Spellman of New York was a favorite target). Some observers believed his 1962 arrest in Chicago was provoked not by his use of dirty words but by his attacks on the Catholic church.

Bruce is revered by fans and many professional comedians today because he enormously expanded the scope of comedy. Sex, politics, and religion became permissible topics in large part because of his pioneering work (although Mort Sahl deserves much credit for pioneering political comedy). Without Bruce the work of George Carlin, Richard Pryor, Eddie Murphy, and a host of others would be unimaginable.[33] In Bruce's hands comedy was a weapon for social change, particularly civil rights and sexual freedom. Yet it is obvious that his scathing and hilarious attacks on the Catholic church, along with many of his routines about Jews and even some of his caricatures of African Americans, met the terms of the Illinois group libel law. One of his routines was to open a performance by asking, "Any spics here tonight? Any kikes? Any niggers?" According to Nat

Hentoff, "the audience froze." But his purpose soon became apparent: to "bring taboos out into the open so you can break them down." One of those taboos was racism, and to make his point Bruce used traditional racist terms and stereotypes.[34] To have curbed his humor under this law would have restricted an important form of political expression.

THE "F WORD" AND THE SUPREME COURT

The "F word" eventually reached the Supreme Court in a series of 1970s cases involving variations on "fuck," "motherfucker," and "white motherfucker." The first and most important arose out of a protest against the Vietnam War. Paul Robert Cohen was arrested and convicted of disturbing the peace for walking through the Los Angeles County courthouse wearing a jacket emblazoned with the words "Fuck the Draft."[35]

The Supreme Court overturned his conviction and, in an opinion by the conservative Justice John Marshall Harlan, established important new protection for offensive speech. Harlan emphasized that Cohen's conviction rested entirely on the content of his speech – that is, the alleged offensiveness of the word "fuck." His only conduct, in fact, was to communicate that word to other people in the courthouse. The facts of the case neatly precluded sustaining the conviction on a number of grounds. His words were not directed at any particular person or persons, and the prosecution made no claim that anyone in the courthouse was violently aroused by his jacket. This also helped eliminate the "captive audience" argument, that people were forced to endure this offensive word against their will. In short, the case turned entirely on the alleged offensiveness of the word "fuck."

The most important aspect of Harlan's opinion was his discussion of the nature of communication. He pointed out that "much linguistic expression serves a dual communicative function." While words have specific meanings, independent of their use in a particular context, they also convey "otherwise inexpressible emotions." "In fact," Harlan continued, "words are often chosen as much for their emotive as their cognitive force."[36]

Recognizing the role of the emotional aspects of verbal communication had enormous implications for the hate speech issue. Many of the political conflicts from the 1960s onward were couched in extreme moral terms. First the civil rights movement, then the Vietnam War, the women's movement, and the abortion controversy (both sides) were seen as great moral struggles. In the *Cohen* case, for example, it is evident that the force of Cohen's opposition to the Vietnam War and the draft would not have been the same had his jacket read "Stop the Draft" or "I Don't Like the Draft." By the same token, the use of the epithets "murderer" and "baby killer" by antiabortion demonstrators in the post–*Roe v. Wade* era, offensive though they might be to their audience, conveys the intensity of the users' feeling that abortion is an enormous crime.[37]

Cohen was quickly followed by other offensive word cases. In 1972 the Court overturned the conviction of another antiwar protester, arrested for saying to a police officer, "White son of a bitch, I'll kill you" and "You son of a bitch, I'll choke you to death." He was convicted under a Georgia law making it a misdemeanor to use "opprobrious words or abusive language, tending to cause of breach of the peace." (He was not charged with threatening the life of the police officer, which would have been a different matter altogether.) The Court overturned the conviction on the grounds that the statute was too broad.[38]

In 1972 the Court made what Harry Kalven called "cultural history of a sort" when it decided three cases involving the word "motherfucker," overturning convictions in all three. Rosenfeld had been convicted for indecent and offensive language for using the term four times at a local school board meeting.[39] Lewis had been convicted of breach of the peace for calling police officers "god damned m — f — ."[40] Finally, Brown had been convicted of violating a law prohibiting the use of obscene or lascivious language in public in the presence of women after calling police officers "m — f — fascist pig cops," and one in particular a "black m — f — pig."[41]

A HISTORICAL NOTE ON RACIAL AND RELIGIOUS EPITHETS

A brief comment about the history of racial epithets in American political discourse is in order at this point. As should be obvious, all the "F word" cases involved the criminal conviction of political dissidents: an opponent of the Vietnam War, an African American militant, and a critic of local school board policy. As First Amendment expert Kent Greenawalt points out, "It is not a coincidence that those less privileged culturally or more radical politically are likely to use words and phrases that might be judged to impair civil discourse."[42] In the absence of real political power, words – extreme, emotionally loaded words – are one of the few devices available to the powerless for capturing attention, dramatizing an issue, and mobilizing people for change. It is also clear that the Court's response was shaped by its sympathy for political dissent and the civil rights movement in particular. As Justice Douglas put it in the 1949 *Terminiello* case, the "F word" cases were instances of speech that "stirs the public to anger . . . or creates a disturbance."[43] Protecting expression of this sort created "breathing room" for civil rights activity.[44]

The increase in offensive language, and racial and religious epithets in particular, in the 1960s was more apparent than real. Terms such as "nigger" and "kike" had long been routine parts of the American language. White southern politicians never blushed at using "nigger" in public – and often used it precisely for pandering to the racism of their constituents. Senator James Eastland of Mississippi, still in the Senate in the 1960s, once attacked African American soldiers by saying, "He has disgraced the flag of his country. He will not fight. He will not work." He opposed voting rights for African Americans on the grounds that "the mental level of those people renders them incapable of suffrage."[45] George Wallace explained his defeat in the 1958 Alabama gubernatorial election by saying that his opponents "out-niggered me that time, but they'll never do it again."[46] Four years later they did not, and Wallace won, launching what became a national political career.

Anti-Semitic comments were blatantly uttered by members of Congress through the 1940s. Perhaps the last notorious offender was Mississippi Representative John Rankin, a prominent member of the House Un-American Activities Committee in the 1940s. He once referred to newspaper columnist Walter Winchell as "a little slime-mongering kike." He also called his colleague Representative L. Emanuel Celler "the Jewish gentleman from New York." When Celler objected, Rankin tauntingly asked whether he objected to being called a Jew or a gentleman.[47] Rankin's comments were typical of much right-wing anti-Communist rhetoric during the Cold War, which saw a vast Jewish/Communist/civil rights conspiracy.[48]

The 1960s were different not because of an increase in racially or religiously offensive language but for the simple reason that white racists and anti-Semites never had to worry about being arrested. What was new in the 1960s was the public use of offensive terms directed at whites by black militants; or in Paul Cohen's case, against the government; or in Lenny Bruce's case, against bigots and the Catholic church. Whereas Mississippi senator Theodore Bilbo could cry "nigger" without fear of arrest, the black militant on the street in the 1960s or 1970s had every reason to fear arrest for using an offensive word. Such words were precisely the excuse a police officer needed to arrest someone for disorderly conduct or some related charge. Accounts of police work are filled with examples of racial epithets used by officers against African American citizens. Until the community relations crisis of the 1960s, northern police departments did not have formal policies prohibiting such language.[49] Even in more recent years, officers rarely face significant discipline solely for using racial epithets.

Civil rights advocates and other dissenters, in short, were the principal beneficiaries of the "breathing room" for offensive speech created by the Supreme Court. Racists and anti-Semites already enjoyed all the space they needed. It was the recognition of this critical protective role of the First Amendment – which allowed organizations to survive and ideas to be expressed – that shaped the libertarian perspective of civil rights leaders and their consequent fear of restrictive speech legislation.

"Dangerous" Organizations

The trend toward greater protection of offensive speech was paralleled by a series of Supreme Court decisions protecting allegedly dangerous organizations. Protection took two forms. One line of decisions, which might be termed the main line of First Amendment cases, protected the right to advocate unpopular ideas, including violent revolution. The other line emerged only in the late 1950s and created a constitutionally protected right to belong to unpopular groups without public exposure. These decisions are relevant to the hate speech question because they established First Amendment protection for organizations that advocate ideas deemed offensive to the majority of society. We should recall that many of the pre–World War II anti-Fascist measures in Europe authorized the government to ban or dissolve political groups.[50] Some of the post–World War II international human rights declarations also proscribe hate groups. Article 4, paragraph b of the International Convention on the Elimination of All Forms of Racial Discrimination states that governments "shall declare illegal and prohibit organizations . . . which promote and incite racial discrimination" and make membership in such organizations a crime.[51] This step follows logically from the first premise: if an idea is forbidden because it threatens the basic values of society, then any organization advocating that idea should be banned.

American law developed in a very different direction. The main line of free speech litigation began with a series of famous 1919 cases upholding the convictions of wartime dissenters.[52] The *Schenck* decision gave birth to the clear and present danger test, which became the standard for First Amendment questions. Between 1937 and 1951 the Court greatly expanded First Amendment protection of political dissent in a series of cases involving Communists. In 1951 the Court drastically limited the clear and present danger test when it upheld the conviction of Communist party leaders in the *Dennis* case.[53] On First Amendment cases not involving Communists, however, the Court continued to expand the protection of offensive speech, as I have already argued. The long line of political speech cases reached its climax in 1969 in the *Brandenburg* case. Because it involved the prosecution of a Ku Klux Klan leader, it had direct relevance to the hate speech question.[54]

The case arose in the midst of the bitterly polarized racial atmosphere of the late 1960s. Brandenburg was a Ku Klux Klan leader who vented his racist views at a Klan rally near Cincinnati. Among other things, he said, "Personally, I believe the nigger should be returned to Africa, the Jew returned to Israel." More relevant to his conviction was a statement that might be interpreted as a call for violent action. In the crucial passage of his speech he said, "We are not a revengent [*sic*] organization, but if our President, our Congress, our Supreme Court, continues to suppress the white, Caucasian race, it's possible that there might have to be some revengeance taken."[55] It was not exactly clear what the semiliterate term "revengeance" meant. Given the historical record of Klan violence, it could have meant violent action against African Americans. Or it could be interpreted as a call for political action against pro–civil rights members of the three branches of the federal government.

Brandenburg was convicted under the Ohio Criminal Syndicalism Law, which made it a crime to advocate violence as a means of accomplishing political change. Criminal syndicalism laws (and their variations: criminal anarchy, etc.) had been the principal weapon against Communists and other radicals since the World War I free speech crisis.[56]

The Court overturned Brandenburg's conviction in a decision that effectively abolished the "clear and present danger" test. The Court held that the First Amendment protected the advocacy of violent revolution as a political doctrine but not direct incitement to an immediate criminal act, such as an assassination or a bombing. With respect to the hate speech question, then, *Brandenburg* established the right to advocate offensive racial or religious ideas – including the deportation of African Americans and Jews – as long as this advocacy did not reach the point of direct incitement to criminal action.

Brandenburg happened to be a Klan case, but it was most relevant for Communists, affording them a degree of protection they had never gained in the many cases involving their own members. There was no small irony in the fact that through most of its history the Communist party had been a vigorous advocate of restricting the rights of the Klan and other racist groups – as in its national campaign to deny speaking permits to Gerald L. K. Smith in the 1940s.[57] There was an even greater and more instructive irony in a series of cases involving the NAACP from 1958 to 1963, which established an extremely important principle of freedom of association under the First Amendment.

FREEDOM OF ASSOCIATION: THE NAACP CASES

The NAACP cases were a series of Supreme Court cases from 1958 to 1963 involving attempts by southern states to restrict the leading African American civil rights organization.[58] The measures in question were adopted in retaliation for the 1954 Supreme Court decision declaring segregated public schools unconstitutional. *Brown v. Board of Education,* it is safe to say, electrified the entire country. It not only outlawed the existing system of public education in the South, but clearly spelled doom for other forms of official segregation. It thrust the Supreme Court into the role of moral and political leadership on the race question and became a beacon of hope for civil rights forces. It is important to recall the political context of the period, in which the Congress was effectively controlled by a segregationist southern bloc and the White House was also neutralized by the political power of anti–civil rights forces. In this context the Supreme Court loomed as the only available avenue of social change.[59]

The South reacted to *Brown* in a variety of ways. Elected officials announced a plan of "massive resistance" to school integration.[60] Southerners in Congress joined other conservatives in an effort to strip the Supreme Court of some of its power.[61] The decision also gave the Ku Klux Klan "a new impetus," and there was a revival of violence against African Americans in the South.[62]

Southern segregationists attacked the NAACP not only because it had argued and won the *Brown* case, but because in most states and communities it was the only organized voice of the civil rights movement.[63] The logic was clear and simple: crush the NAACP and cripple the movement. The result was a series of measures designed to restrict the group's activities. Some were crude, such as the 1959 Arkansas law banning NAACP members from public employment. Other restrictions were more subtle, however, and posed difficult constitutional questions.

The first NAACP case to reach the Supreme Court, *NAACP v. Alabama* (1958), involved the compulsory disclosure of the NAACP membership list.[64] Alabama began by enjoining the NAACP from operating in the state on the grounds that it had not complied with registration requirements for out-of-state corporations. When the NAACP contested this ruling, the state demanded to see its records, including its list of Alabama members. The NAACP produced the other records requested but not the membership list, claiming the state could not compel such disclosure. The NAACP was held in contempt of court, and the case headed for the Supreme Court.

The Supreme Court unanimously upheld the NAACP and affirmed its right not to disclose its members under a new First Amendment principle of freedom of association. Justice John Marshall Harlan wrote that "effective advocacy of both public and private points of view, particularly controversial ones, is undeniably enhanced by group association." Although Alabama had taken "no direct action" to restrict the NAACP members' right to associate, threats to this right were no less serious if they were "unintended." Moreover, the "inviolability of privacy in group association may in many circumstances be indispensable to preservation of freedom of association, particularly where a group espouses dissident beliefs." The underlying issue, of course, was the practical consequences of compulsory disclosure. There was no question what this meant for an NAACP member in the Deep South. Harlan noted the "uncontroverted showing that on past occasions revelation of the identity of its rank-and-file members has exposed these members to economic reprisal, loss of employment, threat of physical coercion, and other manifestation of public hostility."[65]

In reaching this decision the Court had to confront its 1928 ruling in *Bryant v. Zimmerman* upholding the membership disclosure requirement in the New York anti-KKK law.[66] Harlan tried to distinguish between the two cases, arguing that the New York law had been based on a legislative finding about the "particular character" of the Klan's activities – its penchant for violence. Additionally, the Klan had made no effort to comply with the law, whereas the NAACP had supplied most of the information Alabama demanded. Kalven dismissed Harlan's effort here as "surprisingly inept."[67] The two disclosure requirements and their purposes were essentially the same. In a different political and legal context, the Court was willing to do for the NAACP what it had refused to do for the Klan.

Subsequent NAACP cases further extended the freedom of association. Two years later, in *Shelton v. Tucker* (1960), the Court declared unconstitutional an Arkansas requirement that public school teachers disclose the names of all the organizations they belonged to.[68] Here the Court disallowed a seemingly benign if not worthy regulatory measure: one designed to determine the fitness of public school teachers. The Court ruled that the requirement infringed on freedom of association: any regulatory measure, even one with a legitimate purpose, must use the least restrictive alternative. The doctrine of the least restrictive alternative, established in *Shelton,* proved extremely important and was subsequently applied by the Court in a variety of other contexts. This was another of the instances in which the civil rights movement created important new constitutional law doctrine that benefited not just African Americans but society as a whole.[69]

Three years later the Court struck down a Virginia ruling that the NAACP had engaged in the improper solicitation of legal business. In *NAACP v. Button* (1963) the Court held that interest group litigation was a form of political activity protected by the First Amendment.[70] *Button* had far-reaching implications as a virtual charter of freedom for litigation as an agent of social change. Also in 1963, in *Gibson v. Florida Legislative Investigation Committee,* the Court placed significant limits on the power of legislative investigating committees to inquire into political beliefs and associations.[71]

The *Gibson* decision was particularly noteworthy as the Court provided the NAACP a measure of First Amendment protection it had previously denied the Communist party. In general, the measures the southern states used against the NAACP were essentially the same as those used by the federal government and most states against alleged Communist subversion, virtually all of which had been sustained by the Supreme Court. As Kalven pointed out, there were clear parallels between the southern attack on the NAACP and the national anti-Communist crusade. As far as the segregationist South was concerned, the NAACP was nothing less than a "domestic conspiracy aiming at revolution."[72] It was a direct threat to the institutions (segregation) and values (racial superiority) of the majority. Kalven commented cynically that "it is tempting to join the [legal] 'realist' and state the operative principle bluntly: The Communists cannot win; the NAACP cannot lose."[73] Former ACLU legal director Mel Wulf put it even more bluntly: "There were red cases and black cases."[74]

This matter is directly relevant to the hate speech issue because, following the logic of the 1928 *Bryant* decision and the provisions of many of the international human rights statements, the prohibition of hateful ideas leads inevitably to the prohibition of organizations that espouse those ideas. The lesson of the NAACP cases is the importance of a content-neutral protection for all ideas and groups. As the civil rights struggle in the Deep South dramatically illustrated, one community's subversive threat is another community's champion of justice.

The Court's decisions in the NAACP cases were crucial to the survival of both the organization and the larger southern civil rights movement. The impact on the thinking of all civil rights and civil liberties leaders was profound. The defense of group rights, in this case African American rights, depended on the broadest possible protection for individual rights. As much as anything, this explains the growing hostility to group libel or other forms of restrictions on provocative behavior by civil rights forces.

One consequence of the Court's role in supporting the civil rights movement was a near reverence for the Court itself among civil rights leaders. This was perhaps best revealed in a 1968 crisis within the NAACP. Staff attorney Lewis Steel, who happened to be white, published an article in the Sunday *New York Times Magazine* criticizing the Court for its failure to require speedy school integration. Arguing that the Court's members were insensitive to racial justice, Steel labeled them "nine men in black who think white." The NAACP promptly fired Steel. As the organization later explained, his article was an intolerable criticism of the NAACP itself, its many litigation victories, and the Supreme Court.[75] Such was the power of the Court as a symbol of the quest for racial justice in the 1960s.

"The Central Meaning of the First Amendment"

The libertarian thrust of the Warren Court reached its apex in the 1964 *New York Times v. Sullivan.*[76] Fittingly, it was another case arising from the civil rights movement. The decision is significant because, more than in any other case, the Court used it to articulate a coherent theory of the First Amendment. That theory was captured in Justice William Brennan's argument that the United States had made "a profound national commitment to the principle that debate on public issues should be uninhibited, robust, and wide-open." Freedom to criticize government officials was "the central meaning of the First Amendment."[77] Although *Times* was not itself a hate speech case, it had profound implications for the issue.

The *Times* case arose out of the escalating civil rights movement of early 1960. Civil rights leaders placed a full-page advertisement in the *New York Times* on March 29, 1960, with the headline "Heed Their Rising Voices," charging that civil rights demonstrators were facing "an unprecedented wave of terror" and citing various incidents of violence. It did not mention L. B. Sullivan, one of the elected commissioners of the city of Birmingham, but it did refer to certain actions by the police. Sullivan's duties as commissioner included responsibility for the police department, and he claimed that the allegations libeled him. The advertisement included some factual errors, but there was little doubt that the suit against the *Times* was an effort to strike back at what Alabama leaders felt was an unflattering portrayal of their state and the race question by the northern news media. A state court jury awarded Sullivan $500,000 in damages. Few doubted that the award, if ultimately sustained, would inhibit news coverage of the civil rights issue.[78]

The Supreme Court rejected Sullivan's claim, bringing libel within the scope of the First Amendment. This overturned Justice Murphy's holding in *Chaplinsky* that libel was outside the scope of the First Amendment, which had served as the basis of Justice Frankfurter's opinion in *Beauharnais* upholding the constitutionality of the Illinois group libel law. The commitment to "uninhibited, robust, and wide-open" speech that Brennan celebrated included "vehement, caustic, and sometimes unpleasantly sharp attacks on government and public officials." Although the decision was limited to attacks on government officials, it clearly indicated that the Court was committed to protecting speech that offended people's sensibilities. In this respect it followed logically from Justice Douglas's 1950 opinion in *Terminiello* regarding speech that "stirs people to anger" and Justice Harlan's 1971 opinion in *Cohen* holding that the emotional element of speech was central to its overall message.

Finally, and perhaps most important, *Times* was yet another civil rights case. It was one of many in the post–World War II years where the extension of individual rights, and freedom of expression in particular, gave breathing room to civil rights activity. The profound national commitment explicit in *Times* was to keeping open the channels of social change, even at the cost of offensive speech.

Skokie: A Commitment Affirmed

The national commitment to protecting hate speech reached its peak in the celebrated Skokie controversy of 1977–78. The question whether a small group of American Nazis had a right to demonstrate in the predominantly Jewish Chicago suburb, over the intense opposition of that community, attracted national headlines for more than a year. Two years later it was the subject of a network television "docudrama," and eventually there were five books on the affair.[79] In terms of legal doctrine, the Skokie case broke no new ground, essentially ratifying and reaffirming several decades of legal precedent guaranteeing unpopular groups the right to demonstrate on public property. Indeed, when the first telephone call from Nazi leader Frank Collin reached the office of the Illinois ACLU, staff attorney David Goldberger thought it was a routine First Amendment case – one of many such requests that involved settled matters of law and could be disposed of with a relatively quick and easy victory.[80] Ultimately Goldberger was right: the ACLU prevailed in the courts and the Nazis won their right to demonstrate, but not before a national controversy arose, focusing on the scope of the First Amendment.

At the social and political level, however, the Skokie case seemed to portend something new. The ACLU was shocked by the bitter hostility to its defense of the Nazis' rights. One telephone caller told Illinois ACLU executive director David Hamlin, "I spit on you." Other ACLU officials received equally vicious calls and letters. A letter to national ACLU director Aryeh Neier expressed the hope that in the event of another Holocaust he would lead the parade into the crematorium.[81] None of the many previous cases involving the rights of Nazis had generated such a reaction.

The Skokie case was actually only one part of a long-running struggle between Frank Collin's National Socialist Party of America and public officials in the Chicago area. The controversy began in the Marquette Park neighborhood on Chicago's Southwest Side. As African American families began to move into this previously all-white neighborhood, racial tensions rose. Collin seized the opportunity to exploit neighborhood racism and began leading a series of antiblack demonstrations in the summer of 1976. Although his Nazi party was a pathetically small, ragtag group with perhaps two dozen members, he found a responsive audience among the alienated young whites in the neighborhood.[82]

The conflict in Marquette Park was only the latest chapter in the neighborhood-by-neighborhood resistance to black housing opportunity white Chicagoans had waged for decades. In fact the pattern of events was virtually identical to the one in another Chicago neighborhood twenty-five years earlier that resulted in the 1952 *Beauharnais* decision: the racial integration of a previously all-white neighborhood; white resistance; the most prominent role seized by a small white supremacist group; and eventually, a major court case.[83]

After some of the Collin-led demonstrations resulted in violence, Chicago park officials banned all demonstrations in Marquette Park. It then devised a more subtle approach in the form of a new policy requiring groups to post a $250,000 bond for any demonstration. The covert but obvious intent was to prevent demonstrations by small and impecunious groups. Collin turned to the ACLU, which accepted his case and filed suit in federal court, arguing that the requirement violated the First Amendment guarantee of freedom of assembly. These events received almost no publicity. The ACLU's effort on behalf of Collin was greeted with "utter silence," according to David Hamlin, because of the "commonplace nature of the event."[84]

Collin's entire strategy depended on publicity, and so while waiting for the courts to rule on his case he decided to do an end run around the Chicago Park District. He sent letters to more than a dozen suburban communities surrounding Chicago requesting demonstration permits. All but one ignored him. The Village of Skokie responded by advising him he would have to post an insurance bond for $350,000. Had they ignored him as the other communities did, the entire Skokie case might never have occurred. The wily Collin, however, decided to bypass the Skokie park officials by holding a brief demonstration in front of the village hall on May 1, 1977. It would last thirty minutes and involve about fifty people, some of whom would wear Nazi uniforms, with no speeches. No march through town was ever planned. Hoping that the entire affair would pass quickly and quietly, Skokie officials granted the request, hoping to avoid a confrontation that would give Nazis the publicity they sought, the strategy that had dominated the thinking of Jewish leaders since the 1940s.[85]

Village officials, however, did not reckon on the new currents sweeping through the Jewish community. About 40,500 of Skokie's 70,000 residents were Jewish, including an estimated 5,000 Holocaust survivors – apparently one of the largest such groups in the country.[86] Almost immediately there were angry protests from the community, arguing that any Nazi appearance in Skokie was a gross offense to the survivors and the memory of the six million Jews who died in the Holocaust. These protests tapped a new current of Jewish self-consciousness that had been awakened by the 1967 Israeli-Arab Six Day War.[87] In one of the more bizarre ironies of the controversy, it turned out that Nazi leader Collin himself was half Jewish.

In the face of these pressures, the long-standing policy of national Jewish organizations to "quarantine" anti-Semitic rabble-rousers collapsed. Jewish community leaders, in Skokie and at the national level, found it politically impossible to defend the First Amendment rights of the Nazis. In January 1978 the American Jewish Congress reversed its 1960 policy and adopted a resolution supporting restrictions on the proposed Nazi demonstration. A close reading of the resolution, however, revealed that it actually said far less than it appeared to. It declared that under the *Chaplinsky* "fighting words" doctrine "the courts may and should prohibit the [Nazis] from marching through Skokie." The Nazi group had "deliberately" chosen a heavily Jewish community "for the purpose of provoking a violent response." Yet the resolution then went on to say that any limitations needed to be narrowly drawn so as not to violate basic First Amendment rights. It concluded by advocating only a ban on the swastika, on the grounds that it was not the expression of an idea but "an insulting symbol," a fighting word designed only to provoke violence. The Congress's policy "would not prohibit [the Nazis] from marching or parading in the Village of Skokie."[88]

The American Jewish Congress's official statement reflected the agony not just of that organization but of many Jewish leaders as well. It was essentially a political statement designed to appease both sides in a bitter controversy. For over thirty years the Congress had been one of the most activist and libertarian of all the national civil rights groups. In terms of its success in creating new constitutional law doctrine and fostering social change, its record was rivaled only by the NAACP and the ACLU.[89] It had a particularly strong investment in the First Amendment on separation of church and state, since staff attorney Leo Pfeffer was widely regarded as the premier litigator of church-state cases.[90] Theodore R. Mann, chairman of the National Jewish Community Relations Advisory Council, summed up the dilemma: "At war are two parts of our heritage – on the one hand, a profound commitment to the principle of unfettered freedom of expression, and, on the other hand, an anguished collective memory of the Holocaust."[91] Mann effectively expressed the conflicting principles that lie at the heart of the entire hate speech question.

The absence – or small likelihood – of any direct confrontation between demonstrators and Skokie residents proved to be a crucial point in the controversy. The objections to the proposed Nazi demonstration were based on concern for the sensibilities of the Holocaust survivors. No face-to-face personal abuse was likely in Skokie, and any such attacks could be readily avoided. Nor was there initially any likelihood of disorder arising from a confrontation with a hostile audience[92] or even the unpleasantness of being forced to witness a Nazi demonstration. Rather, the idea was that the mere presence of the Nazis in their community would be an intolerable affront. The American Jewish Congress argued for prohibiting only the swastika as a "deliberately provocative and abusive symbol."[93] One of the issues eventually raised by the village of Skokie, but rejected by the courts, was that the demonstration inflicted a "psychic trauma" on the Holocaust survivors.[94] In a separate case, one Jewish leader used this argument in an unsuccessful suit seeking civil damages for "menticide." As many commentators pointed out, however, these same people did not object to the display of the swastika in a television docudrama, *Holocaust,* that NBC broadcast nationwide in March 1978 as the Skokie affair was nearing its climax.[95]

A complex set of legal and tactical maneuvers by both sides ensued. When the village obtained an injunction against the May first demonstration, Collin adroitly announced one for April 30. The village responded by hastily enacting three new ordinances that ultimately became the basis of the principal court case. The first required $300,000 in public liability insurance and another $50,000 in property damage insurance for demonstrations. The second prohibited the "dissemination of any material . . . which promotes and incites hatred against persons by reason of their

race, national origin, or religion, and is intended to do so." The third
prohibited public demonstrations by members of a political group wearing
"military style" uniforms.

The first of these three ordinances was similar to the Chicago Park
District's insurance requirement, which was already being challenged by
Collin and the ACLU. The third was similar to bans on uniforms adopted
by many European countries in the 1930s. The second was the most
important in terms of the hate speech issue, because it was a classic group
libel law and very similar to the 1917 Illinois law upheld by the Supreme
Court in the 1952 *Beauharnais* decision. One of the great ironies of the
Skokie crisis was that the Illinois law no longer existed. Despite the great
victory in the Supreme Court, the state had repealed it in 1961 – an
action that reflected the desuetude it had fallen into after the Supreme
Court's decision.

On May 22, 1978, a little more than a year after the controversy first
arose, the Seventh Circuit Court of Appeals declared all three Skokie
ordinances unconstitutional. The Supreme Court refused to hear an appeal, letting the lower court's opinion stand. The circuit court's opinion
disposed of all the arguments raised by the village of Skokie. Although
public demonstrations could be subjected to reasonable restrictions on
time, place, and manner, the court noted that the village of Skokie had
raised no objections on these grounds. The second and third ordinances
struck directly at "the content of appellees' views and symbols." The
court held that censorship based on the content of an idea was "forbidden" by the First Amendment.[96]

The court ruled that Nazi symbols, and their implied advocacy of
genocide, did not constitute fighting words as defined in *Chaplinsky*. No
face-to-face confrontations were contemplated, and the village of Skokie
conceded there was no threat of responsive violence. The court also
dismissed the village's argument that the Nazi message lacked social
content and contained "false statements of fact." Citing earlier precedents,
the court held that under the First Amendment there was no such thing
as a false idea. It remained for individual citizens, not the government,
"to separate the true from the false for us."[97]

The *Beauharnais* precedent posed a more difficult problem for the
court, since the language of the second ordinance closely paralleled that
of the 1917 Illinois law. The Seventh Circuit held that *Beauharnais* did
not apply, since that opinion "turns quite plainly on the strong tendency

of the prohibited utterances to cause violence and disorder." It again noted that the village did not claim disorder was likely. In passing, the court asked whether, after *Cohen, Gooding,* and *Brandenburg,* "*Beauharnais* would pass constitutional muster today."[98] The greatest threat of disorder, in fact, came from militant Jewish groups. Rabbi Meier Kahane of the Jewish Defense League (JDL) threatened to break the head of any Nazi he saw marching in Skokie.[99] The JDL brought thirty-one people to Skokie for a July 1977 demonstration, many of whom wore helmets and carried clubs. The JDL also picketed the ACLU office in New York, with members carrying baseball bats on one occasion.[100]

Similarly, developments in the area of libel law, principally *Times v. Sullivan,* had invalidated the *Chaplinsky* dictum that libel raised no constitutional problems. The court also addressed the argument that the proposed demonstration would inflict "psychic trauma" on Holocaust survivors. It ruled that even if specific individuals could raise tort claims based on the intentional infliction of emotional distress, the First Amendment did not permit prohibiting an activity "in anticipation of such results."[101] There was no doubt that a Nazi march might disturb some Skokie residents, but this was no justification for prohibiting a peaceful form of expression. The sensitivities of the anticipated audience, in short, could not override the exercise of a fundamental right.

Despite his great victory in the courts, Frank Collin never demonstrated in Skokie. Nor did he demonstrate in Marquette Park, even though the federal courts struck down the Park District's insurance requirement on June 29, 1978.[102] Instead he led a brief demonstration at the Federal Plaza in downtown Chicago on June 24, 1978. Under an agreement negotiated with the Justice Department's Community Relations Service, Chicago police escorted Collin's small group through a crowd of several thousand screaming counterdemonstrators and a large contingent of news media. After fifteen minutes the police led the Nazis away. Collin got what he had wanted all along: an enormous amount of free publicity. After a few more appearances in other cities, he returned to his original obscurity.[103]

The Triumph of a National Policy

Civil libertarians hailed the Skokie affair as a great victory. The federal courts had resoundingly upheld the First Amendment rights of a patently offensive group, reaffirming the commitment to "uninhibited, robust, and wide-open" speech on public matters. Even the ACLU, which had been plunged into a serious financial crisis because of the loss of several thousand members, quickly recovered. A special appeal in 1978 produced an unprecedented flood of contributions and a surge of new members that replaced the losses attributable to Skokie.[104]

The decision reaffirmed a commitment to free speech that had developed over the previous decades. Many observers were surprised that such a seemingly settled issue had aroused so much controversy. Some aspects of the case, however, revealed the ambivalence of many Americans about the hate speech question. The lone dissenter on the Seventh Circuit Court of Appeals pointed out that all the courts dealing with the case (the Illinois supreme court, the federal district court, and the majority on the Seventh Circuit) felt "the need to apologize for its result."[105] Lee Bollinger expanded on this point: it was as if no one liked the result but all felt constrained, if not imprisoned, by the First Amendment.[106] The Seventh Circuit majority members hotly denied that they were apologizing for their decision, arguing that it "was dictated by the fundamental proposition that if these civil rights are to remain vital for all, they must protect not only those society deems acceptable, but also those whose ideas it quite justifiably rejects and despises."[107]

Bollinger asked the pertinent question: Were we "enslaved to freedom"?[108] Did we have to do certain things, such as protect hate speech, because the First Amendment made us? The majority opinion in the Seventh Circuit decision provided the answer. The result in the Skokie case was dictated by a choice about how best to preserve civil rights. If by 1978 the existing body of First Amendment case law "dictated" the result in this case, there had been nothing inevitable about the development of that body of cases. With *Chaplinsky* (1942) and *Beauharnais* (1952) as solid precedents, the law on hate speech could have developed in a very different direction in the twenty-six years from 1952 to 1978. It rejected the option of restricting hate speech because the "lessons" of the civil rights movement were that the interests of racial minorities and powerless groups were best protected through the broadest, most content-neutral protection of speech. The crucial factor was not just that a series of courts and justices embraced that principle, but that the major civil rights groups did so as well, leaving the restriction of hate speech without an effective advocate in the United States.

7 The Campus Speech Codes: Hate Speech in the 1980s and 1990s

Crisis on the Campus

The Skokie affair, which seemed to settle the hate speech issue, was only a prelude to the storm ahead. To the surprise of most First Amendment experts, the controversy made a dramatic and surprising reappearance in the 1980s. Across the country, colleges and universities adopted codes of student conduct restricting offensive speech. The University of Michigan policy, for example, prohibited "any behavior, verbal or physical, that stigmatizes or victimizes an individual on the basis of race, ethnicity, religion, sex, sexual orientation, creed, national origin, ancestry, age, marital status, handicap or Vietnam-era veteran status."[1]

The campus speech code movement was, for a few years anyway, enormously successful. The Carnegie Fund for the Advancement of Teaching estimated that by 1990 60 percent of all colleges and universities had some policy on bigotry or racial harassment, while another 11 percent were considering one.[2] Not all of these policies prohibited hate "speech" as I have defined it; many covered only overt acts of discrimination. Nonetheless, restrictions on offensive speech were widespread, and a number of the student codes were adopted by the leading universities in the country: Michigan, Wisconsin, Stanford, Emory, and others.

The proliferation of restrictive campus speech codes was wholly unprecedented: never had there been such strong support for punishing offensive speech. By comparison the support for group libel laws in the mid-1940s was extremely weak and produced little in the way of tangible legislation. The campus speech code movement enjoyed the advocacy of broad-based coalitions of students, backed by key faculty members.

The attack on hate speech was a response to new political and legal developments in the 1980s, both on and off the campus. There was a shocking resurgence of racism, or at least of publicly expressed racist views, on college campuses. Advocates of restricting hate speech, meanwhile, offered creative new legal arguments for their proposal. The most powerful was that prohibiting hate speech was permissible and perhaps even required under the Fourteenth Amendment. This argument served as a counterweight to opposition based on First Amendment considerations. As one law professor pointed out, the Fourteenth Amendment is "no less a part of the Constitution than the First."[3] Drawing on new legal doctrine related to sexual harassment on the job, advocates also argued that hate speech created a hostile environment that infringed on the constitutionally mandated right to equal access to education.

Civil libertarians expressed great alarm over what they saw as perhaps the most serious threat to free speech and academic freedom since the worst years of the Cold War. They asked whether it would be possible to discuss any sensitive issue related to race or gender without fear of offending someone and facing possible disciplinary charges. Would it, for example, be possible to discuss theories of race or gender differences in intelligence?[4]

The speech codes touched off a wide-ranging national debate over the First Amendment and the problem of American racism. The clash of competing constitutional principles provoked an enormous outpouring of commentary by legal scholars, advocates of civil rights and civil liberties, educators, and journalists. The huge body of literature not only far exceeded that arising from the Skokie affair but was perhaps the intellectually richest dialogue on the meaning of free speech in many years.[5]

The debate was quickly resolved – for the moment, anyway – in the federal courts, where the campus speech codes met a quick and resounding defeat. The first two codes to be challenged – from the Universities of Michigan and Wisconsin – were declared unconstitutional on First Amendment grounds.[6] Then the 1992 Supreme Court decision in the St. Paul cross-burning case, invalidating a hate crimes ordinance under the First Amendment, seemed to spell doom for most of the existing campus speech codes. Justice Scalia's opinion in the cross-burning case was a resounding affirmation of the principle that the First Amendment prohibited content-based restrictions on expression. The government could not single out and curtail racist speech or racial hate speech.[7]

The decisions of the federal courts reaffirmed the national commitment to unrestricted free speech. Although these decisions were based on established doctrine, the outcome was not inevitable. The campus speech codes were justified by novel legal arguments, at least one of which had been sustained by the Supreme Court.[8] The Supreme Court, meanwhile, was dominated by a conservative majority that was unsympathetic to many civil liberties claims and had sanctioned limits on free speech in certain contexts.[9]

This chapter examines the short history of the campus speech codes in the 1980s and early 1990s, focusing on two surprising developments that demand explanation. First, what explained the unprecedented enthusiasm for restricting offensive speech represented by the campus codes? Second, how did a highly conservative Supreme Court reaffirm the national commitment to free speech in the St. Paul cross-burning case?

Campus Racism in the 1980s

The campus hate speech codes were the product of a frightening rash of racist incidents on college and university campuses that peaked in 1986 and 1987. Several of the more grotesque received nationwide publicity and were regularly cited to justify campus speech codes.[10]

At the University of Massachusetts a drunken brawl following the last game of the 1986 World Series evolved into a fight between white Boston Red Sox fans and black New York Mets fans. Reportedly a mob of about three thousand whites chased and beat anyone who was black. The Zeta Beta Tau fraternity at the University of Wisconsin held a mock slave auction. Two white Stanford University freshmen altered a picture of Beethoven, giving him obvious Negroid features, and posted it in a black studies dormitory. An African student at Smith College found a note under her dormitory room door reading, "African Nigger do you want some bananas? Go back to the jungle." An African American student at Brown University found a note under her door saying, "This room is for coloreds only." Someone at the University of Michigan scrawled on a blackboard, "A mind is a terrible thing to waste – especially on a nigger." A Purdue University student found "death nigger" scrawled on his or her dormitory room door. In one of the longest-running and most highly publicized series of events, conservative students at Dartmouth College waged a campaign against African American music professor William Cole. In the climactic incident, four white students physically confronted Cole after class in an apparent attempt to provoke a fight. The National Institute against Prejudice and Violence counted a total of 250 incidents of bigotry on campuses from 1986 to 1989.[11]

The outburst of campus racism was shocking in several ways. Many of the incidents occurred at the best colleges and universities: Stanford, Smith, Brown, Michigan, and Wisconsin. It had always been an article of faith among the educated elite that education was the best antidote to prejudice, with the implicit corollary that only the uneducated lower classes were overt racists. Consequently the series of racist incidents among the most talented students in the nation was truly shocking. Equally unsettling was the crudeness and viciousness of the attacks. The blatant use of the term "nigger" was something educated people associated with the Deep South in the segregation era, not with a contemporary northern university, and certainly not with an elite institution like Stanford or Smith. These incidents were also public events, not privately expressed objections to affirmative action or other civil rights policies. It seemed that some people felt free to act out their racist views. And finally, many of the reported incidents were direct threats – even threats of death.

It is impossible to say definitively whether there was a real increase in racist events on campus or whether simply more were being publicized. There are no systematic data on such cases. Ultimately, however, it was irrelevant whether there was a real increase: the reported incidents themselves were so shocking and so blatant as to be a cause for alarm.

In fact, students of color found that on some campuses they had to worry as much about top administrators as about anonymous bigots. In September 1992, following an attack on an elderly woman by a suspect identified as black, officials at the State University of New York at Oneonta gave the New York state police a list of all African American and Hispanic students on campus. Police officers then questioned minority students in the dormitories, on their jobs, and even in the shower. On the narrowest legal grounds, releasing the names violated the federal Privacy Act; on more general terms it reaffirmed the perception of racial minority students that college campuses were hostile environments.[12]

THE LARGER CONTEXT OF RACISM IN THE 1980s

The racist incidents on campus were part of a general deterioration of American race relations in the 1980s.[13] One of the key episodes of the 1988 presidential election campaign was the Willie Horton issue. Republican candidate George Bush charged that his liberal opponent had granted a furlough to an imprisoned murderer who then raped a woman. Willie Horton was black and the victim was white, and Bush's campaign advertisement exploited white fears of black crime. Two years later North Carolina senator Jesse Helms ran a television ad showing a pair of white hands crumpling a job application, claiming that the job had gone to someone else because of affirmative action. The ad gave a racial twist to white anxieties over shrinking job opportunities in a deteriorating economy.[14]

The increase in racial tensions resulted from a complex mixture of economic factors, crime, and the changing agenda of the civil rights movement. Between the mid-1970s and the 1990s the poor did in fact get poorer, while the rich got much richer and the middle class remained stagnant. The immiseration of the poor produced a new label for those at the bottom: the underclass. The combination of declining income and cuts in social services aggravated other social problems. Crime in underclass neighborhoods worsened while victimization declined for most other Americans.[15] The worst of that crime was drug-related gang violence, as entire neighborhoods were effectively taken over by drugs and gangs. Gang violence led to the deaths of many innocent bystanders, including very young children. Because of needle-based drug abuse, the AIDS epidemic also had a disproportionate effect on the very poor. The profile of the typical HIV-positive person shifted from a professional white male homosexual to a poor nonwhite male drug user.

Not all African Americans suffered from the changing economic patterns. The immiseration of the very poor was paralleled by the growth of a substantial black middle class. During the 1980s the gap between poor and middle-class blacks widened considerably, and the income of two-wage-earner black families nearly matched that of equivalent two-paycheck white families. The problem for both blacks and whites, however, was the decline in the percentage of stable two-paycheck families.[16]

The vast majority of white middle-class and working-class Americans, meanwhile, made almost no economic progress between the mid-1970s and the 1990s, and in many respects they saw their future prospects and those of their children deteriorating. In the context of declining economic opportunity, crime by black Americans became an easy scapegoat. College students were apparently not immune to the temptation.

Contributing to the white backlash, the agenda of the civil rights movement had changed in a very significant way. The classic "civil rights era" in American history that began in the mid-1940s came to an end somewhere in the early 1970s.[17] The central thrust of that movement had been the commitment to equality and the elimination of discriminatory measures. The high ideal was that the Constitution was "color-blind," permitting no distinctions based on race. Gradually, however, civil rights leaders began to argue that eliminating formal barriers did not lead to equality in practice. Thus they began to emphasize positive remedies, particularly affirmative action in employment. But affirmative action was necessarily race conscious rather than color-blind.

The shift from race-neutral to race-conscious programs had several consequences. In terms of formal legal doctrine, it raised the question whether race-conscious remedies violated the equal protection clause of the Fourteenth Amendment and the 1964 Civil Rights Act. The twists and turns of Supreme Court decisions on affirmative action over the past twenty years reflect the complexity of the issue and the dilemma over conflicting constitutional principles – or, in this instance, how to fulfill the constitutional mandate of equal protection. The political impact of affirmative action was even more potent, however. In a stagnant or deteriorating economy, millions of whites resented the idea that some of the few job opportunities would be reserved for racial minorities; white males also resented the prospect that jobs would be reserved for females. That the Democratic Party was so closely identified with the civil rights movement drove many of these whites into the Republican party; they were the much discussed "Reagan Democrats."[18]

Together these new economic, social, and legal factors contributed to the rise of racism among white college students in the 1980s.

The Campus Speech Codes

Students responded to the rash of racist incidents by demanding concrete action from campus officials. One of those demands involved revising codes of student conduct to penalize offensive speech and behavior. It would be misleading to refer to the campus conduct codes as a homogeneous entity: there was tremendous variety, and many covered only overt discriminatory acts. The campus "speech" codes include only those that restricted offensive forms of expression.

The speech codes shared a few common elements, such as the prohibition of demeaning forms of expression and the concept of a hostile environment. Beyond that, however, they varied considerably. Some of the codes were narrowly drawn, often with the assistance of law faculty members who were sensitive to potential First Amendment problems. The University of Wisconsin policy specifically exempted classroom situations so as not to infringe on that aspect of academic freedom.[19] Others, however, were hastily and carelessly drafted. The University of Michigan policy did not exclude the classroom. The University of Connecticut policy prohibited "inappropriately directed laughter [and] inconsiderate jokes" and the "conspicuous exclusion" of people from conversations. The Stanford University policy (officially, the Fundamental Standard Interpretation: Free Expression and Discriminatory Harassment) was possibly the narrowest and most carefully drafted, limited to insults addressed directly to a person and involving "fighting words."[20]

THE POLITICS OF THE SPEECH CODES

The campus speech code movement was the most successful effort in American history to restrict hate speech. The basis of that success is obvious: unlike earlier group libel law proposals, it enjoyed a well-organized set of advocates. The nature of that constituency and the reasons its various members supported restrictions on hate speech are the key to understanding the movement.

The first important factor was the new demographic and political profile of American higher education. Even though enrollment of African American students lagged far behind what many people sought – the enrollment of African American males actually declined in the 1980s – as a group they were still more numerous and better organized politically than before. Enrollment of Hispanic Americans soared from 472,000 in 1980 to 758,000 in 1990, while Asian American and Asian students increased from 286,000 to 555,000 over the decade.[21] Feminism emerged as a powerful force on campuses. In addition to the spread of women's studies programs, feminist faculty members were a strong presence in many established departments. Many of the politically active women students shared the idea advanced by some legal scholars that First Amendment protection of pornography violated the rights of women.[22] This skepticism about the First Amendment led them to urge restrictions on hate speech directed at women. Gay and lesbian students were also an active presence on many campuses.

Restrictive speech codes were demanded by coalitions representing students of color, feminists, and gay and lesbian students. Generally they were joined by other politically active students – white, male, heterosexual – committed to equality and diversity. The student advocates of restrictive speech codes did not necessarily represent all the members of their respective groups. As always, most students took little interest in campus politics regardless of color or gender. In any event, there was little organized (as opposed to unorganized and silent) student opposition to the proposed speech codes.

In this respect the speech code movement was remarkably successful because campuses represented minirepublics where left-liberal coalitions dominated the political agenda. Conservative critics of higher education, in fact, were particularly agitated by what they saw as a left-wing "takeover" of the campuses.[23] As we shall see, however, the campus coalitions were remarkably unsuccessful in the larger world – namely, the federal courts.

From the perspective of the history of American higher education, it was truly astonishing to find students asking administrators to curb outrageous student conduct. This was a complete reversal of the traditional pattern of campus life where successive younger generations shocked their elders – parents, faculty, administrators, trustees – with new forms of behavior. One of the pivotal moments in the campus political upheavals of the 1960s, after all, was the Free Speech Movement on the Berkeley campus of the University of California.[24]

Although most faculty members may have opposed the campus speech codes out of traditional fear of restricting academic freedom, there was crucial support from one influential segment of the faculty. This included a group of law professors, the most prominent of whom were members of racial minority groups. The three most important were Charles Lawrence III, Mari Matsuda, and Richard Delgado. Their law review articles were the most widely cited and persuasive statements on behalf of restricting offensive speech.[25] The three taught at some of the leading law schools and published their articles in the top law reviews. Thus their arguments carried all the prestige and authority normally associated with Stanford, Wisconsin, and the *Michigan Law Review*. They were joined by a number of white legal scholars who advocated restricting offensive speech based on other doubts about an absolutist approach to free speech and other constitutional rights.

The role of the law professors was critical in several respects. First, they contributed specific language to some of the campus codes, producing far more carefully drafted provisions than had only students and administrators written them. Second, their published articles on behalf of restricting offensive speech provided the kind of sophisticated arguments about the First and Fourteenth Amendments that helped to persuade or at least neutralize other faculty members and administrators.

Another factor in the spread of the speech codes was the relative weakness of the opposition on the campuses (the federal courts were a different story altogether). With few exceptions, university administrators were receptive to proposed codes. President Benno Schmidt of Yale and President Derek Bok of Harvard, in contrast, were notable for their strong public statements that the proposed codes threatened academic freedom. Many college administrators had a genuine concern about equal educational opportunity and the need to increase the enrollment of racial minorities. There was considerable alarm in the mid-1980s over the decline in the enrollment of African American males, and so creating and maintaining an open and tolerant atmosphere on campus became one of the principal rationales for the speech codes.[26] Cynics suggested that college administrators simply wanted to avoid trouble and that acceding to the demands of minority students was the line of least resistance. A number of campuses did experience disruptive sit-ins over charges that the officials had not done enough in the way of affirmative action for both student and faculty recruitment.

Many individual faculty members, along with off-campus free speech advocates, expressed strong objections to the proposed codes because of the threat to academic freedom and free speech. On some campuses these objections opened up a vigorous debate that prevented the adoption of any new speech codes. On many others, however, the opposition failed. To a great extent the advocates of restricting hate speech held the moral and political high ground within the context of college and university campuses: there did appear to be a frightening upsurge of racism. Campus racism posed another of the classic "hard cases" where the free speech advocates are forced to defend the rights of some with utterly despicable points of view. As First Amendment authority Rodney Smolla put it, hate speech posed "the hardest free speech question of all,"[27] and many of the liberal faculty members undoubtedly concluded that this was not the issue on which to take an unpopular stand. The threats of violence in some of the incidents added an element of crisis that, for many, probably tipped the balance in favor of the codes. For uncertain faculty members, the law professor advocates provided sophisticated scholarly arguments that the codes were not inconsistent with the First Amendment.

At the national level the organized voice of the faculty, the American Association of University Professors (AAUP) issued a strong statement against restrictive speech codes in June 1992: "Freedom of thought and expression is essential to any institution of higher learning," the AAUP declared, and "a college or university sets a perilous course if it seeks to differentiate between high-value and low-value speech." Such distinctions "are neither practicable nor principled." Free speech is not merely one part of the higher education but is "the very precondition of the academic enterprise itself."[28] The official AAUP statement, however, was not adopted until 1992, somewhat late in the short history of the campus speech codes.

The role of the ACLU reflected its organizational weaknesses and strengths. From a national perspective, campuses appeared to be an ACLU stronghold. Along with lawyers, professors constituted one of the largest single groups of ACLU members. Organizationally, however, the ACLU had no strong network of campus chapters; its strength lay off campus in the statewide affiliate offices.[29] And it was the affiliates in Michigan and Wisconsin that brought the successful suits against the Michigan and Wisconsin codes. There was also an important division of opinion within the ACLU. As we shall see, a significant minority argued that properly and narrowly drafted codes of conduct did not violate the First Amendment.

New Rationales for an Old Idea

The campus speech codes began with the same basic premise as the old group libel laws – that society had a right to restrict speech that harmed others – but added a number of new rationales. Some of these were revived versions of old arguments, while others were wholly new.

The first significant change was an expanded list of protected groups. Whereas the old group libel laws generally covered race, ethnicity, and religion, most campus speech codes also covered sex, sexual orientation, age, and physical capacity. The University of Michigan policy added "Vietnam-era veteran status." This expanded list reflected the impact of the "rights revolution" that began in the 1960s. One of the major consequences of the civil rights movement was an expanded awareness of the exclusion of so many groups from full participation in American society.

A second change was specific language encompassing more than speech and publication. Although they were generally referred to as "speech" codes, most covered a broader range of behavior. The University of Michigan policy specified "any behavior, verbal or physical"; the University of Wisconsin code embraced "comments, epithets or other expressive behavior." This language reflected contemporary understanding of the nature of communication as recognized by legal scholars and courts.[30]

The primary rationale underlying the speech codes was a revived version of the old fighting words doctrine. Although the 1942 *Chaplinsky* decision had not been formally reversed by the mid-1980s, its scope had been drastically narrowed by a series of decisions, to the point where many legal scholars did not believe there was anything left in the way of viable doctrine. The speech code advocates attempted to breathe new life into the fighting words doctrine by reviving Justice Murphy's two-tiered analysis of the First Amendment. As a number of scholars pointed out, American law was far less "absolutist" on the First Amendment than civil libertarians were willing to admit. There were many forms of speech or expression that did not enjoy constitutional protection: bribery, fraud, criminal conspiracy, and some forms of libel.[31]

One approach viewed hate speech as a form of assault. Richard Delgado led the way on this point with a widely cited article arguing for encompassing hate speech within the tort of infliction of emotional distress.[32] Others went even further, arguing that racist speech was not really "speech" at all: it was not the expression of an idea, entitled to First Amendment protection, but an assault. Lawrence argued that "the invective is experienced as a blow, not as a proffered idea." It was designed to end discussion, not initiate it: "Assaultive racist speech functions as a preemptive strike"; "once the blow is struck, a dialogue is unlikely to follow."[33]

In an admittedly content-based distinction, Lawrence and others singled out racist speech as a special evil: "Racist speech inflicts real harm, and . . . this harm is far from trivial."[34] The harm was immediate and personal; hate speech assaulted the dignity of the individual and caused feelings of inferiority and unworthiness. Others emphasized the international and historical dimensions of racism. The author of one law review article asserted that "racism is unique"; the central theme of world history was the "catastrophic historical experience with racism."[35] Thus racism in all its manifestations, including speech and other forms of propaganda, could and should be prohibited by law. A similar rationale underlay the prohibitions on racist propaganda in the various international human rights declarations.[36]

This content-based exception to the First Amendment was in many respects a new version of the special case exception argument that had been around since the 1920s. In slightly different versions it underpinned the pre–World War II anti-Fascist legislation, David Riesman's argument for group libel legislation, and Justice Felix Frankfurter's opinion in *Beauharnais* upholding the Illinois group libel law.

Lawrence also advanced the novel argument that the historic *Brown v. Board of Education* decision outlawing segregated schools was really a *speech* case.[37] Segregated schools communicated a message of unworthiness to black children. Lawrence's reference to *Brown* was part of a far more important development in thinking about rights: that limiting hate speech was necessary to fulfill the mandate of the Fourteenth Amendment. Restricting hate speech was not merely permissible but constitutionally required. This was an extremely powerful argument because it recast the hate speech debate. For decades the issue had always been approached in terms of the First Amendment alone. The immediate question was whether this particular restriction (say, group libel) infringed on First Amendment rights. Cast in these terms, free speech advocates occupied the constitutional high ground – or, as Lawrence saw it, the "moral high ground."[38] Introducing the Fourteenth Amendment's guarantee of equal protection produced a level constitutional playing field.

Some feminists had made a similar argument with respect to pornography. Andrea Dworkin and Catherine MacKinnon had argued that pornography was a form of sex discrimination, introducing egalitarian principles to counter the First Amendment argument on behalf of freedom of expression.[39] A proposed antipornography ordinance in Minneapolis was ultimately defeated, and an Indianapolis ordinance based on their ideas was declared unconstitutional.[40]

The emphasis on the special evil of racism was part of a new approach to legal reasoning. Along with a number of other scholars, Lawrence, Matsuda, and Delgado introduced a personal element into legal writing. They wrote in a personal voice, recounted personal experiences, and argued that more weight should be given to personal experience in all reasoning about the law. The problem with traditional legal reasoning – which included First Amendment jurisprudence – was that it was too abstract and impersonal. Speaking for all victims of discrimination, Lawrence argued, "We see a different world."[41] Matsuda called for new methods, "grounded in the particulars of . . . social reality and experience." It was especially important to explore the experience of the historical victims of racism in order "to know history from the bottom." Her major article, subtitled "Considering the Victim's Story," began with several examples of racism, including a personal experience: "As a young child I was told never to let anyone call me a J–p." Her parents' warning "transmitted a message of danger, that the word was a dangerous one, tied to violence."[42] Lawrence expressed his dismay "that we have not listened to the real victims – that we have shown so little understanding of their injury."[43] Harvard Law professor Derrick Bell's analysis of civil rights law, *And We Are Not Saved,* was a series of narratives or "chronicles" told by Geneva Crenshaw, a character of Bell's creation.[44]

Civil libertarians had always objected to using people's sensibilities as a standard for defining limitations on speech. In particular, it gave the audience a powerful veto over anything it deemed offensive: war veterans were offended by flag-burning; Christian moralists were offended by homosexuality; Catholics were offended by attacks on the church over abortion or gay rights; and so on. It represented the vagueness problem run amok: What words or expression gave offense? Who would determine which were harmful and to what degree?

Using victims' sensibilities as a standard also introduced the question of which groups qualified as the victims of discrimination. Some advocates candidly argued that restrictive speech codes should apply only to the "historical" victims of racism. Professor Kent Greenawalt, who is white, concluded that religious slurs were far less serious than racial and ethnic slurs. Moreover, he argued that people of color were entitled to a higher degree of protection than whites: the term "'honkey' hurts a lot less than 'nigger.'"[45] This was a new version of Riesman's contextualized approach: some kinds of offensive speech were more harmful than others; what should be tolerated in one country and one time may be too dangerous in another.[46] Mari Matsuda elaborated on this point and, in the process, exposed the elusiveness of the definition of who was a victim. Addressing the question of "Zionist" speech, she argued that it depended on the speaker and the audience. On one hand, "angry, survivalist expression, arising out of the Jewish experience of persecution and without resort to the rhetoric of white supremacy" was protected under what she called the "victim's privilege." But a Zionist lost the privilege by indulging in any expression of white supremacy over "brown or black people." In her judgment, "the various subordinated communities are best equipped to analyze and condemn hate speech within their midst." Earlier she had argued that "the appropriate standard" was "the recipient's community standard." Thus only "victim" groups would be protected, and each victim group could determine what was offensive. This was the civil libertarian's proverbial slippery slope in the extreme.[47]

The most important aspect of the position advanced by Lawrence and Bell was their profound pessimism about the state of racial justice and the effect of the law in achieving equality. The title of Bell's book said it all: *And We Are Not Saved: The Elusive Quest for Racial Justice.*[48] The law – at least litigation based on race-neutral egalitarian principles – had not achieved racial justice. From their perspective the great gains of the civil rights movement and of civil rights litigation amounted to nothing. More than anything else, this pessimism separated Lawrence and Bell (and others who shared their view) from previous generations of civil rights leaders. The earlier opposition to restricting hate speech, I have argued, was driven by the exhilarating experience of making great gains through constitutional litigation. From the vantage point of the 1980s, Lawrence and Bell saw nothing but unfulfilled promises. Race-conscious measures were now required, including both affirmative action and content-based restrictions on hate speech.[49] By 1992 Bell was even more pessimistic, declaring in his latest book that blacks would "never" achieve full equality in America.[50]

This mood of despair led Lawrence to a fatalistic assumption of inevitable defeat when confronted with hateful words. "In most situations," he wrote, "members of minority groups realize that they are likely to lose if they fight back, and are forced to remain silent and submissive."[51] This represented an entirely different approach from that taken by several prominent African American members of the ACLU Board of Directors who opposed any restrictions on hate speech. Board member Gwen Thomas, for example, began with the assumption of African American assertiveness, a readiness to engage the offensive speaker and gain self-respect from the struggle. "We have to teach [our young people] how to deal with adversarial situations," she argued. "They have to learn how to survive with offensive speech they find wounding and hurtful."[52] Thomas and fellow ACLU board member Michael Meyers expressed contempt for those who shrank from the struggle and sought the refuge of protective and, in their minds, paternalistic legislation. This combative mode expressed an implicit optimism about the possibilities of change through law. Where Lawrence and Bell saw inevitable defeat, Thomas and Meyers saw at least a fighting chance.

Perhaps the most creative new element attributed to the harm caused by hate speech was the relatively new concept of the hostile working environment. The University of Michigan policy, for example, prohibited expressive behavior that "creates an intimidating, hostile, or demeaning environment for educational pursuits, employment or participation in University sponsored extra-curricular activities" (section 1.C).[53] Similar language was found in other campus policies.

The concept of the hostile environment had developed out of the law on sex discrimination. Feminist legal scholar Catherine MacKinnon developed the argument that on-the-job sexual harassment was a form of sex discrimination under Title VII of the 1964 Civil Rights Act.[54] The Supreme Court endorsed this idea in the 1986 *Meritor Savings Bank* decision, holding that a hostile environment was a form of sex discrimination and that an employer who knew about the offending practices and failed to take remedial action was liable.[55]

Applying this principle to the college campus, speech code advocates argued that maintaining a nonhostile campus environment was necessary to achieve the goal of equal educational opportunity: the victims of attack would tend to drop out of school or not enroll at all. Racist speech communicated a message of exclusion. This claim gave added weight to the point about the psychic harm of hate speech. In the challenges to their speech codes, both the University of Michigan and the University of Wisconsin argued that they had a legal mandate to provide equal educational opportunity and that their speech codes were a legitimate and necessary means to that end.[56]

The introduction of Fourteenth Amendment considerations into the hate speech debate was part of a much broader current of thought among legal scholars and some social critics. From a number of different perspectives – feminist, leftist, African American, conservative, and moderate liberal – there was a new criticism of the weight given to individual rights in American law and policy at the expense of either group rights or the interests of society as a whole. Some feminists, for example, argued that a purely individualist approach to rights left women disadvantaged in the real world. Catherine MacKinnon's argument that pornography constituted a form of sex discrimination reflected discontent with an approach that gave the First Amendment automatic priority.[57]

Support for restricting hate speech also came from a new movement known as communitarianism.[58] Several organizations and social commentators began to argue that the "rights revolution" had gone too far in emphasizing individual rights and that more attention should be given to individual responsibilities and the needs of society as a whole. One group was led by sociologist Amitai Etzioni, who founded and edited the journal *The Responsive Community* as a voice for communitarianism.[59] It was joined by the American Alliance for Rights and Responsibilities and by theologian Richard John Neuhaus's Institute on Religion and Public Life. Harvard law professor Mary Ann Glendon criticized the American preoccupation in her book *Rights Talk* and decried "the missing language of responsibility."[60] Communitarians stressed children and families, arguing that there should be less emphasis on each member's right to happiness and self-fulfillment, which frequently led to divorce, and more on parents' obligations to their children.[61] Etzioni cited sobriety checkpoints as an example of a minor intrusion on individual rights that benefited the general public.

With respect to hate speech, the communitarian platform endorsed freedom of speech but called for individual self-restraint: even though you had the right to call someone a name, you should not exercise that right.[62] Civility and the common good were more important than unlimited individual rights. In many respects the communitarians were reviving the old "balancing test" that had been the focal point of debates over the First Amendment in the late 1950s and early 1960s – the rights of the individual needed to be balanced against the interests of society as a whole.

Some prominent legal scholars endorsed official restriction of hate speech on related grounds. Cass Sunstein argued that the "core" value embodied in the First Amendment was not free speech for its own sake but "rational deliberation, especially about democratic values." Reviving the argument originally made by Alexander Meiklejohn, he said the central purpose of free speech was "the exchange of ideas about some question of public importance."[63] From this perspective, some kinds of speech had little if any value. Sunstein pointed out, as did Lawrence, that the protection of free speech was far less "absolutist" than many civil libertarians wanted to admit. Many forms of speech were subject to criminal penalties: bribery, fraud, libel, pornography, and more recently certain kinds of sexual harassment.[64] If these forms of speech had no social value and were not entitled to First Amendment protection, why couldn't racist speech be prohibited as well?

THE DEBATE AMONG THE CIVIL LIBERTARIANS

The campus speech codes provoked an immediate response from the ACLU and other free speech advocates. Many saw the codes as the most serious threat to freedom of expression and to academic freedom since the worst years of the Cold War. Initially, however, the ACLU was not entirely of one mind on this issue. A significant minority within the organization supported some limited measures to restrict racist speech on campus.

Fourteenth Amendment considerations weighed heavily on the minds of many members. The ACLU had a strong organizational commitment to racial equality. In addition to its own affirmative action policy on staff employment, it had litigated major school desegregation cases, was arguably the principal litigator of voting rights cases that had empowered black voters across the South (and in some nonsouthern states as well), and had taken a prominent role in fighting police misconduct, which was for all practical purposes a civil rights issue.[65] ACLU legal director john a. powell[66] expressed his personal belief that too often the First Amendment had been allowed to trump the Fourteenth. Mary Ellen Gale, a member of the national Board of Directors and leader of the powerful Southern California affiliate, reminded her colleagues that the Fourteenth Amendment is "no less a part of the Constitution than the First."[67]

The outcome of the debate, whatever role the ACLU might play in the campus speech code controversy, was not insignificant. The ACLU had defended the free speech rights of offensive groups since the 1920s. The 1934 statement on the free speech rights of domestic Nazis, as I have argued, was the seminal document in the development of national policy. And ultimately, ACLU affiliates in Michigan and Wisconsin brought the two successful challenges to the campus speech codes. Endorsement by the ACLU of some form of hate speech restriction on campus could conceivably have a substantial impact on the outcome of the controversy.

Support for some limited restriction on hate speech was centered in the three California ACLU affiliates.[68] They were a powerful presence within the organization, since their combined membership far exceeded that of any other state. The Southern California affiliate in particular had opposed national ACLU policies on a variety of issues: it had its own policy on economic rights, for example. The three California affiliates adopted their own policies on the campus speech codes. Under the ACLU's federal structure, affiliates may adopt policies that differ from national policy or may adopt a policy in the absence of national policy. In the Supreme Court, however, only the national policy can be presented in the name of the ACLU.[69] Southern California has a very comprehensive policy on economic rights, for example, while the Michigan ACLU adopted a policy on surrogate parenting and took a case even before the national Board of Directors considered the issue.

The division of opinion within the ACLU on hate speech paralleled divisions on other issues. The ACLU minority perspective gave much greater weight to egalitarian and social justice considerations than did the majority. The ACLU minority, for example, favored limits on political campaign financing, in the interests of equality, while the ACLU majority opposed them on First Amendment grounds. The ACLU minority also favored expanding the scope of civil liberties to include economic rights, as in the right to the necessities of life such as food, shelter, and employment.[70] In several respects, then, the ACLU minority position was closer to the general thrust of the international human rights statements than was official ACLU policy.[71]

The conflict within the ACLU came to a head in California when the University of California (UC) adopted a harassment policy on September 21, 1989. A new part of section 51 of the code of student conduct stated that students could be disciplined for using "fighting words," defined as words that were "personally abusive," were "directly addressed to any ordinary person," and were "in the context used and as a matter of common knowledge, inherently likely to provoke a violent reaction whether or not they actually do so." Additionally, fighting words constituted harassment when they created "a hostile and intimidating environment" and "interfere[d] with the victim's ability to pursue effectively his or her education."[72]

The California ACLU affiliates responded by adopting their own policies that endorsed some very limited grounds for restricting hate speech. Because the nine UC campuses covered the jurisdictions of all three affiliates, they eventually agreed on a common policy, which began by acknowledging a commitment to the two conflicting civil liberties principles: "The ACLU has always been committed to protecting freedom of speech to guarantee the free exchange of ideas," including "the protection of speech which expresses unpopular or abhorrent ideas." But the ACLU was also "committed to the proposition that on college campuses, full participation in the educational process must be available on a nondiscriminatory basis to all." This meant that college and university administrators "are obligated to take all steps necessary within constitutional bounds to minimize and eliminate a hostile educational environment which impairs access of protected minorities to equal educational opportunities." Any limitations on speech, however, had to "be carefully drawn" and "focus on speech or expression used as a weapon to harass specific victims on the basis of their protected status." This included only speech or expression that "is specifically intended to and does harass an individual or specific individuals" on the basis of their protected status; "is addressed directly to the individual or individuals whom it harasses"; and "creates a hostile and intimidating environment." It then added a number of important due process considerations related to the enforcement of any harassment policy. These points included the right to notice and a hearing, a list of "specific illustrations" of the kind of behavior covered by any policy, penalties "proportionate to the gravity of the violation," and no prior restraint of any expression.[73]

The California ACLU policy provoked considerable controversy. To the casual reader there appeared to be no conflict between it and the UC harassment policy. Some observers thought the ACLU had endorsed potentially sweeping restrictions on speech. In a series of articles, journalist

Nat Hentoff accused the California affiliates of "retreating" on the First Amendment. "What's happening to the ACLU?" he asked.[74] Hentoff's was a voice to be reckoned with. He was a lifelong civil libertarian, a former member of the ACLU Board of Directors, and one of only two newspaper columnists who regularly wrote on civil liberties issues.[75]

Hentoff grossly exaggerated the scope of the California ACLU policy and the conflict within the organization. In fact, the California ACLU affiliates regarded the UC code as unconstitutional and quickly launched protracted negotiations with the university.[76] The ACLU affiliates argued that the university had given the term "fighting words" too broad a meaning and that a speaker had no way of knowing what words might be covered. The phrase about interfering with a student's ability to effectively pursue an education was impermissibly vague. The three ACLU affiliates asked whether "interference" would be determined by the "sensitivities of the victim" or by some objective standard. If the latter, what was that standard and how would a speaker know what it was?[77] Also, the policy did not explicitly require that the offending words be intended to harass.

These were not merely hypothetical issues: one of the requirements of any criminal code is that it specify the prohibited conduct. The questions raised by the California ACLU affiliates dramatized the fact that the vagueness problem could not be wished away. Narrow as it was, the UC policy left a number of important questions unanswered. And as we will see shortly, a federal judge declared the University of Michigan policy unconstitutional in part because the university had given conflicting interpretations of its application. In the judge's words, it did not know what its own policy was and was simply making it up as it went along.[78]

Negotiations between the University of California and ACLU representatives dragged on for over a year with no satisfactory resolution. At one point a clearly frustrated UC staff counsel asked the ACLU affiliates to submit their own "model policy." The affiliates declined.[79] No suit challenging the policy was filed, however. Apart from one potential case that was rejected because of a bad set of facts, the three California ACLU affiliates remained without a client.[80] It was not entirely clear whether this was due to the nonenforcement of the harassment code or whether no disciplined students wanted to contest their punishment. The history of the hate speech issue suggested that it was the former. The principal state group libel laws – Illinois (1917), New Jersey (1934), and Massachusetts (1943) – were rarely if ever enforced. Nor is there any indication that the many European laws against racist propaganda are enforced more than occasionally.[81]

The national ACLU slowly moved toward developing a policy on the campus speech codes. The 1989 biennial conference, attended by lay members and leaders, featured a major debate between Charles Lawrence and future ACLU president Nadine Strossen.[82] Their presentations were subsequently expanded and published in the *Duke Law Journal*, with Lawrence's article becoming one of the major defenses of restricting hate speech.[83] Strossen responded with the traditional civil libertarian arguments opposing content-based restrictions, citing the vagueness problem and the proverbial danger of the "slippery slope." To these points she added that prohibiting racist speech could even "aggravate the underlying problem of racism" because it would focus on one of the symptoms of racism without addressing the causes. Moreover, it would inevitably grant enormous discretion in enforcement to officials who could then use it against racial minority leaders who used inflammatory language. She cited instances where the British Race Relations Act had been used against black leaders. Strossen concluded with the traditional civil libertarian prescription for offensive speech: more speech. Government officials should condemn racism and racist speech, and "private individuals and groups should exercise their first amendment rights by speaking out against racism."[84]

While the national ACLU debated, two affiliates acted. The Michigan affiliate challenged the University of Michigan policy and won a ruling declaring it unconstitutional in September 1989. The Wisconsin affiliate won its challenge to the University of Wisconsin policy in 1991.

The ACLU's national Board of Directors finally considered the campus speech code issue in October 1990 and unequivocally reaffirmed its support for freedom of speech. The new policy on Free Speech and Bias on College Campuses began by rejecting the alternatives of either restricting speech or allowing "bias to be unremedied." It declared that the ACLU "opposes all campus regulations which interfere with the freedom of professors, students and administrators to teach, learn, discuss and debate or to express ideas, opinions or feelings in classroom, public or private discourse." It added that "this policy does not prohibit colleges and universities from enacting disciplinary codes aimed at restricting acts of harassment, intimidation and invasion of privacy." It quickly explained that "the fact that words may be used in connection with otherwise actionable conduct does not immunize such conduct." The phrase "otherwise actionable" in effect meant that college and university administrators could punish assaults as traditionally defined in criminal statutes but not words or expressive behavior alone.[85]

The problem of racism on campus, the ACLU policy continued, should be dealt with through affirmative steps to enhance equal opportunity in education. The ACLU called on college and university administrators to communicate "commitment to the elimination of all forms of bigotry on campus"; to develop "comprehensive plans" for reducing prejudice; to pursue affirmative action recruitment efforts; and to offer and consider requiring courses in the history and meaning of prejudice.

In the end, the ACLU debate over hate speech on campus was anticlimactic. There was no sharp division of opinion as the organization reaffirmed its commitment to defending the free speech rights of racists. The 1990 policy on campus speech was little more than an elaboration of the position first articulated in the ACLU's 1934 pamphlet *Shall We Defend Free Speech for Nazis in America?*[86]

THE HYDE BILL: CONSERVATIVES DISCOVER FREE SPEECH

One of the more curious responses to the campus speech controversy was a bill in Congress to protect freedom of speech at private colleges and universities. The bill was introduced by Rep. Henry Hyde, a conservative Illinois Republican who was most famous for the Hyde Amendment prohibiting the use of federal funds for abortion services. Hyde's Collegiate Speech Protection Act would allow students at private educational institutions receiving federal funds to challenge campus conduct codes on First Amendment grounds.[87]

The ACLU cosponsored the Hyde bill, bringing the organization into a coalition with one of its bitterest enemies. Hyde himself admitted he had "made a career out of battling the ACLU," and even some ACLU members were uneasy about the alliance.

The bill had several extraordinary aspects. It was a radical departure from traditional conservative opposition to federal regulation. The pursuit of social policies through regulations tied to federal funding was an established liberal strategy and one of the bêtes noirs of conservatives. Extending federal regulation to private institutions was an even more serious departure from conservative doctrine. Not surprisingly, the Hyde bill was opposed by the National Association of Independent Colleges and Universities, which charged that it would interfere with their efforts to "create a climate of civility" on their campuses.[88]

Finally, the bill marked a rare and almost unprecedented move by a conservative politician to institutionalize protection of free speech. In the entire history of the hate speech controversy there were no other examples of leading conservatives rising to the defense of offensive speech. Nor did the larger history of the First Amendment contain many instances of conservative support for free speech. The major exception was the challenge to the 1974 amendments to the Federal Election Campaign Act, *Buckley v. Valeo*, featuring Republican senator James Buckley and a bizarre coalition of liberal, leftist, and conservative groups.[89]

Hyde's discovery of free speech was probably motivated less by the hate speech issue itself than by the conservative belief that leftists had taken over the universities. This issue became known as the "PC" (political correctness) controversy. According to conservatives, leftist faculty and students had imposed their own political orthodoxy on college campuses. Anyone who disagreed with the "politically correct" agenda was vilified, or worse. Closely related to this was the furious battle over the curriculum. Conservatives believed that high academic standards, institutionalized in the "canon" of classic works, were being replaced by a politically driven curriculum. As its own subtitle ("A Response to the New Intolerance in the Academy") suggested, the Hyde bill was essentially a political statement about higher education.[90]

The Campus Speech Codes in the Federal Courts

When the campus speech codes finally reached the federal courts, they met a quick and resounding defeat. The first and only two to be challenged were declared unconstitutional on First Amendment grounds. These decisions reaffirmed the commitment to the protection of provocative and offensive speech. They were soon followed by the Supreme Court's 1992 decision in the St. Paul cross-burning case, which appeared to doom most of the remaining speech codes.

The University of Michigan's policy was the first to reach the courts. It arose out of a series of racist incidents on campus in 1987. On January 27 some unknown people distributed a racist leaflet declaring "open season" on African Americans, referring to them as "saucer lips, porch monkeys, and jigaboos." A week later the campus radio station broadcast some racist jokes. When students demonstrated to protest these events, someone displayed a Ku Klux Klan costume from a dormitory window. The university president responded with a public statement expressing his outrage at these incidents and reaffirming the university's commitment to a racially and culturally diverse campus. The state legislature entered the picture when the chairman of the House Subcommittee on Higher Education of the Appropriations Committee held public hearings on campus racism. Students, meanwhile, formed a United Coalition against Racism and threatened to file a class-action suit against the university for failing to maintain a nonracist atmosphere on campus.[91]

Responding to this extraordinarily tense situation, the university regents began working on a student code of conduct in early 1988. After much debate they adopted a policy on April 14, to be effective May 31, 1988. The Policy on Discrimination and Discriminatory Harassment of Students in the University Environment prohibited "any behavior, verbal or physical, that stigmatizes or victimizes an individual on the basis of race, ethnicity, religion, sex, sexual orientation, creed, national origin, ancestry, age, marital status, handicap or Vietnam-era veteran status." This included any "express or implied threat to an individual's academic efforts, employment, participation in University sponsored extra-curricular activities or personal safety" or anything that interfered with those activities or "create[d] an intimidating, hostile, or demeaning environment for educational pursuits, employment or participation in University sponsored extra-curricular activities." A second section, with nearly identical wording, prohibited "sexual advances, requests for sexual favors," or other stigmatizing behavior based on gender or sexual orientation. In August the university suddenly withdrew the section relating to a hostile environment but not, for some unexplained reason, the identical section relating to sexual harassment.[92]

There were two aspects of the policy that immediately created alarm among civil libertarians. First, it did not explicitly require that an offensive expression be directed at an individual. Second, it did not specifically exempt classroom situations. Even worse was the university's attempt to explain how it might be applied. In fall 1989 its Office of Affirmative Action published an interpretive guide, *What Students Should Know about Discrimination and Discriminatory Harassment by Students in the Uni-*

versity Environment. It included some examples of behavior that violated the policy: distributing a flier containing racist threats; a male student's commenting in class that "women students just aren't as good in this field as men"; a dormitory party to which everyone is invited except a student others believe to be a lesbian. Whereas the first example clearly involved a threat, the second represented a statement that could legitimately arise in a discussion of gender differences; the third involved private group behavior rather than speech. A few months later the university withdrew the guide, although without informing anyone on campus, leaving the terms of the policy completely ambiguous. Only later did the university state that the information in the guide was "not accurate."[93]

The policy was challenged by a graduate student in biopsychology who argued that it infringed on his freedom to teach. Some of the theories in his field relating to biologically based differences between races and genders might prompt in-class discussions that would be perceived as violating the policy. The Michigan ACLU affiliate agreed to take the case.

On September 22, 1989, the federal district court declared the policy unconstitutional on grounds of vagueness and overbreadth. The first issue confronting the court was whether the policy applied to classroom discussions. It found ample evidence in both the legislative history and its application showing that it did. It cited three instances where students had been disciplined or threatened with discipline under the policy for comments in class. One involved a social work graduate student who said he believed homosexuality was a disease and had counseled clients accordingly. A formal hearing ruled that he did not violate the policy. A second case concerned a business student who read a limerick in a class exercise that ridiculed a famous athlete because of his alleged sexual orientation. This case was settled informally, with the student agreeing to write a letter of apology and attend a gay rap group. The third involved an orientation session in predentistry in which a student commented that he had heard minorities had great difficulty in the course and were not treated fairly. The complaint was filed by a racial minority professor who argued that the comment was unfair and had hurt her chances for tenure. The student was counseled informally and persuaded to write a letter to the professor.

The court accepted the ACLU's argument that the policy was unconstitutionally vague. When asked during the oral argument how he would distinguish between merely offensive speech, which he conceded was protected, and speech that was prohibited by the policy, the university's attorney answered, "very carefully."[94] The court concluded that there was no consistency between the legislative history of the policy, the record of its administration, and the interpretation offered in court. Citing the withdrawal of the explanatory guide and the "eleventh hour" suspension of the section on hostile environment, the court concluded that "the University had no idea what the limits of the Policy were and . . . was essentially making up the rules as it went along."[95]

Several possible remedies for discriminatory and harassing behavior were available to the university. What it could not do – and what this policy did – however, was to prohibit "certain speech because it disagreed with ideas or messages sought to be conveyed." The most recent decision cited in support of this prohibition on content-based restrictions had been delivered by the Supreme Court only three months earlier. In one of the most controversial First Amendment cases in years, the Court upheld the right to burn the American flag. Although burning the American flag was profoundly offensive to millions of Americans, the Court held that to punish that act was to make a distinction based on the content of the message.[96] The flag-burning decision – and the decision the following year overturning the new flag protection act[97] – was extremely relevant to the campus speech code controversy. It is fair to say that many if not most of the students supporting the restriction on hate speech would defend the right of a political radical to burn the flag as a form of protest. The conjunction of the flag-burning and speech-code decisions within a few months of each other in 1989 dramatized once again the earlier lesson of the civil rights movement: that any measure designed to protect powerless groups could easily be used to restrict the political activity of the powerless.

Two years later a federal district court in Wisconsin ruled that the University of Wisconsin code violated the First Amendment. The Policy and Guidelines on Racist and Discriminatory Conduct was notable in that it had been drafted with the help of law professor Richard Delgado, whose article on tort remedies for racist speech and other harmful speech was one of the most influential and widely cited items advocating restrictions.[98] Formally adopted on June 9, 1989, the policy covered "racist or discriminatory comments, epithets or other expressive behavior directed at an individual" where those comments "demean the race, sex, religion, color, creed, disability, sexual orientation, national origin, ancestry or age of the individual or individuals" or "create an intimidating, hostile or demeaning environment for education" or other university-related activity.[99]

The Wisconsin policy was much clearer and more narrowly drafted than Michigan's in several respects – and thus more likely to survive a First Amendment challenge. First, it explicitly applied only to direct attacks on an individual. Second, the policy itself included illustrative examples: calling someone an offensive name, placing demeaning material in someone's living quarters or workplace, destroying property, and so forth. Most important, it exempted classroom situations: "A student would not be in violation if, during a class discussion, he or she expressed a derogatory opinion concerning a racial or ethnic group." The university also published an explanatory pamphlet with additional examples. This included two classroom situations. In one a male student expresses the view that women are "by nature better equipped to be mothers" and should not be employed in upper-level management positions. The university explained that this was not covered by the policy because it involved "an expression of opinion, contains no epithets, and is not directed to a particular individual." In the second example a faculty member states that certain ethnic groups seem to be genetically predisposed to alcoholism. This was also not covered because the policy did not apply to faculty members. Wisconsin students, in short, had a much clearer picture of what kinds of behavior were forbidden and what ones were not.[100]

Although it was far more carefully drafted than the Michigan policy, the federal district court found the University of Wisconsin policy unconstitutional. The court rejected the university's argument that the policy properly covered only fighting words as defined by *Chaplinsky* and held that the first prong of the *Chaplinsky* definition (words likely to inflict injury) was "defunct" and that the policy exceeded the scope of the surviving second prong because it was not limited to words that had a tendency to incite an immediate breach of the peace. Moreover, because it singled out racist speech, the policy was an impermissible content-based restriction on speech. The university had argued that it regulated only speech that had harmful effects and minimum social value. The court held that such a balancing test was permissible only in content-neutral regulations.[101]

The court also rejected the university's arguments based on the two most important new rationales for prohibiting hate speech. It rejected the argument that the university had a compelling interest under the

Fourteenth Amendment in increasing the diversity of the student body, noting that the university had offered no evidence that it was not "providing education on equal terms." It also ruled that the concept of a hostile environment did not apply because the *Meritor* decision applied to employment and not to education. Students are not the responsible agents of the university in the same sense that employees are, and consequently the university was not liable for their conduct as was the employer in *Meritor*. The court added that Title VII of the 1964 Civil Rights Act was a statute and could not supersede the First Amendment.[102]

Finally, the university's policy was found to be unconstitutionally vague. It was not clear whether it was sufficient for the offending speaker to merely intend to demean the listener (without necessarily accomplishing that end) or whether the words had to actually do so. Along the lines of the decision in the Michigan case, the court cited the inconsistency between the language of the rule and the cases adjudicated to date. The policy stated that words must have the effect of demeaning, whereas the illustrative examples indicated no need to prove that the words in question had any effect on the listener or the educational environment. Nine months later the board of regents formally repealed the policy.[103]

The Michigan and Wisconsin decisions appeared to doom most of the remaining campus speech codes. Two federal district courts had reaffirmed the principle of uninhibited free speech, without content-based restrictions. Moreover, they had rejected the new argument that the prohibition of racist speech was necessary to fulfill the mandate of the Fourteenth Amendment. These were only district court opinions, and it was still possible that higher courts, including the Supreme Court, might reverse one of the two and give new life to the campus speech code movement. It was not to be. Eight months after the decision in the Wisconsin case the Supreme Court gave content-based restrictions on hate speech an even deadlier blow.

Cross Burning as Hate Speech

The St. Paul cross-burning case arose in response to the same rise in racist acts that spawned the campus speech codes. In the 1980s there appeared to be a resurgence of violent acts directed at racial minorities (particularly cross burnings), Jews (in the desecration of synagogues and Jewish cemeteries), and homosexuals (in assaults on gay persons, or "gay bashing"). Like campus racist incidents, these acts occurred across the country, even in some unlikely places. Dubuque, Iowa, for example, was the scene of a series of cross burnings in the early 1990s.

In response, virtually every state enacted "hate crimes" legislation or strengthened existing laws.[104] The Anti-Defamation League was particularly active in lobbying for such legislation. Hate crimes laws took several forms. Some created new crimes relating to racial assaults or desecration of religious property. Others enhanced penalties for criminal acts that involved race, religion, or some other protected class. Thus a felonious assault might incur a harsher penalty if the attack was racially motivated. As with the campus speech codes, there was tremendous variety in these laws: some were narrowly drafted but others contained very broad language that raised serious First Amendment issues. Such was the case with the St. Paul ordinance.

The St. Paul Bias-Motivated Crime Ordinance made it a misdemeanor to place "on public or private property a symbol, object, appellation, characterization or graffiti" that "arouses anger, alarm or resentment in others on the basis of race, color, creed, religion or gender." The ordinance specifically mentioned "a burning cross or Nazi swastika" as examples of such symbols or objects. The law extended very broadly, covering the mere display of symbols, with no requirement that they be directed toward a specific individual, be intended to harass that person, or be likely to incite a breach of the peace. The prohibition of displays on private property clearly limited what people could do in their own front yards.[105]

A challenge to the law reached the Supreme Court in the context of worsening racial tension, highlighted by the Rodney King incident. Nine months before the oral argument, Los Angeles police officers had savagely beaten King. A videotape of the beating was broadcast innumerable times over the next year, offering unprecedented visual evidence of a seemingly unnecessary act of police brutality. The decision in the cross-burning case came a month after the acquittal of four police officers accused in the beating. The verdict sparked one of the worst riots in American history. For black Americans, the verdict compounded the message of the original King beating: that they could expect no justice in the American legal system. A Supreme Court decision overturning the cross-burning conviction, coming on the heels of the two campus speech code decisions, could reinforce that perception.

There was considerable uncertainty among court watchers about how the justices would rule. This was not the Warren Court, with its commitment to uninhibited speech. The Burger and Rehnquist Courts had found sufficient justification to limit First Amendment rights in a number of special contexts: high-school newspapers, the military, and prisons.[106] In these situations the Court had been willing to defer to the expressed needs of administrative officials. On the other hand, it had sustained free speech rights in some cases concerning very offensive forms of expression that involved public speech about public figures or issues. Most relevant were the two flag-burning cases of 1990 and 1991. And the crucial factor in those decisions was that Justices Scalia and Kennedy, two of the most conservative members of the Court, had agreed that flag burning was a protected form of expression under the First Amendment.[107] Also relevant was the *Hustler* decision, where the Court had overturned a libel award against *Hustler* magazine for a parody attacking Moral Majority leader Rev. Jerry Falwell. The parody was grossly obscene or hilariously funny, depending on one's political perspective. Offensive or not, the Court had ruled that it was fair comment on a public figure.[108]

The St. Paul case itself involved a relatively low level of violence. A group of teenagers, including Robert Viktora, put together a crudely made cross and burned it on the front lawn of a black family who lived across the street. In some respects the incident was a run-of-the-mill juvenile prank. But there was no mistaking the meaning of the burning cross, the traditional symbol of the Ku Klux Klan. It was a racist incident and, in the context of similar incidents across the country, a matter to be taken seriously. Viktora was charged in juvenile court under the Bias-Motivated Crimes Ordinance. Because he was a juvenile at the time of the original action, he was referred to as R.A.V. – hence the name of the ultimate court case.[109]

In what many regarded as a surprising decision, the Supreme Court declared the St. Paul ordinance unconstitutional. The law represented a prohibition on expression based on its content and, Justice Scalia wrote, "that is precisely what the First Amendment forbids."[110] The decision was unanimous, but the justices disagreed sharply over the rationale. The most surprising aspect of the division of opinion was that the more conservative justices were in the majority, striking down the ordinance on broader grounds than the more moderate justices. Scalia, widely regarded as the most conservative of all, wrote the majority opinion.

The St. Paul ordinance was unconstitutional on its face because it prohibited only certain kinds of speech based on their content. It covered fighting words related to race, color, creed, religion, or gender but not similar words related to, for example, "political affiliation, union membership, or homosexuality." Even worse, Scalia argued, the ordinance discriminated among particular viewpoints. The advocate of racial or religious tolerance could use many forms of invective, but that speaker's opponents could not.

Four justices agreed that the ordinance was unconstitutional, but for different reasons. Justices White, O'Connor, Blackmun, and Stevens were generally regarded as the more moderate members of the Rehnquist Court. They argued that the law was unconstitutional because of its breadth. This particular ordinance went too far, they argued, but a prohibition on fighting words that did not involve the exchange of ideas and were used only "to provoke violence or to inflict injury" was compatible with the First Amendment. There was a surprising reversal of roles in this split. The more conservative justices offered the most sweeping, doctrinaire defense of free speech. The moderates, who wanted to preserve some limited basis for restricting hate speech, criticized this approach as "arid, doctrinaire" and "mischievous" – precisely the terms conservatives had used to criticize the activist libertarianism of the Warren Court.[111]

Coming only weeks after the Los Angeles riots and a heightening of racial polarization, the decision confounded many civil rights activists. Did the First Amendment bar any action against racially motivated cross burning? Some of their complaints resembled the traditional arguments of conservatives angered by constitutional barriers to the social policies they preferred. Scalia anticipated these criticisms and addressed them in the first paragraph of his opinion. The actual cross burning in this case "could have been punished under any of a number of laws," he wrote, citing Minnesota laws on terrorist threats, arson, and criminal damage to property.[112] The decision by no means completely settled the matter: many states had hate crimes laws that were far more narrowly drafted than the St. Paul ordinance. In all likelihood the Court would soon have to consider a case where the distinction between expression and pure conduct was much narrower.

A Commitment Strengthened

From the perspective of the history of the hate speech issue, *R.A.V. v. St. Paul* did not mark the end of an era. Rather, it reaffirmed an American tradition that had developed over the previous half century. On the issue of hate speech, that tradition afforded broad First Amendment protection for offensive and even hateful forms of expression. The depth and strength of that tradition were dramatized in that a unanimous Supreme Court struck down the St. Paul ordinance. The most conservative of the justices affirmed the principle that the First Amendment forbade distinctions based on content – an idea that had been a radical notion only half a century earlier.

8 Hate Speech and
the American Community

By the 1990s the protection of hate speech under the First Amendment was more firmly established in the law than ever before. In the international context, the contrast between American law and policy and that of the rest of the world was also greater than ever. Other countries had steadily moved in the opposite direction, toward the formal prohibition of racial and religious propaganda.

Few Americans were aware of just how unusual their country was on this issue, and not many understood how the commitment to free speech had come to pass. Many assumed it began with the ratification of the First Amendment in 1791. Others thought it was something imposed by the Supreme Court – what Robert Bork has called the "imperial judiciary."[1] The specifics of how this commitment developed, and particularly how recently it occurred, were understood only by specialists in First Amendment law. Many Americans found the protection of hate speech very troubling, asking why the Bill of Rights compelled us to put up with distasteful things.

The answer is that the First Amendment itself did not force us to do anything. The First Amendment came to protect hate speech because we chose to interpret it that way. "We" in this context refers to the entire body of people who ever spoke or wrote on the subject: in public debate, policy statements, law review articles, briefs and arguments in court, and court decisions over the course of nearly seventy years. To be sure, these people were not the mass of average Americans. The key actors were members of a policy-making elite: judges, lawyers, activists. But though this collective decision generated protests over the years, it never sparked a full-scale revolt. To a remarkable extent, Americans have acquiesced in the development of a free speech tradition that protects extreme forms of offensive speech. Movements to strip the Supreme Court of its powers – in the late 1950s and with the "social agenda" of the Moral Majority in the 1980s – never succeeded.

As this book has argued, moreover, the outcome of the long history of the First Amendment was not inevitable: American law and policy could have gone in a very different direction. The Supreme Court gave its blessing to an alternative approach in 1942 and 1952, yet those invitations were rejected.

There must be a reason for this broad acquiescence in a social policy committed to uninhibited free speech. I have argued in this book that the protection of provocative and even offensive speech served broad social and political needs. In particular, provocative speech was a crucial weapon for the civil rights movement and the struggle for racial equality. With civil rights leaders committed to free speech, outlawing hate speech was an idea without an advocate, a virtual orphan in the political arena.

Civil rights forces reached that conclusion because in the midst of so many specific controversies – school integration in the Deep South in the 1950s, the struggle for racial justice in northern cities in the 1960s and 1970s – the success if not the very survival of civil rights activity depended on the protection of provocative, sometimes offensive, and occasionally even hateful speech. For the powerless and the excluded, speech was often the only resource available. The only hope lay – in the words of Justice William O. Douglas – in words that arouse, offend, "induce a condition of unrest, create dissatisfaction with things as they are, or even stir people to anger."[2] Reflecting on the role of the law in advancing civil rights, Eleanor Holmes Norton, professor of Law at Georgetown University and former chairwoman of the Equal Employment Opportunity Commission, commented that "there was always the First Amendment."[3]

Telling the Tale: Constitutional Narratives

One of the notable aspects of the recent debate over hate speech on college campuses is that several prominent legal scholars who are advocates for racial justice have chosen to reject the "lessons" of the First Amendment that an earlier generation of civil rights advocates felt were so important.

Derrick Bell, Charles Lawrence, Mari Matsuda, Richard Delgado, Patricia Williams, and others see the failure of the legal system to ensure full racial equality. Their criticisms of the legal system and the traditional mode of legal thinking extend to the dominant civil libertarian approach to First Amendment issues.

The view of civil rights history that these critics advance speaks directly to one of the current trends in legal scholarship. They emphasize the importance of the personal voice: legal issues should be considered not just in abstract terms but from the perspective of personal experience – particularly the experience of racial minorities and the victims of injustice. Their preferred mode of writing is the "narrative" that expresses the personal voice. Richard Delgado frames the hate speech controversy in terms of "constitutional narratives in collision," a clash between a First Amendment narrative and an equal protection one.[4] He very ably illuminates the extent to which the conventional civil libertarian approach to hate speech is shaped by the telling of a story. In this case it is a dramatic and compelling story that includes the suppression of free speech during World War I, the first tentative victories for free speech in the Supreme Court in the 1930s, the terrible years of the Cold War, and the great triumph of free speech under the Warren Court. The dramatic and emotional power of this story or narrative shapes people's responses as much as (if not more than) the purely rational arguments about the scope of the First Amendment.[5] He counters this with an alternative narrative emphasizing the principle of equality and its denial to people of color.

The narrative approach offers a useful perspective on the history of the hate speech issue I have presented in the preceding chapters. This account is indeed a narrative. It is a tale that has led to a definite conclusion: the protection of offensive speech has been critical to the pursuit of racial equality, along with defense of the rights of other powerless groups – the Jehovah's Witnesses, Vietnam War protesters, and others. This is a somewhat different narrative about race and racism than the one favored by Delgado and his colleagues. They have, in fact, engaged in sleight of hand by positing a neat duality of only two "constitutional narratives." They admit no distinctions or differences within either side and present their own version of the equal protection narrative.

Actually, there are a number of possible narratives on each side. Delgado concludes that "our system's winners have a stake in liberal, marketplace interpretations of law and politics," which includes the established content-neutral approach to First Amendment jurisprudence.[6] Not necessarily. This book has revived a different narrative, one that an earlier generation of civil rights leaders preferred to tell. In it, the liberal, market-oriented, content-neutral approach to the law was the most powerful weapon in the cause of racial justice. Society's "winners" were the ones who sought to suppress free speech. It was those on the outside who were demanding to be admitted to full citizenship.

The genius of constitutional litigation over the past half century has been to take the high-sounding promises of the Bill of Rights and force the majority to honor them. Derrick Bell gives some acknowledgment to this but prefers to frame it in a different narrative, one that emphasizes the failures of civil rights litigation.[7] Perhaps he is right. But the narrative game is one that all can play: there are many tales to be told. Even the First Amendment narrative has some important variations. This book offers one that leads to a different conclusion than do the narratives of Bell, Delgado, Lawrence, and their colleagues.

Hate Speech and the American Community

The history of the hate speech issue offers a new perspective on the relation of free speech to the question of inclusion in American society. Since the crisis over the suppression of civil liberties during World War I – the turning point in the development of First Amendment law – many justifications have been offered for free speech. The first rationale, advanced by Justice Oliver Wendell Holmes and elaborated by Alexander Meiklejohn, is that free speech is the core aspect of democracy.[8] It allows all ideas to be heard so that the people may freely choose which course of action to pursue. Later the idea of personal fulfillment was added. Freedom of expression is a necessary element of allowing all individuals to fully express their own identity. Freedom of speech also helps to ensure equality, guaranteeing that those in power cannot completely monopolize public discourse and forbid certain ideas.[9] Out of the Vietnam War and Watergate crises emerged an appreciation of the "checking" value of free speech. It is a tool that helps the people control the now massive and often secretive government bureaucracy.[10]

The history of the hate speech issue offers a variation on some of these justifications. The protection of free speech has helped to ensure the participation of different groups in American society, particularly the powerless. It does not guarantee equality as a result – that is Derrick Bell's complaint – but it does ensure participation in the political struggle. The point was best made in the crucial NAACP cases, where the First Amendment gave vital "breathing room" to the leading civil rights organization. In effect, it guaranteed its right to survive and continue its work. By the same token, the many cases affording protection to the Jehovah's Witnesses in the late 1930s and 1940s gave that hated religious sect breathing room.

The Witness cases in particular dramatize the ramifications of constitutionally protected breathing room. The broader message is that these people are legitimate members of the American community, as entitled to its rights and privileges as all others. The message was one of tolerance: that is the primary value communicated by the First Amendment.[11] And to the hated Witnesses in their time, that was more important than the specific holding about First Amendment rights in any particular case. The NAACP cases communicated a similar message of tolerance in a different time and place.

By the same token, free speech ensures inclusion in contemporary society.[12] The advocates of restricting hate speech on college campuses argue that it must be prohibited in order to achieve the inclusion of the historical victims of discrimination. But the history of the hate speech issue, as presented in this book, supports just the opposite argument. The inclusion of the powerless and the historical victims of discrimination has been aided (not fully achieved, of course) by the broadest content-neutral protection of offensive speech.

The Continuing Controversy

To be sure, the First Amendment has not eliminated racism or hate in American society. No one would seriously presume that it could. The past decade has in fact witnessed an alarming rise in the public expression of racist sentiments. Despite the great gains in civil rights over the past half century, some things appear to be getting worse. The profound pessimism expressed by Derrick Bell and others has some foundation in fact. At the same time, however, the events of the past few years – indeed, events that occurred while I was writing this book – dramatize how the protection of offensive speech protects the powerless and the victims of discrimination.

Almost every month it seems there is a new example of an assault on the sensibilities of a group or the attempted suppression of such speech. One could write an entire book just about the free speech battles of the past few years. In fact, Nat Hentoff has. His recent book *Free Speech for Me – but Not for Thee* is a vivid account of the threats to free speech from all portions of the political spectrum.[13]

I can supplement his chapters with a few other examples. One particularly useful one illustrates the ever changing nature of language itself. One of the more militant gay rights groups is an organization called Queer Nation. The term "queer," of course, is a long-standing epithet for homosexuals. Under the terms of virtually all of the campus speech codes, it would be prohibited. And yet militant gay and lesbian people have now embraced that hateful term as their own.[14]

The meanings of words change. Yesterday's respectful term is today an embarrassment. There is a wonderful Jules Feiffer cartoon from the 1960s on the evolution of the accepted and acceptable term for African Americans: from "black" to "colored" to "Negro" to "black." And in the interim it has evolved to African American. This exposes the problem inherent in the enforcement of any law or regulation banning offensive epithets: a word that is offensive one day is proudly used the next day; the former epithet becomes a badge. How is a speech code to cope with such radical changes in meaning and usage? Can a word be offensive coming from one person but not from another? In the case of Queer Nation, the choice of words is deliberate. The hateful term has become a political weapon. To restrict its use in one context would require restricting it in another.

The same process has occurred with the word "nigger." It is, of course, the most hateful racist term. A few years ago, however, there appeared on the music scene a rap group known as NWA – short for Niggers with Attitude. It was enormously popular, selling several million copies of its album with no air play on mainstream Top Forty radio stations. The "N word" was repeated in the title of the album *Niggazforlife*. To protect the sensibilities of readers – and in recognition of the power of the word – the album title was often published backward, as *Efilrofzaggin*. As with "queer," the most hateful term has been proudly embraced and turned into a political weapon. The same danger also arises: to prohibit the word in one context limits its possible use in another.

The First Amendment at City University

On the campus of the City University of New York (CUNY), meanwhile, the issue of offensive racial propaganda has been played out in a way that almost seemed deliberately scripted to dramatize the importance of protecting free speech. On one side stands philosophy professor Michael Levin, who had published at least three items asserting that blacks were, on average, "significantly less intelligent" than whites. He argued that this had been "amply confirmed" by research and that intellectual deficiency, not discrimination and poverty, was responsible for the small numbers of blacks in certain intellectually demanding fields. Black students protested, and some disrupted his classes. The university established a committee to investigate his views and offered a parallel course as an alternative to one he taught.[15]

Not to be outdone on the issue of racial superiority, the chairman of the CUNY African Studies Department, Leonard Jeffries, made a speech alleging a "conspiracy" on the part of Jews and the Mafia (meaning Italian Americans) to bring about the "destruction of black people."[16] His speech provoked outraged charges of anti-Semitism, and demonstrations. The university removed him as chairman of the department. The statements by both Levin and Jeffries represented their personal views, were made outside the classroom, and in no sense involved the indoctrination of students.

Certain aspects of both cases ended up in court over First Amendment issues. Professor Levin won a ruling that the university had violated his First Amendment rights by threatening him with disciplinary action based on statements made outside the classroom. In short, the university could not punish him for his beliefs. Even the threat of discipline, through an investigating committee, had a "chilling effect" on his freedom of expression. Almost exactly a year later a court ruled that the university had violated Professor Jeffries's First Amendment rights by removing him as department chairman – that is, by punishing him solely based on his views.[17]

A law professor seeking to illustrate the role of the First Amendment in protecting offensive speech would have had a hard time proposing two hypothetical cases more apposite than the ones that developed at CUNY. The First Amendment protected the offensive views of both sides in the bitter conflict between Jews and African Americans. The practical effect was that neither side could use its political power to punish someone for expounding views it found hateful. To be sure, the result was that some extremely offensive, uninformed, and frankly erroneous views found protection under the First Amendment. Some observers would argue that this only further poisoned the already hostile racial and ethnic atmosphere of CUNY and New York City. The only alternative, however, seems to be that university officials, responding to the changing winds of political pressure, would be in the business of determining which ideas were acceptable. The New York courts in the two CUNY cases instead adopted the far wiser course prescribed by Justice Robert Jackson in the 1943 flag salute case. "The very purpose of the Bill of Rights," he wrote, "was to withdraw certain subjects from the vicissitudes of political controversy." And in a passage that spoke directly to university officials fifty years later, Jackson declared that "if there is any fixed star in our constitutional constellation, it is that no official, high or petty, can prescribe what shall be orthodox in politics, nationalism, religion, or other matters of opinion.[18]

The Jeffries case produced another free speech case with a wonderfully ironic twist. Outraged by his anti-Semitic remarks, a militant Jewish group, Kahane Chai, decided to picket Jeffries's home. Kahane Chai was named after the late Rabbi Meir Kahane, founder of the Jewish Defense League. During the Skokie affair, Kahane and the JDL had threatened to physically attack any Nazis who demonstrated in the village. It happened that Jeffries lived in Teaneck, New Jersey, and at that very moment this racially mixed community was in the midst of a bitter conflict over the fatal shooting of a black teenager by a white police officer. Hoping to avoid violence, the township of Teaneck denied Kahane Chai's application for a parade permit. The militant Jewish group promptly sought the assistance of the New Jersey ACLU, which filed a suit charging a violation of freedom of assembly. With no comment, Judge Alfred M. Wolin ordered Teaneck to grant the parade permit.[19]

The irony of the Teaneck case almost surpasses belief. The very group that had denounced the ACLU fourteen years earlier now sought its assistance. An organization that had vehemently argued that a group it did not like had no First Amendment right to demonstrate over the objections of the community now demanded that same right for itself.

The CUNY and Teaneck cases summed up the various themes of the seventy-year history of the hate speech issue. First, it was clear that there was no end to racial, religious, and ethnic prejudice and hatred. Second, however, it was equally clear that the First Amendment had become one of the major instruments – perhaps even the principal instrument – for managing those conflicts. The decisions that emanated from courts across the land in the late 1980s and 1990s – in the CUNY cases, the university speech code cases, the flag burning and cross burning cases – illustrated the depth and strength of First Amendment values. The evolution of those values since the first controversies in the 1920s was one of the most important developments in modern American history.

Third, as I have argued in this book, First Amendment values triumphed because they had powerful advocates who, over the course of many years, were able to persuade those who were at first skeptical. The idea of restricting offensive speech, by the same token, has never had an equally effective advocate. Even the writings of the various law professors in the 1980s, who made the most powerful argument in American history on behalf of restricting speech, ultimately failed to carry the day. Their case was weak for reasons that were clear in many of the campus controversies: often it was the member of a minority group who was threatened with punishment for expressing an offensive idea. It is in the protection of all ideas that the history of the hate speech issue demonstrates the true meaning of the First Amendment.

Notes

Chapter One: Hate Speech in American History

1. Sandra Coliver, ed., *Striking a Balance: Hate Speech, Freedom of Expression and Non-discrimination* (London: Article 19, 1992).

2. *West Virginia State Board of Education v. Barnette*, 319 U.S. 624 (1943).

3. *New York Times v. Sullivan*, 376 U.S. 254 (1964).

4. This memorable phrase comes from Justice Oliver Wendell Holmes's last great dissent in a free speech case: *U.S. v. Macintosh*, 283 U.S. 605 (1931).

5. Rodney Smolla, *Free Speech in an Open Society* (New York: Alfred A. Knopf, 1992), p.151.

6. There is now a substantial body of literature on this point. The best starting place is Charles Lawrence III, "If He Hollers Let Him Go: Regulating Racist Speech on Campus," *Duke Law Journal*, June 1990, pp.431–83. See the reply by the president of the ACLU, Nadine Strossen, "Regulating Racist Speech on Campus: A Modest Proposal?" *Duke Law Journal*, June 1990, pp.484–573.

7. Mary Ellen Gale, "On Curbing Racial Speech," *Responsive Community* 1 (Winter 1990–91): 55. This is a shortened version of Mary Ellen Gale, "Reimagining the First Amendment: Racist Speech and Equal Liberty," *St. John's Law Review* 65 (Winter 1991): 119–85.

8. *R.A.V. v. City of St. Paul*, 505 U.S. ___, L. Ed. 2d 305, 112 S. Ct. ___ (June 22, 1992).

9. *Doe v. University of Michigan*, 721 F. Supp. 852 (E.D. Mich. 1989); *UWM Post v. Board of Regents of the University of Wisconsin*, 774 F. Supp. 1163 (E.D. Wis. 1991).

10. Nat Hentoff, "A Startling Triumph for Free Speech," *Village Voice*, July 28, 1992, pp.18–19.

11. Scalia was joined by Chief Justice Rehnquist and Justices Kennedy, Souter, and Thomas. Justices White, Blackmun, O'Connor, and Stevens agreed with the result but not the rationale.

12. *Beauharnais v. Illinois*, 343 U.S. 250 (1952). The decision and its surprising aftermath are discussed in chapter 5.

13. Human Rights Watch, *"Hate Speech" and Freedom of Expression: A Human Rights Watch Policy Paper* (New York: Human Rights Watch, 1992), p.7. The qualifying adjective "valid" is extremely important. There are many laws on the books, but most would not survive a constitutional challenge, particularly after the decision in the St. Paul cross-burning case.

14. Kevin Boyle, "Overview of a Dilemma: Censorship versus Racism," in Coliver, *Striking a Balance*, p.4.

15. The examples are drawn from Boyle, "Overview."

16. Eric Stein, "History against Free Speech: The New German Law against 'Auschwitz' – and Other 'Lies,'" *Michigan Law Review* 85 (November 1986): 277–324.

17. Kathleen Mahoney, "The Constitutional Approach to Freedom of Expression in Hate Propaganda and Pornography," *Law and Contemporary Problems* 55 (Winter 1992): 77–105.

18. For a comprehensive collection, see Ian Brownlie, ed., *Basic Documents on Human Rights*, 2d ed. (Oxford: Clarendon Press, 1981).

19. When the United States Senate ratified the International Covenant in 1992, it attached the "reservation" that article 20 "does not authorize or require legislation or other action by the United States that would restrict the right of free speech and association protected by the Constitution and laws of the United States."

20. For a general discussion of these limitations, see Alexandre Charles Kiss, "Permissible Limitations on Rights," in *The International Bill of Rights: The Covenant on Civil and Political Rights*, ed. Louis Henkin (New York: Columbia University Press, 1981), pp.290–310.

21. Andrew Hacker, *Two Nations: Black and White, Separate, Hostile, Unequal* (New York: Charles Scribner's Sons, 1992).

22. National Institute against Prejudice and Violence, *Campus Ethnoviolence ... and the Policy Options* (Baltimore: NIAPV, 1990). See chapter 7 for a fuller discussion of campus racism in the 1980s.

23. The best summary of American race relations is National Research Council,

A Common Destiny: Blacks and American Society (Washington, D.C.: National Academy Press, 1989). See also Hacker, *Two Nations.*

24. See, for example, the University of Michigan policy declared unconstitutional in *Doe v. University of Michigan,* 721 F. Supp. 852 (E.D. Mich. 1989).

25. The most important contributions to this debate are discussed in chapter 7. The literature continues to grow apace; for the most recent items consult the *Index to Legal Periodicals.*

26. Thomas Emerson, *The System of Freedom of Expression* (New York: Vintage Books, 1970); Franklyn S. Haiman, *Speech and Law in a Free Society* (Chicago: University of Chicago Press, 1981); Smolla, *Free Speech;* Kent Greenawalt, *Speech, Crime, and the Uses of Language* (New York: Oxford University Press, 1989).

27. Lawrence, "If He Hollers Let Him Go"; Mari J. Matsuda, "Public Response to Racist Speech: Considering the Victim's Story," *Michigan Law Review* 87 (August 1989): 2320–81; Gale, "On Curbing Racial Speech."

28. In one of the more valuable contributions to this subject, Harry Kalven, Jr., observed in the mid-1960s that the African American civil rights movement had not made group libel legislation one of its goals. Harry Kalven, Jr., *The Negro and the First Amendment,* Phoenix ed. (Chicago: University of Chicago Press, 1966), pp.11–12.

29. See, for example, the University of Michigan Policy on Discrimination and Discriminatory Harassment of Students in the University Environment, which was held unconstitutional in *Doe v. University of Michigan,* 721 F. Supp. 852 (E.D. Mich. 1989). See the discussion in chapter 7.

30. Human Rights Watch, *"Hate Speech" and Freedom of Expression.*

31. Smolla, *Free Speech in an Open Society,* p.152.

32. Haiman, *Speech and Law in a Free Society,* chaps. 3, 4, 5.

33. The benchmarks in documenting this process are Zechariah Chafee, Jr., *Free Speech in the United States* (Cambridge: Harvard University Press, 1981); Emerson, *System of Freedom of Expression;* Haiman, *Speech and Law in a Free Society;* and Smolla, *Free Speech in an Open Society.*

34. Anti-Defamation League, *Hate Crimes Statutes: A 1991 Status Report* (New York: ADL, 1991).

35. *R.A.V. v. City of St. Paul,* 505 U.S. ___, L. Ed. 2d 305, 112. S. Ct. ___ (1992).

36. *State v. Mitchell,* 485 N.W.2d 807 (1992). The U.S. Supreme Court declared the law unconstitutional: *Wisconsin v. Mitchell,* 61 U.S.L.W. 4575 (June 11, 1993).

37. Paul L. Murphy, *World War I and the Origin of Civil Liberties in the United States* (New York: W. W. Norton, 1979); Samuel Walker, *In Defense of American Liberties: A History of the* ACLU (New York: Oxford University Press, 1990).

38. *Stromberg v. California*, 283 U.S. 359 (1931): *Near v. Minnesota*, 283 U.S. 697 (1931).

39. On the significance of the two 1931 decisions, see Paul. L. Murphy, *The Meaning of Freedom of Speech: First Amendment Freedoms from Wilson to FDR* (Westport, Conn.: Greenwood Press, 1972). There is some disagreement among scholars as to the first decision affirming free speech rights. Norman Dorsen and Franklyn Haiman have reminded me that *Fiske v. Kansas*, 274 U.S. 380 (1927), in 1927 was really the first – a point made in Chafee, *Free Speech in the United States*, pp.351–52. I have chosen to follow Paul Murphy's argument that the 1931 decisions are the real turning point.

40. Walker, *In Defense of American Liberties*, pp.115–18.

41. *Terminiello v. Chicago*, 337 U.S. 1 (1949).

42. David Rabban, however, has persuasively demonstrated that a vigorous First Amendment jurisprudence existed before the World War I crisis: David A. Rabban, "The First Amendment in its Forgotten Years," *Yale Law Journal* 90 (January 1981): 516–97. Nonetheless, free speech did not assume a central place in American politics until World War I.

43. John P. Roche, "American Liberty: An Examination of the 'Tradition' of Freedom," in *Aspects of Liberty*, ed. Milton R. Konvitz and Clinton Rossiter (Ithaca: Cornell University Press, 1958), p.137.

44. Murphy, *World War I and the Origin of Civil Liberties*. On civil liberties jurisprudence in the pre–World War I years, see Mark A. Graber, *Transforming Free Speech: The Ambiguous Legacy of Civil Libertarianism* (Berkeley: University of California Press, 1991); Rabban, "First Amendment," pp.516–97.

45. A biography of Marshall is in preparation by Mark Tushnet. In the interim, see Richard Kluger, *Simple Justice* (New York: Vintage Books, 1977).

46. This point is explicit in Walker, *In Defense of American Liberties*, but it can be gleaned from a cursory glance at the dates of important court decisions on individual rights to be found in any constitutional law casebook.

47. The current state of public attitudes toward freedom of speech is itself a complex matter. My view is that there has been a substantial growth in public awareness of and support for civil liberties principles since the 1950s. The principal benchmarks recording that growth are Samuel Stouffer, *Communism, Conformity, and Civil Liberties* (New York: Doubleday, 1955), and Herbert McCloskey and

Alida Brill, *Dimensions of Tolerance: What Americans Believe about Civil Liberties* (New York: Russell Sage Foundation, 1983).

48. On the "imperial judiciary," see Robert Bork, *The Tempting of America* (New York: Free Press, 1990).

49. See particularly Murphy, *Meaning of Free Speech.*

50. Gerald N. Rosenberg, *The Hollow Hope: Can Courts Bring about Social Change?* (Chicago: University of Chicago Press, 1991).

51. Lee Epstein and Joseph F. Kobylka, *The Supreme Court and Legal Change: Abortion and the Death Penalty* (Chapel Hill: University of North Carolina Press, 1992).

52. At present there is no history of the concept of the right to privacy in America. See Alan F. Westin, *Privacy and Freedom* (New York: Atheneum, 1967).

53. With respect to abortion and the death penalty, see Epstein and Kobylka, *Supreme Court and Legal Change.*

54. Walker, *In Defense of American Liberties.*

55. Kluger, *Simple Justice.*

56. Several scholars have emphasized the contribution of the civil rights movement to the development of American constitutional law, with enormous benefits to all Americans: for example, Kalven, *Negro and the First Amendment;* Derrick Bell, *And We Are Not Saved: The Elusive Quest for Racial Justice* (New York: Basic Books, 1987), chap. 2, "The Benefits to Whites of Civil Rights Litigation."

57. The group libel issue usually does not appear in the published histories of the major civil rights organizations. If it is mentioned, it is only in passing. See Naomi W. Cohen, *Not Free to Desist: The American Jewish Committee, 1906–1966* (Philadelphia: Jewish Publication Society of America, 1992). On the program of the Anti-Defamation League in the 1950s, see Arnold Forster, *A Measure of Freedom* (New York: Doubleday, 1950). On the NAACP, see Kluger, *Simple Justice.*

58. The United Kingdom does have its free speech advocate, the National Council for Civil Liberties (NCCL). But the NCCL has never been as large or as influential as the ACLU in the United States. See Norman Dorsen, "A Transatlantic View of Civil Liberties in the United Kingdom," in *Civil Liberties 1984* (ed. Peter Wallington (Oxford: Martin Robertson, 1984); Mark Lilly, *The National Council for Civil Liberties: The First Fifty Years* (London: Macmillan, 1984).

Chapter Two: Origins of the Hate Speech Issue

1. The classic popular account, which established the stereotypes of the decade, remains Frederick Lewis Allen, *Only Yesterday* (New York: Harper, 1931). See

also Geoffrey Perrett, *America in the Twenties: A History* (New York: Simon and Schuster, 1982).

2. John Higham, *Strangers in the Land* (New Brunswick, N.J.: Rutgers University Press, 1955); C. Vann Woodward, *The Strange Career of Jim Crow,* 3d ed. (New York: Oxford University Press, 1974).

3. Lobbying by Catholic clerics was the primary force behind the motion picture production code in 1934, and Catholic lobbying blocked congressional efforts to repeal federal restrictions on the dissemination of birth control literature and devices. See Samuel Walker, *In Defense of American Liberties: A History of the* ACLU (New York: Oxford University Press, 1990), pp.98–100.

4. *Encyclopedia of Associations,* 26th ed. (Detroit: Gale Research, 1992).

5. Walker, *In Defense of American Liberties.* The ACLU did have a predecessor, the Free Speech League, organized in 1902. Owing in large part to the personality and objectives of its leader, Theodore Schroeder, the League never developed into a permanent organization.

6. *Bryant v. Zimmerman,* 278 U.S. 63 (1928). See below.

7. Norman Cohn, *Warrant for Genocide: The Myth of the Jewish World-Conspiracy and the Protocols of the Elders of Zion* (London: Eyre and Spottswoode, 1967).

8. *The International Jew: The World's Foremost Problem,* 3 vols. (Dearborn, Mich.: Dearborn Independent, 1920–21); Albert Lee, *Henry Ford and the Jews* (New York: Stein and Day, 1980); Seymour Martin Lipset and Earl Raab, *The Politics of Unreason: Right-Wing Extremism in America, 1790–1977,* 2d ed. (Chicago: University of Chicago Press, 1978), pp.135–38; Gustavus Myers, *History of Bigotry in the United States* (New York: Random House, 1943), pp.333–69.

9. *International Jew,* passim.

10. Jerold S. Auerbach, *Unequal Justice: Lawyers and Social Change in Modern America* (New York: Oxford University Press, 1976).

11. Restrictive covenants were declared unconstitutional in *Shelley v. Kraemer,* 334 U.S. 1 (1948). The Rehnquist incident is recounted in David G. Savage, *Turning Right: The Making of the Rehnquist Supreme Court* (New York: John Wiley, 1992), p.21.

12. Lee, *Henry Ford and the Jews,* pp.34–35.

13. Richard Maxwell Brown, *Strain of Violence* (New York: Oxford University Press, 1975).

14. *Schenck v. United States,* 249 U.S. 47 (1919).

15. ACLU, *Annual Report, 1920–1921* (New York: Arno Press, 1970); Walker, *In Defense of American Liberties,* chap. 3.

16. ACLU form letter, March 28, 1921, NAACP Papers, I/C-192, Library of Congress.

17. ACLU, "Report on Civil Liberty Situation, April 18, 1921," NAACP Papers, I/C-192.

18. City membership totals are given in Kenneth T. Jackson, *The Ku Klux Klan in the City, 1915–1930* (New York: Oxford University Press, 1967), table 9, p.239. See also David M. Chalmers, *Hooded Americanism: The History of the Ku Klux Klan* (Chicago: Quadrangle Books, 1968). Myers, *History of Bigotry in the United States,* pp.282–313.

19. The decision in *Pierce v. Society of Sisters,* 268 U.S. 510 (1925) held that the law infringed on parents' freedom to control the education of their children. *Pierce* and a related case, *Meyer v. Nebraska,* 262 U.S. 390 (1923), had little immediate impact on legal doctrine but resurfaced in the 1960s as precedent for the constitutional right to privacy.

20. Robert K. Murray, *The 103rd Ballot: Democrats and the Disaster in Madison Square Garden* (New York: Harper and Row, 1976), pp.153–64.

21. Albert DeSilver [ACLU codirector], "The Ku Klux Klan," *Nation,* September 14, 1921; pamphlet reprinted by the ACLU.

22. See, for example, ACLU, "Report on Civil Liberty Situation for the Week Ending August 15, 1921," NAACP Papers, I/C-192.

23. Letter, Milner (ACLU) to mayor, Cudahay, Wis., December 24, 1925; ACLUP/1925/291; ACLU Papers, Princeton University, *New York Times,* December 20, 1925.

24. Note, "Antimask Laws: Exploring the Outer Bounds of Protected Speech under the First Amendment – State v. Miller, 260 Ga. 669, 338 S.E. 2d 547 (1990)," *Washington Law Review* 66 (1991): 1139–58.

25. *State v. Miller,* 398 S.E. 2d 547 (1990).

26. "Antimask Laws," 1145, n.46.

27. *Milwaukee Publishing Co. v. Burleson,* 255 U.S. 407 (1921).

28. Letter, DeSilver to James Weldon Johnson (NAACP), January 10, 1921; ACLUP/1921/168.

29. Walker, *In Defense of American Liberties,* p.62.

30. See the discussion in chapter 5.

31. *Boston Evening Transcript,* January 25, 1923; clipping in ACLUP/1923/228; Chalmers, *Hooded Americanism,* p.271.

32. Letter, Curley to Codman, ACLU, October 4, 1923; Chafee Papers, box 30, Harvard Law School Library (hereafter HLS).

33. Letter, Codman to Curley, October 11, 1923; Chafee Papers, box 30, HLS.

34. *Hague v. CIO,* 307 U.S. 496 (1939).

35. Letter, Curley to Codman, 3/25/25; Chafee Papers, box 30, HLS.

36. *Bryant v. Zimmerman,* 278 U.S. 63 (1928). The decision was overturned in *NAACP v. Alabama,* 357 U.S. 449 (1958). New York successfully used the law in 1939 against the German-American Bund. Susan Canedy, *America's Nazis: A Democratic Dilemma* (Menlo Park, Calif.: Markgraf Publications, 1990), pp.180–82.

37. *NAACP v. Alabama,* 357 U.S. 449 (1958).

38. *Brown v. Board of Education,* 347 U.S. 483 (1954). For a general discussion of the NAACP cases, see Harry Kalven, Jr., *The Negro and the First Amendment,* Phoenix ed. (Chicago: University of Chicago Press, 1966).

39. See the valuable discussion of the First Amendment issues raised by these measures in Harry Kalven, Jr., *A Worthy Tradition* (New York: Harper and Row, 1988), chaps. 17–22.

40. On the different handling of the Communist and the NAACP cases by the Supreme Court, see Kalven, *Negro and the First Amendment.* Former ACLU legal director Mel Wulf commented that there were "red cases and there were black cases"; quoted in Walker, *In Defense of American Liberties,* p.240.

41. David Rabban, "The First Amendment in Its Forgotten Years," *Yale Law Journal* 90 (January 1981): 516–97.

42. Felix Frankfurter and Nathan Greene, *The Labor Injunction* (New York: Macmillan, 1930).

43. *Abrams v. United States,* 250 U.S. 616 (1919); *Whitney v. California,* 274 U.S. 357 (1927). Zechariah Chafee, Jr., *Free Speech in the United States* (Cambridge: Harvard University Press, 1941).

44. Chafee, *Free Speech in the United States,* p.362.

45. *Stromberg v. California,* 283 U.S. 359 (1931).

46. George W. Kirchway, *A Survey of the Workings of the Criminal Syndicalism Law of California* (Los Angeles: ACLU of Southern California, 1926).

47. *Stromberg v. California,* 283 U.S. 359 (1931).

48. Chafee, *Free Speech in the United States.*

49. Walker, *In Defense of American Liberties,* chap. 4.

50. *Near v. Minnesota,* 283 U.S. 697 (1931).

51. The best account of the case is Fred W. Friendly, *Minnesota Rag* (New York: Vintage Books, 1982).

52. For a colorful account of local corruption in 1903, see Lincoln Steffens, "The Shame of Minneapolis," in *The Shame of the Cities* (New York: McClure, Phillips, 1904).

53. Quotations from Friendly, *Minnesota Rag.*

54. *Near v. Minnesota,* 283 U.S. 697, 716 (1931); *New York Times Co. v. United States,* 403 U.S. 713 (1971); Sanford J. Ungar, *The Papers and the Papers* (New York: Dutton, 1972).

55. The real change in the Court's posture on political and civil rights came in 1937–38, notably in *Palko v. Connecticut,* 302 U.S. 319 (1937), and *United States v. Carolene Products,* 304 U.S. 144 (1938), esp. n.4.

56. Paul L. Murphy, *The Meaning of Freedom of Speech: First Amendment Freedoms from Wilson to FDR* (Westport, Conn.: Greenwood Press, 1972). A study of political crises over the Supreme Court did not even mention the two 1931 decisions: see William Lasser, *The Limits of Judicial Power* (Chapel Hill: University of North Carolina Press, 1988).

57. Kenneth L. Karst, *Belonging to America: Equal Citizenship and the Constitution* (New Haven: Yale University Press, 1989).

58. Some historians argue that the NAACP won its first significant victory in helping to defeat the nomination of John J. Parker to the Supreme Court in 1930: Richard Kluger, *Simple Justice* (New York: Vintage Books, 1977), pp.141–44.

59. Stephen Jay Gould, *The Mismeasure of Man* (New York: Norton, 1981).

60. Higham, *Strangers in the Land,* chap. 6, "Toward Racism: The History of an Idea."

61. Higham, *Strangers in the Land.*

62. Walker, *In Defense of American Liberties,* chap. 2.

63. For the best treatment of the connection between anti-immigrant sentiment and the suppression of dissent during World War I, see William Preston, *Aliens and Dissenters: Federal Suppression of Radicals, 1903–1933* (New York: Harper and Row, 1966).

64. Paul Berman, *Debating PC* (New York: Dell, 1992).

65. Horace M. Kallen, "Democracy versus the Melting Pot," *Nation* 100 (February 18, 1915): 190–94; (February 25, 1915): 217–20; idem, *Culture and Democracy in the United States* (New York, 1924). On Kallen's career, see Milton R. Konvitz, ed., *The Legacy of Horace M. Kallen* (Rutherford, N.J.: Fairleigh Dickinson University Press, 1987). See also John Higham, *Send These to Me: Jews and Other Immigrants in Urban America* (New York: Atheneum, 1975), chap. 10, "Ethnic Pluralism in Modern American Thought," pp.196–230.

66. Kallen, *Culture and Democracy,* p.124.

67. This view of American legal history is argued in greater detail in Samuel Walker's *The Rights Revolution: Rights and Community in Modern America* (New York: Oxford University Press, forthcoming).

68. It is fair to say that the Supreme Court's decisions on school prayer and Bible reading effectively changed routine practices in the public schools. It is worth noting that in his book arguing that the Court is ineffective in changing social policy, Gerald Rosenberg ignores all First Amendment issues: Gerald Rosenberg, *The Hollow Hope* (Chicago: University of Chicago Press, 1991). A more balanced view might be that the Court is extremely weak on some issues, notably school integration, but very effective on others, especially First Amendment ones.

69. A richly detailed account of American vigilantism, which places it in a broader theoretical framework, is found in Richard Maxwell Brown, *Strain of Violence* (New York: Oxford University Press, 1975).

Chapter Three: Free Speech for Nazis?

1. Travis Hoke, *Shirts!* (New York: ACLU, 1934). For the estimate of three hundred see Ludwig Lore, "Nazi Politics," *Nation*, November 29, 1933, pp.615–17. Susan Canedy, *America's Nazis: A Democratic Dilemma* (Menlo Park, Calif.: Markgraf Publications, 1990).

2. Martha Glasser, "The German-American Bund in New Jersey," *New Jersey History* 92 (1974): 33–49. The estimate of 60,000 is found in Hoke, *Shirts!* Canedy, *America's Nazis*, is a history of the German-American Bund.

3. Lore, "Nazi Politics."

4. Allan Brinkley, *Voices of Protest: Huey Long, Father Coughlin, and the Great Depression* (New York: Vintage Books, 1983).

5. Glaser, "German-American Bund."

6. ACLU, press release, October 30, 1937; ACLUP/1937/999.

7. Robert Lacey, *Little Man: Meyer Lansky and the Gangster Life* (Boston: Little, Brown, 1991), p.113; Jim Marrs, *Crossfire: The Plot That Killed Kennedy* (New York: Carroll and Graf, 1989), p.382. The involvement of both Lansky and Ruby is entirely probable. Both started out as street level thugs involved in labor union violence. Lansky's account is suspect, however, because it originates in a 1971 interview with an Israeli journalist at a time when he was seeking Israeli citizenship to avoid United States prosecution. Thus he had compelling reasons for exaggerating his Jewish identity.

8. ACLU, Board of Directors, Minutes, June 27, 1938.

9. These incidents are summarized briefly in the ACLU annual reports. See, for example, ACLU, *Annual Report,* 1939, p.38, 40; and 1940, p.37. Samuel Walker, *In Defense of American Liberties: A History of the* ACLU (New York: Oxford University Press, 1990).

10. Glaser, "German-American Bund," p.35; ACLU, *Shall We Defend Free Speech for Nazis in America?* (New York: ACLU, 1934).

11. See the extensive correspondence from critics to ACLUP/1934/700 and ACLUP/1939/2147. See the form letter sent to critics, ACLU, "To Members and Friends," May 9, 1934, ACLUP/1934/718.

12. See Norman Hapgood, *Professional Patriots* (New York: Albert and Charles Boni, 1927).

13. Letter, Baldwin to C. Burlingham, January 11, 1934, ACLUP/1934/718.

14. Roger N. Baldwin, "Voting Red in Austria," *Nation,* June 15, 1927, pp.663–64.

15. Arthur Garfield Hays, "Men in the Shadow of Death," *Modern Monthly,* January 1934, pp.708–12.

16. The ACLU's allegedly "absolutist" positions on censorship, particularly regarding pornography, and on separation of church and state did not solidify until the late 1950s and early 1960s; see Walker, *In Defense of American Liberties.*

17. Letter, M. DeSilver to Ernst, ca. April 1934, ACLUP/1934/718. "Hitlerism or Americanism?" *New York Post,* March 31, 1934, p.4. Robert C. Cottrell, *Izzy: A Biography of I. F. Stone* (New Brunswick, N.J.: Rutgers University Press, 1992), p.94.

18. Hoke, *Shirts!*

19. Hoke, *Shirts!* p.19. On Pelley, see Leo P. Ribuffo, *The Old Christian Right: The Protestant Far Right from the Great Depression to the Cold War* (Philadelphia: Temple University Press, 1983), pp. 25–79.

20. ACLU, *Shall We Defend?* On the special committee, see ACLU, Board of Directors, Minutes, April 30, 1934.

21. For a strong argument that racist speech represents a special case because of the "catastrophic historical experience with racism," see David Kretzmer, "Freedom of Speech and Racism," *Cardozo Law Review* 8 (1987): 458.

22. *Terminiello v. Chicago,* 337 U.S. 1, 37 (1949).

23. See the article listing the Jews active in the ACLU: Mary D. Brite, "The Jew in Civil Liberties," *Hebrew Union College Monthly,* June 1931, pp.13–14, 36. In the Skokie affair, some of the most vicious attacks on the ACLU were directed by Jews at ACLU officials who were Jewish. See the reply in Aryeh Neier, *Defending My Enemy* (New York: Dutton, 1979).

24. Walker, *In Defense of American Liberties,* chaps. 1, 2.

25. The ACLU had been very explicit: after being pilloried by a congressional investigating committee for supporting Communists, it issued ACLU, *The Right to Advocate Violence* (New York: ACLU, 1931).

26. ACLU, press release, November 13, 1935, ACLUP/1935/142.

27. Years later the ACLU reversed itself on this point, arguing that appearing in public in any kind of disguise or costume was protected by the First Amendment.

28. ACLU, *Why We Defend Free Speech for Nazis, Fascists – and Communists* (New York: ACLU: 1939). The most important change in the 1939 version was the naming of Communists in the title, along with some explanatory comments in the text. This change was entirely a result of the bitter factionalism within the ACLU Board of Directors over the question of participation by Communists in the ACLU itself. A conservative faction wanted the ACLU on record as opposing Communism. It eventually succeeded in banning Communists from leadership positions and removing Elizabeth Gurley Flynn from the Board of Directors. None of this controversy, however, produced any change in the arguments on the basic question of free speech for unpopular political groups. See Walker, *In Defense of American Liberties,* pp.127–33.

29. ACLU, *The Case against Legal Restraints on Racial Libels and Anonymous Publications* (New York: ACLU, 1946).

30. ACLU, *Why the American Civil Liberties Union Defends Free Speech for Racists and Totalitarians* (New York: ACLU, 1978).

31. ACLU, "Hate Speech on Campus" (1992). Briefing Paper.

32. John Haynes Holmes, "Should a Law Be Enacted against Incitement to Race and Religious Prejudice?" transcript, debate sponsored by National Lawyers Guild, December 20, 1938; copy in Tamiment Library, New York University.

33. *Smith v. Collin,* 436 U.S. 953 (1978). See chapter 6 for a full discussion of the Skokie affair.

34. *R.A.V. v. City of St. Paul,* 505 U.S. ___, L. Ed. 2d 305, 112 S. Ct. ___ (June 22, 1992).

35. Hadley Cantril, ed., *Public Opinion, 1935–1946* (1951) (Westport, Conn.: Greenwood Press, 1978), p.381.

36. David S. Wyman, *Paper Walls: America and the Refugee Crisis, 1938–1941* (New York: Pantheon Books, 1985); Davis S. Wyman, *The Abandonment of the Jews: America and the Holocaust, 1941–1945* (New York: Pantheon Books, 1984).

37. Karl Loewenstein, "Militant Democracy and Fundamental Rights, I," *American Political Science Review* 31 (June 1937): 417–32; idem, "Militant Democracy and Fundamental Rights, II," *American Political Science Review* 31

(August 1937): 638–58. His articles anticipated the similar and much more detailed analysis by David Riesman, "Democracy and Defamation," *Columbia Law Review* 42 (1942): 729–80, 1085–1123, 1282–1318. Reisman's article is discussed in chapter 5.

38. Reisman, "Democracy and Defamation."

39. Loewenstein, "Militant Democracy," p.423.

40. *Terminiello v. Chicago*, 337 U.S. 1, 37 (1949).

41. Loewenstein, "Militant Democracy," p.424.

42. For a contemporary version of the same argument, emphasizing the "catastrophic" impact of worldwide racism, see Kretzmer, "Freedom of Speech and Racism," pp.445–513.

43. See, for example, Richard E. Morgan, *Disabling America: The "Rights Industry" in Our Time* (New York: Basic Books, 1984), and the communitarian movement that emerged in the 1990s: Amitai Etzioni, *The Spirit of Community* (New York: Crown Books, 1993).

44. The concept of "militant democracy" is embodied in the constitution of the Federal Republic of Germany: see Rainer Hoffman, "Incitement to National and Racial Hatred: The Legal Situation in Germany," in *Striking a Balance*, ed. Sanda Coliver, pp.159–70 (London: Article 19, 1992).

45. Loewenstein, "Militant Democracy," p.430.

46. Hoffman, "Incitement to National and Racial Hatred," pp.159–70.

47. Loewenstein, "Militant Democracy," p.432.

48. Ibid.

49. Ibid.

50. *Abrams v. United States*, 250 U.S. 616 (1919); Zechariah Chafee, Jr., *Free Speech in the United States* (Cambridge: Harvard University Press, 1981).

51. Walker, *In Defense of American Liberties*; Paul L. Murphy, *World War I and the Origin of Civil Liberties in the United States* (New York: W. W. Norton, 1979).

52. David P. Shannon, *The Socialist Party of America: A History* (New York: Macmillan, 1955).

53. Melvin Dubofsky, *We Shall Be All* (Chicago: Quandrangle Books, 1969).

54. Walker, *In Defense of American Liberties*, chap. 3.

55. This part of his argument is contained in part 2 of his series in *American Political Science Review* 31 (August 1937): 638–58.

56. Ibid., p.644.

57. Ibid.

58. Ibid., p.645.

59. Ibid., p.646.

60. Ibid., p.649.

61. Ibid., p.651.

62. Gerald D. Anderson, *Fascists, Communists, and the National Government: Civil Liberties in Great Britain, 1931–1937* (Columbia: University of Missouri Press, 1983).

63. Loewenstein, "Militant Democracy," pp.638–39.

64. Ibid., p.641.

65. Ibid., p.642.

66. Mark Lilly, *The National Council for Civil Liberties: The First Fifty Years* (London: Macmillan, 1984). An NCCL had existed during World War I but disbanded. It was recreated in large part because of the assaults on civil liberties arising out of labor disputes in the mid-1930s.

67. On the ACLU's view of the law, see Lucille B. Milner, "Fighting Fascism by Law," *Nation* 146 (January 15, 1938): 65–67; Anderson, *Fascists, Communists, and the National Government*, pp.169–202. On the current status of the Public Order Act, see Fund for Free Expression, *Restricted Subjects: Freedom of Expression in the United Kingdom* (New York: Human Rights Watch, 1991).

68. Anderson, *Fascists, Communists, and the National Government*, pp.192–93, 198, 202. Alan Brinkley reaches a similar conclusion in his study of right-wing extremist movements in the early 1930s: Brinkley, *Voices of Protest*.

69. Glaser, "German-American Bund." See the discussion below.

70. Correspondence, ACLUP/1937/1001. On the New York bill, see ACLU, Board of Directors, Minutes, April 30, 1934, ACLUP. Carl J. Austrian, chairman, American Jewish Committee, Legal Advisory Committee, letter to ACLU, March 1, 1937, ACLUP/1937/1001. Canedy, *America's Nazis*, pp.180–82.

71. ACLU, Board of Directors, Minutes, December 12, 1938; ACLU, Report of Special Committee on Legislation to Curb Fascist Activities, January 21, 1938, ACLUP/1938/1079.

72. Baldwin, letter to *Passaic News*, August 20, 1935, clipping in Alexander Meiklejohn Papers, Wisconsin Historical Society.

73. See the table on meetings and arrests in Anderson, *Fascists, Communists, and the National Government*, p. 193. For the ACLU perspective on the law, see the article by the organization's secretary, Milner, "Fighting Fascism by Law."

74. Milner, "Fighting Fascism by Law."

75. Memos, ACLUP/1923/234; ACLU, *Shall We Defend?* (1934).

76. ACLU, Report of the Special Committee, January 21, 1938; ACLUP/1938/1079.

77. Anderson, *Fascists, Communists, and the National Government.*

78. ACLU, Board of Directors, Minutes, April 25, 1938.

79. Glaser, "German-American Bund."

80. Ibid.

81. This point is discussed at length in chapter 4.

82. ACLU, press release, November 13, 1935, ACLU/1935/845. In another instance the ACLU offered to represent Ferdinand Hepperle, of West New York, New Jersey, threatened with prosecution for printing anti-Semitic pamphlets, but apparently nothing came of the issue: ACLU, *Civil Liberties Quarterly,* December 1938.

83. Elliott M. Rudwick, *Race Riot at East St. Louis, July 2, 1917* (Cleveland: World Publishing, 1966).

84. *Bevins v. Prindable,* 39 F. Supp. 708 (E.D. Ill., 1941).

85. *Beauharnais v. Illinois,* 343 U.S. 250, 282 (1952).

86. Glaser, "German-American Bund."

87. *State v. Klapprott,* 22 A. 2d 877 (1941). Frankfurter did not find the ruling in *Klapprott* applicable to the Illinois law struck down in *Beauharnais v. Illinois,* 343 U.S. 250, 266, n.23 (1952).

88. *Cantwell v. Connecticut,* 310 U.S. 296 (1940).

89. Walker, *In Defense of American Liberties.*

90. *State v. Klapprott,* 22 A. 2d 877, 881 (1941). See papers related to the ACLU brief in Arthur Garfield Hays Papers, Mudd Library, Princeton University.

91. HUAC was formally a temporary committee in 1938 and had to be reauthorized each year. In 1945 Congressman John Rankin (D-Miss.) managed to have it converted into a permanent committee. See Walter Goodman, *The Committee* (New York: Farrar, Straus, and Giroux, 1968), pp.175–99.

92. Jerold S. Auerbach, *Labor and Liberty* (Indianapolis: Bobbs-Merrill, 1966).

93. The best summary is in Telford Taylor, *Grand Inquest: The Story of Congressional Investigations* (New York: Simon and Schuster, 1955).

94. The leading anti-Communist within the ACLU, the now-controversial Morris L. Ernst, always stressed the importance of enhancing the amount of information available to the public. Thus, in his view legislative investigations were entirely consistent with civil liberties principles. For the same reason, he felt that civil libertarians should seek to break up monopolies in the communications industry. See Walker, *In Defense of American Liberties.*

95. See the defense of this power in Felix Frankfurter, "Hands off the Investigations," *New Republic,* May 21, 1924, pp.329–31.

96. Goodman, *Committee,* pp.3–24.

97. His list of forty-six suspected Nazis was published in the *New York Times,* July 28, 1937.

98. Goodman, *Committee.*

99. Brinkley, *Voices of Protest.*

Chapter Four: The Hateful and the Hated

1. Sandra Coliver, ed., *Striking a Balance: Hate Speech, Freedom of Expression and Non-discrimination* (London: Article 19, 1992).

2. Ian Brownlie, ed., *Basic Documents on Human Rights* (Oxford: Clarendon Press, 1981).

3. Herbert Garfinkel, *When Negroes March* (Glencoe, Ill.: Free Press, 1959).

4. This point is argued in Samuel Walker, *In Defense of American Liberties: A History of the ACLU* (New York: Oxford University Press, 1990), pp.104–14.

5. The crisis over the Witnesses began and ended with changes in the group's tactics. The period began in 1931 and ended roughly twenty years later. The last major Supreme Court case involving the Witnesses was decided in 1951 (*Niemotko v. Maryland,* 340 U.S. 268 [1951]).

6. The most detailed account is in David Manwaring, *Render unto Caesar: The Flag-Salute Controversy* (Chicago: University of Chicago Press, 1962), pp.163–86.

7. Henry J. Abraham, *Freedom and the Court,* 5th ed. (New York: Oxford University Press, 1988), pp.297–98.

8. Harry Kalven, Jr., *The Negro and the First Amendment,* Phoenix ed. (Chicago: University of Chicago Press, 1966).

9. *West Virginia Board of Education v. Barnette,* 319 U.S. 624 (1943); Manwaring, *Render Unto Caesar.*

10. *Chaplinsky v. New Hampshire,* 315 U.S. 358 (1942). In 1981 Franklyn Haiman commented that "without explicitly saying so, the Supreme Court seems to have chopped off the first branch of the *Chaplinsky* definition of fighting words." Franklyn S. Haiman, *Speech and Law in a Free Society* (Chicago: University of Chicago Press, 1981), pp.134–35.

11. Joseph F. Rutherford, *Enemies* (Brooklyn, N.Y.: Watchtower Bible and Tract Society, 1937).

12. M. James Penton, *Apocalypse Delayed: The Story of the Jehovah's Witnesses* (Toronto: University of Toronto Press, 1985), p.129.

13. Penton, *Apocalypse Delayed,* pp.55–56.

14. Walker, *In Defense of American Liberties,* p.58.

15. The name Jehovah's Witnesses was officially adopted on July 26, 1931, at 4:00 P.M. Penton, *Apocalypse Delayed,* p.62.

16. James A. Beckford, *The Trumpet of Prophecy: A Sociological Study of Jehovah's Witnesses* (Oxford: Basil Blackwell, 1975), p.42.

17. *Lovell v. Griffin*, 303 U.S. 444 (1938).

18. *Schneider v. Irvington*, 308 U.S. 147 (1939).

19. *De Jonge v. Oregon*, 299 U.S. 353 (1937).

20. *Herndon v. Lowry*, 301 U.S. 242 (1937).

21. *Hague v. CIO*, 307 U.S. 496 (1939).

22. *Martin v. Struthers*, 319 U.S. 141 (1943).

23. *Cox v. New Hampshire*, 315 U.S. 569 (1941).

24. *Cantwell v. Connecticut*, 310 U.S. 296 (1940).

25. Ibid.

26. *State v. Klapprott*, 22 A. 2d 877, 882 (1941).

27. Abraham, *Freedom and the Court*, pp.38–117.

28. *Engel v. Vitale*, 370 U.S. 421 (1962); *Abington School District v. Schempp*, 374 U.S. 203 (1963).

29. *Chaplinsky v. New Hampshire*, 315 U.S. 568 (1942).

30. Ibid.

31. The controversy and the cases are examined in detail in Manwaring, *Render unto Caesar.*

32. *West Virginia State Board of Education v. Barnette*, 319 U.S. 624 (1943).

33. Manwaring, *Render unto Caesar*, p.11.

34. Ibid.

35. *Minersville School District v. Gobitis*, 310 U.S. 586 (1940).

36. *Hague v. CIO*, 25 F. Supp. 127, 152 (1938).

37. *Minersville School District v. Gobitis*, 310 U.S. 586 (1940).

38. Manwaring, *Render unto Caesar.* On the ACLU's demands for federal intervention to prosecute vigilantes, see Walker, *In Defense of American Liberties*, pp.108–10.

39. *Olmstead v. United States*, 277 U.S. 438 (1928).

40. Manwaring, *Render unto Caesar.*

41. *Jones v. Opelika*, 316 U.S. 584, 623–24 (1942).

42. Manwaring, *Render unto Caesar*, pp. 148–62, 193–94.

43. *West Virginia State Board of Education v. Barnette*, 319 U.S. 624 (1943).

Chapter Five: The Curious Rise and Fall of Group Libel

1. For the best survey of developments in the period, see Joseph Tanenhaus, "Group Libel," *Cornell Law Quarterly* 35 (winter 1950): 261–302.

2. *Beauharnais v. Illinois,* 343 U.S. 250 (1952).

3. The American Jewish Congress repudiated group libel legislation at its biennial conference, 1960. See AJC, Commission on Law and Social Action, *Cases and Materials,* AJC Library, New York City.

4. On the contribution of the civil rights movement to American constitutional law, in ways that extended far beyond the immediate concerns of the movement itself, see Harry Kalven, Jr., *The Negro and the First Amendment,* Phoenix ed. (Chicago: University of Chicago Press, 1966); Derrick Bell, *And We Are Not Saved* (New York: Basic Books, 1987), chap. 2, "The Benefits to Whites of Civil Rights Litigation."

5. Ian Brownlie, ed., *Basic Documents on Human Rights,* 2d ed. (Oxford: Clarendon Press, 1981).

6. David Riesman, "Democracy and Defamation," *Columbia Law Review* 42 (1942): 729–80, 1085–1123, 1282–1318.

7. On the evolution of Riesman's intellectual career, see the essays collected in David Riesman, *Individualism Reconsidered* (Glencoe, Ill.: Free Press, 1954).

8. Karl Loewenstein, "Militant Democracy and Fundamental Rights, I," *American Political Science Review* 31 (June 1937): 417–32; "Part II," Ibid. 31 (August 1937): 638–58.

9. Riesman, "Democracy and Defamation," p.1318.

10. Ibid, p.1301.

11. Ibid, p.1306.

12. Ibid, p.1313.

13. Ibid, p.1313.

14. Ibid, p.1312–13.

15. Most importantly in *R.A.V. v. City of St. Paul,* 505 U.S. ___, L. Ed. 2d 305, 112 S. Ct. ___(June 22, 1992).

16. Mari J. Matsuda, "Public Response to Racist Speech: Considering the Victim's Story," *Michigan Law Review* 87 (August 1989): 2320–81, esp. p. 2364.

17. The best survey of existing legislation at the time is Tanenhaus, "Group Libel," p. 279.

18. *Beauharnais v. Illinois,* 343 U.S. 250 (1952).

19. American Jewish Congress, Commission on Law and Social Action, *Cases and Materials,* AJC Library.

20. "Group Libelling," *Massachusetts Law Quarterly* 28 (December 1943): 104. This item is only a reprint of a brief article in the *Boston Herald,* not a legal commentary.

21. Civil Liberties Union of Massachusetts, Executive Committee, Minutes, January 5, 1944, ACLUP/1944/2541.

22. Note, "A Consideration of the Massachusetts Group Libel Statute," *Boston University Law Review* 32 (November 1952): 414–18, reexamines the law in the wake of the *Beauharnais* decision, arguing that it would probably be found constitutional. This brief note, however, did not cite any prosecutions over the previous ten years.

23. Sandra Coliver, ed., *Striking a Balance: Hate Speech, Freedom of Expression and Non-discrimination* (London: Article 19, 1992), particularly Coliver, "Hate Speech Laws: Do They Work?" pp.363–74; but see the chapters on individual countries as well.

24. ACLU, Board of Directors, Minutes, February 28, 1944.

25. Tanenhaus, "Group Libel," p.281.

26. Ibid., pp. 284–85.

27. Note, "Statutory Prohibition of Group Defamation," *Columbia Law Review* 47 (May 1947): 595–613.

28. United States House of Representatives, Subcommittee of the Committee on the Post Office and Post Roads, Hearings on H.R. 2328 and H.J. 49, November 15 and 16, 1943, 78th Cong., 1st sess. (1943).

29. A. L. Wirin to Clifford Forster, ACLU legal director, January 2, 1945; and subsequent correspondence, ACLUP/1945/2565.

30. Hearings, pp. 5–20. See also Nathan D. Perlman and Morris Ploscowe, "False, Defamatory, Anti-racial and Anti-religious Propaganda and the Use of the Mails," *Lawyers Guild Review* 4 (January–February 1944): 13–23. Perlman, chairman, American Jewish Congress, memorandum, November 15, 1943, ACLUP/1944/2580. See reply on behalf of the ACLU: Arthur Garfield Hays, letter to Perlman, December 27, 1943, ibid.

31. Hearings, part 2, February 15 and March 16 and 17, 1944, 78th Cong., 2d sess., pp.128–47 (testimony of Clifford Forster, ACLU staff counsel, and Morris L. Ernst, ACLU general counsel).

32. Samuel Walker, *In Defense of American Liberties: A History of the ACLU* (New York: Oxford University Press, 1990), passim.

33. *Hannegan v. Esquire,* 327 U.S. 146 (1946).

34. Hearings, part 2, p. 190; ACLU, *Bulletin,* March 20, 1944, ACLUP/1944/2580.

35. Resolution of December 13, 1944, cited in ACLUP/1944/2580.

36. U.S. House of Representatives, Committee on the Post Office, Hearings (1943).

37. Hearings, part 2, pp.138–47. Walker, *In Defense of American Liberties,* p.104.

38. Walker, *In Defense of American Liberties,* pp.84–86, 104, 240. *U.S. v. One Book Called Ulysses,* 5 F. Supp. 182 (1933). Ernst's first important anticensorship book was Morris L. Ernst and William Seagle, *To the Pure . . . : A Study of Obscenity and the Censor* (New York: Viking, 1929).

39. For this reason Ernst supported in principle legislative investigations of political groups, even though the ACLU consistently called for the abolition of the House Un-American Activities Committee. See Walker, *In Defense of American Liberties,* pp.128–30.

40. President's Committee on Civil Rights, *To Secure These Rights* (New York: Simon and Schuster, 1947), p.164; Walker, *In Defense of American Liberties,* p.104.

41. Perlman and Ploscowe, "False, Defamatory, Anti-racial and Anti-religious Propaganda."

42. U.S. House of Representatives, Committee on Un-American Activities, *Guide to Subversive Organizations and Publications,* rev. ed. (Washington, D.C.: Government Printing Office, 1961), p.121. On the Guild in the Cold War, see Ann Fagan Ginger and Eugene M. Tobin, eds., *The National Lawyers Guild: From Roosevelt through Reagan* (Philadelphia: Temple University Press, 1988).

43. Norman Cousins, editor of the *Saturday Review of Literature,* published a 1947 editorial in the form of an open letter to New York state legislators, asking for a debate on the group libel question. He received letters from Judge Learned Hand, Senator Arthur H. Vandenberg, financier Bernard Baruch, and a few others, but the issue immediately disappeared. Norman Cousins, "Group Libel," *Saturday Review of Literature* 30 (February 1, 1947): 20; letters, ibid., 30 (March 15, 1947): 23–24.

44. Ian Brownlie, ed., *Basic Documents on Human Rights,* 2d ed. (Oxford: Clarendon Press, 1980); Coliver, *Striking a Balance.* Mary Ann Glendon, *Rights Talk* (New York: Free Press, 1991), p.7.

45. Dennis J. Driscoll, "The Development of Human Rights in International Law," in *The Human Rights Reader,* rev. ed. Walter Laqueur and Barry Rubin, eds., 41–56 (New York: New American Library, 1989).

46. For a general discussion of limitations, see Alexandre Charles Kiss, "Permissible Limitations on Rights," in *The International Bill of Rights: The Covenant on Civil and Political Rights,* ed. Louis Henkin, 290–310 (New York: Columbia University Press, 1981).

47. Ineke Boerefijn and Joanna Oyediran, "Article 20 of the International Covenant on Civil and Political Rights," in Coliver, *Striking a Balance,* pp.29–32.

48. Ibid., p.31.

49. Coliver, *Striking a Balance,* "Annexe B: Reservations and Declarations concerning Racist Speech and Advocacy of Racial and Religious Hatred," p.394; American Association for the Advancement of Science, *Report on Science and Human Rights,* Spring 1992, p.5.

50. K. J. Partsch, "Racial Speech and Human Rights: Article 4 of the Convention on the Elimination of All Forms of Racial Discrimination," in Coliver, *Striking a Balance,* pp.21–28.

51. Natan Lerner, *The U.N. Convention on the Elimination of All Forms of Racial Discrimination* (Rockville, Md: Sijthoff and Nordhoff, 1980), p.43.

52. Coliver, *Striking a Balance,* "Annexe B," p.394.

53. Brownlie, *Basic Documents on Human Rights;* Coliver, *Striking a Balance.*

54. Glendon, *Rights Talk,* 159. Anthony Lester, "The Overseas Trade in the American Bill of Rights," *Columbia Law Review* 88 (1988): 537.

55. For a spirited critique of the emphasis on individual rights in contemporary America see Glendon, *Rights Talk.* In 1991 *Harper's* magazine sponsored a symposium on a "bill of duties," prompted by the argument that American society had gone too far in emphasizing individual rights and that as a corrective more emphasis should be given to duties and community responsibilities. One participant, law professor Christopher Stone, pointed out, however, that the entire discussion was immediately framed in terms of the rights of children – that is, in terms of individual rights. See comments by Stone in "Who Owes What to Whom?" *Harper's* 282 (February 1991): 48.

56. The exception is the section of ACLU policy 318 on homelessness, adopted in 1989, which holds that it is unconstitutional for the government to adopt policies that reduce housing for the poor while enhancing housing opportunities for others. See ACLU, *Policy Guide* (New York: American Civil Liberties Union, n.d.), policy 318.

57. Walker, *In Defense of American Liberties,* pp.313–14, 376–78.

58. Some answers to these questions may be gleaned from a history of one of the international documents, Lerner, *U.N. Convention.*

59. Kiss, "Permissible Limitations on Rights."

60. *Beauharnais v. Illinois,* 343 U.S. 250 (1952).

61. Elliot M. Rudwick, *Race Riot at East St. Louis, July 2, 1917* (Carbondale: Southern Illinois University Press, 1964).

62. Chicago Commission on Race Relations, *The Negro in Chicago: A Study of Race Relations and a Race Riot* (Chicago: University of Chicago Press, 1922); Allan H. Spear, *Black Chicago: The Making of a Negro Ghetto, 1890–1920* (Chicago: University of Chicago Press, 1967).

63. Arnold R. Hirsch, *Making the Second Ghetto: Race and Housing in Chicago, 1940–1960* (New York: Cambridge University Press, 1983).

64. Hirsch, *Making the Second Ghetto.*

65. National Commission on the Causes and Prevention of Violence, *The History of Violence in America* (New York: Bantam Books, 1969).

66. *Chaplinsky v. New Hampshire,* 315 U.S. 568 (1942); *Beauharnais v. Illinois,* 343 U.S. 250, 255–58 (1952).

67. Ibid., 266.

68. *State v. Klapprott,* 22 A. 2d 882 (1941); *Beauharnais v. Illinois,* 343 U.S. 250, 266, n. 23.

69. Ibid., 258–59.

70. The balancing test was framed in a debate between Justices John Marshall Harlan and Hugo Black. See particularly *Konigsberg v. State Bar of California,* 366 U.S. 36 (1961). See the discussion in Harry Kalven, Jr., *A Worthy Tradition* (New York: Harper and Row, 1988), pp.548–87.

71. *Beauharnais v. Illinois,* 343 U.S. 250, 281 (1952).

72. Ibid., 269.

73. Ibid., 286–87.

74. Ibid., 304–5.

75. *Terminiello v. Chicago,* 337 U.S. 1 (1949).

76. Tanenhaus, "Group Libel."

77. Joseph Tanenhaus, "Group Libel and Free Speech," *Phylon* 13, no. 3 (1952): 219.

78. Gordon W. Allport, *The Nature of Prejudice* (Reading, Mass.: Addison-Wesley, 1954), p.469; see chap. 29, "Ought There to Be a Law?"

79. David Riesman, "The 'Militant' Fight Against Anti-Semitism," *Commentary* 11 (1951): 11–19; reprinted in Riesman, *Individualism Reconsidered* (Glencoe, Ill.: Free Press, 1954) pp.139–52.

80. Riesman, letter to Norman Dorsen (president of the ACLU), September 1, 1978, Dorsen Papers, New York University Law School.

81. Biennial conference resolution, 1960; American Jewish Congress, Commission on Law and Social Action, *Cases and Materials,* American Jewish Congress Library.

82. This was not an isolated move. In 1962 the ACLU also adopted a new and stronger policy against censorship, ending many years of uncertainty about where it stood on allegedly obscene forms of expression: Walker, *In Defense of American Liberties.*

83. Theodore R. Mann, "The Nazis and the First Amendment," *Congress Monthly* 45 (February 1978): 6. Mann was then (1978) chairman of the NJCRAC. See Aryeh Neier, *Defending My Enemy* (New York: E. P. Dutton, 1979), pp.30–31.

84. Charles H. Bowman, "The Illinois Criminal Code of 1961," *Illinois Bar Journal* 50 (September 1961): 34–40.

85. The Model Penal Code was not formally completed until 1962, but work on it had begun in 1952, and the various deliberations and drafts already had an influence on legal thought. See Herbert Wechsler, "The Challenge of a Model Penal Code," *Harvard Law Review* 65 (May 1952): 1097–1133; American Law Institute, *Proceedings* (1952–62); and American Law Institute, *Model Penal Code* (1962).

86. Neier, *Defending My Enemy.* See the full discussion of Skokie in chapter 6 below.

Chapter Six: Free Speech Triumphant

1. *New York Times Co. v. Sullivan*, 376 U.S. 254 (1964).

2. *Collin v. Smith*, 578 F. 2d 1197 (1978). There is a sizable literature on the Skokie affair. This account is based on Samuel Walker, *In Defense of American Liberties: A History of the ACLU* (New York: Oxford University Press, 1990), pp.323–31. For other works see the text and notes below.

3. Archibald Cox, *The Warren Court* (Cambridge: Harvard University Press, 1968), p.1.

4. William Lasser, *The Limits of Judicial Power: The Supreme Court in American Politics* (Chapel Hill: University of North Carolina Press, 1988).

5. Ian Brownlie, ed., *Basic Documents on Human Rights* (Oxford: Clarendon Press, 1981).

6. Anthony Dickey, "English Law and Race Defamation," *New York Law Forum* 14 (Spring 1968): 9–32. Sandra Coliver, ed., *Striking a Balance: Hate Speech, Freedom of Expression and Non-discrimination* (London: Article 19, 1992), chaps. 27, 28, 29. On the first serious race riots, see Lord Scarman, *The Scarman Report: The Brixton Disorders 10–12 April 1981* (New York: Penguin Books, 1982).

7. Coliver, *Striking a Balance.*

8. Hugh Davis Graham, *The Civil Rights Era* (New York: Oxford University Press, 1990). Graham's account begins with 1960 and focuses on the major legislative accomplishments in Congress. There is a voluminous literature on the earlier years. The turning point was 1954, the year that marked the decision in *Brown v. Board of Education,* 347 U.S. 483 (1954), in May and the Senate's censure of Senator Joseph McCarthy in December. This point is argued in more detail in Walker, *In Defense of American Liberties,* pp.211–14.

9. For the program of the Anti-Defamation League in the early 1960s, see Benjamin R. Epstein and Arnold Forster, *"Some of My Best Friends..."* (New York: Farrar, Straus and Cudahy, 1962).

10. An important qualification needs to be entered here. The "major" civil rights groups include the NAACP, the Urban League, the American Jewish Congress, the Anti-Defamation League, the American Jewish Committee, the ACLU, the National Council of Churches, and several of the more liberal labor unions such as the United Automobile Workers. A number of the minor civil rights groups, particularly left-oriented ones, did not share the same commitment to unrestricted free speech. The National Lawyers Guild, the Jewish War Veterans, and some of the smaller left-wing labor unions generally supported group libel legislation.

11. For an initial assessment of the civil rights coalition, see [Norman Redlich], "Private Attorneys General – Group Action in the Fight for Civil Liberties," *Yale Law Journal* 58 (1949): 574–98. On the relations between the major Jewish groups, see Howard M. Sachar, *A History of the Jews in America* (New York: Alfred A. Knopf, 1992), pp.672–712.

12. Will Maslow, interview with author.

13. The national civil rights coalition began to unravel in the 1970s over the question of affirmative action, which, in contrast, sought to advance group rights through group-based remedies. The members of the civil rights coalition lined up according to whether they thought affirmative action did or did not violate the principle of strict adherence to individual rights. Opponents of formal quotas rejected that approach as a form of reverse discrimination. For the best indication of the lineup of groups, see the amicus briefs filed in *Regents of Univ. of California v. Bakke,* 438 U.S. 265 (1978).

14. Lee Bollinger, *The Tolerant Society* (New York: Oxford University Press, 1986), pp.29–30.

15. Walker, *In Defense of American Liberties,* pp.323–31.

16. Aryeh Neier, *Defending My Enemy* (New York: Dutton, 1979), pp.11–22.

17. In declaring unconstitutional a Virginia statute that had been used to restrict the NAACP, the Supreme Court held that "there thus inheres in the statute the gravest danger of smothering all discussion": *NAACP v. Button,* 371 U.S. 415 (1963).

18. *Chaplinsky v. New Hampshire,* 315 U.S. 568 (1942).

19. *Terminiello v. Chicago,* 337 U.S. 1 (1949).

20. On the policy and its partial demise in the Skokie affair, see Donald Alexander Downs, *Nazis in Skokie: Freedom, Community and the First Amendment* (Notre Dame, Ind.: Notre Dame University Press, 1985), pp.44–46, 114–15. See also Theodore R. Mann, "The Nazis and the First Amendment," *Congress Monthly* 45 (February 1978): 6–7.

21. On the program of the Anti-Defamation League, see Arnold Forster, *Anti-Semitism in the United States* (New York: ADL, 1947); idem, *A Measure of Freedom* (New York: Doubleday, 1950).

22. Glen Jeansonne, *Gerald L. K. Smith: Minister of Hate* (New Haven: Yale University Press, 1988). On the ACLU's defense of Smith's free speech rights, see Walker, *In Defense of American Liberties,* pp.185, 229.

23. Arnold Forster and Benjamin Epstein, *The Trouble-Makers* (Garden City, N.Y.: Doubleday, 1952), pp.225–26; Neier, *Defending My Enemy,* pp.30–31. It is evident that these criticisms of militant tactics were prompted in part by a strong desire to distance the major Jewish groups from the Communist party.

24. David Riesman, "The 'Militant' Fight against Anti-Semitism," *Commentary* 11 (1951): 11–19.

25. *Terminiello v. Chicago,* 337 U.S. 1 (1949).

26. *Feiner v. New York,* 340 U.S. 315 (1951).

27. *Edwards v. South Carolina,* 372 U.S. 229 (1963).

28. *Cox v. Louisiana,* 379 U.S. 536 (1965).

29. Harry Kalven, Jr., *The Negro and the First Amendment,* Phoenix ed. (Chicago: University of Chicago Press, 1966), pp.11–12.

30. *Gregory v. Chicago,* 394 U.S. 111 (1969).

31. Neier, *Defending My Enemy,* p.142.

32. Nat Hentoff, *Free Speech for Me—but Not for Thee* (New York: Harper Collins, 1992), pp.315–35, "Obscenity and How It Did in Lenny Bruce." See also Frank Kofsky, *Lenny Bruce: The Comedian as Social Critic and Secular Moralist* (New York: Pathfinder Press, 1974); William Karl Thomas, *Lenny Bruce: The Making of a Prophet* (Hamden, Conn.: Archon Books, 1989).

33. In the 1980s a new group of comedians emerged whose humor was directed largely at feminists and gay people; many women and gay people objected. Some

of these comedy routines might even have fallen under the terms of some of the campus speech codes. Yet apart from the specific targets, this brand of humor was little different from Lenny Bruce's material twenty-five years earlier.

34. Hentoff, *Free Speech for Me,* p.328.

35. *Cohen v. California,* 403 U.S. 15 (1971).

36. Ibid.

37. *Roe v. Wade,* 410 U.S. 113 (1973). ACLU Reproductive Freedom Project, *Preserving the Right to Choose: How to Cope with Violence and Disruption at Abortion Clinics* (New York: ACLU, 1986), pp.18–22.

38. *Gooding v. Wilson,* 405 U.S. 518 (1972).

39. *Rosenfeld v. New Jersey,* 408 U.S. 901 (1972).

40. *Lewis v. New Orleans,* 408 U.S. 913 (1972).

41. *Brown v. Oklahoma,* 408 U.S. 914 (1972).

42. Kent Greenawalt, *Speech, Crime, and the Uses of Language* (New York: Oxford University Press, 1989), p.298.

43. *Terminiello v. Chicago,* 337 U.S. 1 (1949).

44. The phrase "breathing room" appears in one of the Court's opinions protecting the NAACP from onerous restrictions: *NAACP v. Button,* 371 U.S. 415 (1963).

45. Quoted in Robert Sherrill, *Gothic Politics in the Deep South: Stars of the New Confederacy* (New York: Grossman, 1968), pp.210–11.

46. Ibid., p.267.

47. These incidents are recounted in Walter Goodman, *The Committee* (New York: Farrar, Straus, and Giroux, 1968), p.182.

48. Forster and Epstein, *Trouble-Makers.*

49. President's Commission on Law Enforcement and Administration of Justice, *Task Force Report: The Police* (Washington, D.C.: Government Printing Office, 1967), pp.180–81.

50. See chapter 3 above.

51. International Convention on the Elimination of All Forms of Racial Discrimination (1966), cited in Brownlie, *Basic Documents on Human Rights,* pp. 150–63.

52. *Schenck v. United States,* 249 U.S. 47 (1919); *Frohwerk v. United States,* 249 U.S. 204 (1919); *Debs v. United States,* 249 U.S. 211 (1919); *Abrams v. United States,* 250 U.S. 616 (1919).

53. *Dennis v. United States,* 341 U.S. 494 (1951).

54. *Brandenburg v. Ohio,* 395 U.S. 444 (1969).

55. Ibid.

56. Zechariah Chafee, Jr., *Free Speech in the United States* (Cambridge: Harvard University Press, 1941); Harry Kalven, Jr., *A Worthy Tradition: Freedom of Speech in America* (New York: Harper and Row, 1988).

57. On the anti–civil libertarian positions of the Communist party, see Walker, *In Defense of American Liberties.*

58. Kalven cites six major cases involving the NAACP as an organization: Kalven, *Negro and the First Amendment,* pp.65 ff.

59. On *Brown v. Board of Education,* 347 U.S. 483 (1954), see Richard Kluger, *Simple Justice* (New York: Vintage Books, 1977). For a critique of the traditional view of the impact of *Brown,* see Gerald Rosenberg, *The Hollow Hope* (Chicago: University of Chicago Press, 1991).

60. Numan V. Bartley, *The Rise of Massive Resistance* (Baton Rouge: Louisiana State University Press, 1969).

61. This effort gained greater momentum after a series of 1957 Court decisions protecting the rights of criminal suspects and limiting some anti-Communist measures. The "court-stripping" effort of 1958 ultimately failed. That may have been because for many northern members of Congress court stripping was already discredited by its association with segregation. See C. Herman Pritchett, *Congress versus the Supreme Court,* 1957–1960 (Minneapolis: University of Minnesota Press, 1961).

62. David M. Chalmers, *Hooded Americanism: The History of the Ku Klux Klan* (Chicago: Quadrangle Books, 1968), p.343.

63. Given the proliferation of civil rights groups, especially after 1960, it is difficult to appreciate today how completely the NAACP dominated civil rights efforts, especially in the South, during this period.

64. *NAACP v. Alabama,* 357 U.S. 449 (1958).

65. Ibid.

66. *Bryant v. Zimmerman,* 278 U.S. 63 (1928); see chapter 2, above.

67. Kalven, *Negro and the First Amendment,* p.94.

68. *Shelton v. Tucker,* 364 U.S. 479 (1960).

69. Derrick Bell, *And We Are Not Saved: The Elusive Quest for Racial Justice* (New York: Basic Books, 1987), chap. 2, "The Benefits to Whites of Civil Rights Litigation."

70. *NAACP v. Button,* 371 U.S. 415 (1963).

71. *Gibson v. Florida Legislative Investigation Commission,* 372 U.S. 539 (1963).

72. Kalven, *Negro and the First Amendment,* p.66.

73. Kalven, *Worthy Tradition*, p.259.

74. Wulf, quoted in Walker, *In Defense of American Liberties*, p.240.

75. Lewis Steel, "Nine Men in Black Who Think White," *New York Times Magazine* 13 (October 1968): 56. The episode is recounted in Bell, *And We Are Not Saved*, pp.60–61.

76. *New York Times v. Sullivan*, 376 U.S. 254 (1964). For an excellent account of the case, see Anthony Lewis, *Make No Law* (New York: Random House, 1991).

77. *New York Times v. Sullivan*, 376 U.S. 254 (1964).

78. Lewis, *Make No Law*.

79. The Skokie case has inspired a rather large body of literature. Firsthand accounts by participants include [ACLU executive director] Aryeh Neier, *Defending My Enemy*, and [Illinois ACLU executive director] David Hamlin, *Nazi/Skokie Conflict* (Boston: Beacon Press, 1980). Some academic studies of the controversy are James L. Gibson and Richard D. Bingham, *Civil Liberties and Nazis: The Skokie Free-Speech Controversy* (New York: Praeger, 1985); Downs, *Nazis in Skokie;* and a major essay on the First Amendment, Bollinger, *Tolerant Society*.

80. Hamlin, *Nazi/Skokie Conflict*, chap. 1.

81. Ibid, p.65; Neier, *Defending My Enemy*, p.1.

82. Hamlin, *Nazi/Skokie Conflict;* Neier, *Defending My Enemy*.

83. Nicholas Lemann, *The Promised Land* (New York: Vintage Books, 1992), pp.70–77.

84. Hamlin, *Nazi/Skokie Conflict*, p.19.

85. On the change among national Jewish organizations, see Neier, *Defending My Enemy*, pp.30–31; on the Village of Skokie, Hamlin, *Nazi/Skokie Conflict*, pp.34–39. See also chapter 5, above.

86. The five thousand figure is cited in Howard M. Sachar, *A History of the Jews in America* (New York: Alfred A. Knopf, 1992), p.792.

87. See the vivid firsthand testimony in Charles Silberman, *A Certain People* (New York: Summit Books, 1985).

88. American Jewish Congress, resolution, January 8, 1978; reprinted in *Congress Weekly* 45 (February 1978): 9; interviews with Will Maslow and Norman Redlich.

89. [Redlich], "Private Attorneys General," pp.574–98.

90. James E. Wood, ed., *Religion and the State: Essays in Honor of Leo Pfeffer* (Waco, Tex.: Baylor University Press, 1985); Pfeffer, interview with author; Will Maslow, interview with author.

91. Mann, "Nazis and the First Amendment," p.6.

92. As the national controversy increased, the Jewish Defense League threatened to hold a counterdemonstration, including thinly veiled threats of anti-Nazi violence.

93. American Jewish Congress, resolution, January 8, 1978, reprinted in *Congress Monthly* 45 (February 1978): 9.

94. *Collin v. Smith,* 578 F. 2d 1197, 1205–6 (7th Cir. 1978).

95. Hamlin, *Nazi/Skokie Conflict,* pp.111, 154–55.

96. *Collin v. Smith,* 578 F. 2d 1197, 1201, 1202 (7th Cir. 1978).

97. Ibid., 1203.

98. Ibid., 1204.

99. In yet another irony related to the case, Kahane had moved to Israel and was elected to its parliament as the leader of the right-wing and racist anti-Palestinian Kach party. Because of its racist ideas, the Kach party was first removed from the ballot and then, when that move was overturned, was subjected to a series of legal restrictions. None of these measures would have been possible in the United States under the First Amendment principles that Kahane opposed in the Skokie case.

100. Neier, *Defending My Enemy,* pp.32–33, 50–51.

101. *Collin v. Smith,* 578 F. 2d 1197, 1206 (7th Cir. 1978).

102. *Collin v. O'Malley,* 452 F. Supp. 577 (1978).

103. Hamlin, *Nazi/Skokie Conflict,* pp.163–77.

104. Walker, *In Defense of American Liberties,* pp.323–31.

105. *Collin v. Smith,* 578 F. 2d 1197, 1211 (7th Cir. 1978).

106. Bollinger, *Tolerant Society,* pp.29–30.

107. *Collin v. Smith,* 587 F. 2d 1197, 1210 (7th Cir. 1978).

108. This is the title of chapter 1 of Bollinger, *Tolerant Society.*

Chapter Seven: The Campus Speech Codes

1. *Doe v. University of Michigan,* 721 F. Supp. 852 (E.D. Mich. 1989).

2. Carnegie Fund for the Advancement of Teaching, *Campus Life* (New York, 1990). The survey was based on replies from 355 colleges and universities.

3. Mary Ellen Gale, "On Curbing Racial Speech," *Responsive Community* 1 (Winter 1990–91): 55. A longer version appeared as Mary Ellen Gale, "Reimagining the First Amendment: Racist Speech and Equal Liberty," *St. John's Law Review* 65 (Winter 1991):119–85.

4. This was precisely the point raised by the plaintiff, a graduate student in psychology, in the challenge to the University of Michigan policy: *Doe v. University of Michigan,* 721 F. Supp. 852 (E.D. Mich. 1989). The most persistent public criticisms of the campus speech codes were in journalist Nat Hentoff's newspaper columns. These were revised and republished in Hentoff, *Free Speech for Me–but Not For Thee* (New York: Harper Collins, 1992), pp.146–92; but see the other chapters for closely related free speech issues.

5. I will not attempt to cite the entire body of literature here. Interested readers may consult the *Index to Legal Periodicals* and the *Reader's Guide to Periodical Literature.* The most important items are cited throughout the text in this chapter.

6. *Doe v. University of Michigan,* 721 F. Supp. 852 (E.D. Mich. 1989); UWM *Post v. Board of Regents of the University of Wisconsin,* 774 F. Supp. 1163 (E.D. Wis. 1991). On the reaction to the University of Michigan decision, see "Symposium: Campus Hate Speech and the Constitution in the Aftermath of Doe v. University of Michigan," *Wayne Law Review* 37 (Spring 1991).

7. *R.A.V. v. City of St. Paul,* 505 U.S. __, L. Ed. 2d 305, 112 S. Ct. __ (June 22, 1992).

8. That a hostile environment is a form of sexual harassment in violation of title 7 of the 1964 Civil Rights Act: *Meritor Savings Bank, FSB v. Vinson,* 477 U.S. 57 (1986).

9. David Savage, *Turning Right: The Making of the Rehnquist Supreme Court* (New York: John Wiley, 1992); Herman Schwartz, *Packing the Courts: The Conservative Campaign to Rewrite the Constitution* (New York: Charles Scribner's Sons, 1988).

10. There is an enormous body of literature reporting these incidents. A comprehensive list is in National Institute against Prejudice and Violence, *Campus Ethnoviolence . . . and the Policy Options* (Baltimore: National Institute, 1990), pp.41–72. Incidents are cited in the important articles advocating speech codes: Charles Lawrence III, "If He Hollers Let Him Go: Racist Speech on Campus, *Duke Law Journal* June 1990, 431–83. Mari J. Matsuda, "Public Response to Racist Speech: Considering the Victim's Story," *Michigan Law Review* 87 (August 1989): 2320–81. Richard Delgado, "Words That Wound: A Tort Action for Racial Insults, Epithets and Name-Calling," *Harvard Civil Rights–Civil Liberties Law Review* 17 (Spring 1982): 133–81; idem, "Campus Antiracism Rules: Constitutional Narratives in Collision," *Northwestern University Law Review* 85 (1991): 343.

11. The most comprehensive list is in National Institute against Prejudice and Violence, *Campus Ethnoviolence,* pp.41–72.

12. "Anger over List of Names Divides Blacks from Their College Town, " *New York Times,* September 27, 1992.

13. National Institute against Prejudice and Violence, *Campus Ethnoviolence,* "The Societal Context," pp.5–10.

14. Andrew Hacker, *Two Nations: Black and White, Separate, Hostile, Unequal* (New York: Charles Scribner's Sons, 1992), pp.179–80, 202; Thomas Byrne Edsall and Mary D. Edsall, *Chain Reaction: The Impact of Race, Rights, and Taxes on American Politics* (New York: W. W. Norton, 1991), pp.222–24, 275; income trends are reported in "Income Data Show Years of Erosion," *New York Times,* September 7, 1992.

15. Wilson Julius Wilson, *The Truly Disadvantaged: The Inner City, the Underclass, and Public Policy* (Chicago: University of Chicago Press, 1987); U.S. Bureau of Justice Statistics, *Criminal Victimization,* 1992 (Washington, D.C.: Government Printing Office, 1993).

16. Hacker, *Two Nations,* chaps. 6, 7.

17. The 1978 *Bakke* case involving affirmative action probably marked the end of the historical civil rights coalition: *Regents of University of California v. Bakke,* 438 U.S. 265 (1978).

18. Edsall and Edsall, *Chain Reaction.*

19. UWM *Post v. Board of Regents of the University of Wisconsin,* 774 F. Supp. 1163 (E.D. Wis. 1991).

20. Lawrence, "If He Hollers Let Him Go," 450–51. See especially the spirited defense of the Stanford policy by Cass Sunstein, "Ideas, Yes; Assaults, No," *American Prospect,* summer 1991, pp.35–39. This was a reply to ACLU leader Franklyn Haiman, "The Remedy Is More Speech," ibid., pp.30–35.

21. Enrollment of African American males fell from 464,000 in 1980 to 436,000 in 1986 and then rose to 476,000 in 1990. U.S. Department of Education, cited in *Chronicle of Higher Education,* August 26, 1992, p.11.

22. Catherine MacKinnon, "Pornography, Civil Rights, and Speech," *Harvard Civil Rights–Civil Liberties Law Review* 20 (1985): 1.

23. Dinesh D'Souza, *Illiberal Education* (New York: Free Press, 1991).

24. Michael V. Miller and Susan Gilmore, *Revolution at Berkeley: The Crisis in American Education* (New York: Dial Press, 1965). See, for example, the criticism of the younger generation for its bizarre haircuts and outrageous ideas and behavior – in 1911! "A Letter to the Rising Generation," *Atlantic Monthly* 107 (February 1911): 149.

25. Lawrence, "If He Hollers Let Him Go"; Matsuda, "Public Response to Racist Speech"; Delgado, "Words That Wound"; idem, "Campus Antiracism Rules."

26. This argument was made by both the University of Michigan and the University of Wisconsin in the suits over their policies.

27. Rodney V. Smolla, *Free Speech in an Open Society* (New York: Alfred A. Knopf, 1992), p.151.

28. American Association of University Professors, "On Freedom of Expression and Campus Speech Codes," resolution approved by Committee A, June 1992; published in *Academe,* July–August 1992, pp.30–31.

29. For a guide to descriptions of the ACLU, see Samuel Walker, *The American Civil Liberties Union: An Annotated Bibliography* (New York: Garland, 1993).

30. Franklyn S. Haiman, *Speech and Law in a Free Society* (Chicago: University of Chicago Press, 1981).

31. Kent Greenawalt, *Speech, Crime, and the Uses of Language* (New York: Oxford University Press, 1989).

32. Delgado, "Words That Wound." See the reply by Marjorie Heins, "Banning Words: A Comment on 'Words That Wound,'" *Harvard Civil Rights–Civil Liberties Law Review* 18 (Summer 1983): 585–92; and the rejoinder by Delgado, ibid., pp.593–97.

33. Lawrence, "If He Hollers Let Him Go"; Delgado, "Campus Antiracism Rules."

34. Charles R. Lawrence III, "Acknowledging the Victim's Cry," *Academe,* November–December 1990, p.10.

35. David Kretzmer, "Freedom of Speech and Racism," *Cardozo Law Review* 8 (1987): 445–513.

36. Sandra Coliver, ed., *Striking a Balance: Hate Speech, Freedom of Expression and Non-discrimination* (London: Article 19, 1992).

37. Lawrence, "If He Hollers Let Him Go," pp.438–49.

38. Ibid., p.436.

39. Catherine MacKinnon, *Only Words* (Cambridge: Harvard University Press, 1993); Andrea Dworkin, *Pornography: Men Possessing Women* (New York: Perigee, 1981).

40. *American Booksellers Association v. Hudnut,* 771 F. 2d 323 (7th Cir. 1985). For an account of the history of antipornography ordinances in Minneapolis and Indianapolis, see Donald Alexander Downs, *The New Politics of Pornography* (Chicago: University of Chicago Press, 1989).

41. Lawrence, "If He Hollers Let Him Go," p.435; Delgado, "Campus Antiracism Rules"; the subtitle of the article is "Constitutional Narratives in Collision."

42. Matsuda, "Public Response to Racist Speech," pp.2327–29.

43. Lawrence, "Acknowledging the Victim's Cry," p.10.

44. Derrick Bell, *And We Are Not Saved: The Elusive Quest for Racial Justice* (New York: Basic Books, 1987).

45. Greenawalt, *Speech, Crime, and the Uses of Language,* p.147.

46. Ibid, p.148.

47. Matsuda, "Public Response to Racist Speech," p.2364.

48. Bell, *And We Are Not Saved.*

49. A similar pessimism about the law pervades the arguments of some feminist legal scholars: that the law has been and is likely to remain an instrument of patriarchy. This assumption undergirds gender-conscious remedies.

50. Derrick Bell, *Faces at the Bottom of the Well* (New York: Basic Books, 1992).

51. Lawrence, "Acknowledging the Victim's Cry," p.13.

52. ACLU, Board of Directors, Minutes, October 13, 1990. Thomas is also quoted in Nat Hentoff, "The ACLU Does the Right Thing," *Village Voice,* November 13, 1990; Hentoff, *Free Speech for Me,* p.162.

53. *Doe v. University of Michigan,* 721 F. Supp. 852 (E.D. Mich. 1989).

54. Catherine A. MacKinnon, *Sexual Harassment of Working Women* (New Haven: Yale University Press, 1979).

55. *Meritor Savings Bank, FSB v. Vinson,* 477 U.S. 57 (1986).

56. *Doe v. University of Michigan,* 721 F. Supp. 852 (E.D. Mich. 1989); *UWM Post v. Board of Regents of the University of Wisconsin,* 774 F. Supp. 1163 (E.D. Wis. 1991).

57. MacKinnon, *Only Words.*

58. Note, "A Communitarian Defense of Group Libel Laws," *Harvard Law Review* 101 (January 1988): 682–701.

59. See the communitarian movement's official platform in Amitai Etzioni, *The Spirit of Community* (New York: Crown Publishers, 1993), pp. 253–67.

60. Mary Ann Glendon, *Rights Talk: The Impoverishment of Political Discourse* (New York: Free Press, 1991).

61. Symposium, "Who Owes What to Whom?" *Harper's* 282 (February 1991): 43 ff.

62. *Responsive Community,* vol. 2.

63. Sunstein, "Ideas, Yes; Assaults, No"; Alexander Meiklejohn, *Free Speech and Its Relation to Self-Government* (New York: Harper and Row, 1948).

64. Greenawalt, *Speech, Crime, and the Uses of Language.*

65. Samuel Walker, *In Defense of American Liberties: A History of the* ACLU (New York: Oxford University Press, 1990). The record is also summarized by future ACLU president Nadine Strossen in "Regulating Racist Speech on Campus: A Modest Proposal?" *Duke Law Journal,* June 1990, 551–53.

66. Mr. powell spells his name with lowercase letters.

67. Gale, "On Curbing Racial Speech," p.55.

68. Northern California (San Francisco); Southern California (Los Angeles); and San Diego and Imperial Valley (San Diego).

69. ACLU, *Policy Guide of the American Civil Liberties Union* (New York, n.d.), policy 523.

70. Walker, *In Defense of American Liberties,* pp.313–14, 376–78. The debate can be followed best in the materials from the ACLU biennial conferences from 1968 onward; ACLU Papers, Princeton University.

71. Ian Brownlie, ed., *Basic Documents on Human Rights,* 2d ed. (Oxford: Clarendon Press, 1981).

72. Letter, David Gardner, president, University of California, to colleagues, September 21, 1989.

73. ACLU of Southern California, policy, March 21, 1990; revised version adopted May 15, 1991. Queries to the University of California about its policy were cosigned by the directors of all three ACLU affiliates, representing a common ACLU affiliate policy and a common set of objections to the university policy. Subsequent decisions by the California affiliates resulted in three slightly different policies by 1992.

74. See, among others, Hentoff's column in the *Village Voice,* May 15, 1990; May 22, 1990; June 5, 1990; June 12, 1990; June 19, 1990; and September 18, 1990; *Washington Post,* October 27, 1990; Hentoff, *Free Speech for Me,* pp.146–92.

75. The other was Harvard law professor Alan Dershowitz, who also made a habit of tweaking the ACLU. Both Hentoff and Dershowitz had been members of the ACLU Board of Directors and were not reelected some years earlier. Hentoff had also concluded that there was no constitutional right to an abortion and was mounting an unrelenting attack on the ACLU on that issue.

76. "The ACLU . . . has concluded that the policy infringes on the First Amendment rights of University of California students": letter, Ripston (ACLU-SC), Ehrlich (ACLU-NC), Hills (ACLU-SDIC), et al. to Gardner, August 8, 1990. See also letter, Ripston, Ehrlich, Hills to Gardner, January 12, 1990.

77. Letter, Ripston, Ehrlich, Hills to Gardner, November 22, 1989.

78. *Doe v. University of Michigan*, 721 F. Supp. 852 (E.D. Mich. 1989).

79. Letter, Gary Morrison, deputy general counsel, University of California, to Paul Hoffman, ACLU-SC, August 29, 1990; letter, Hoffman to Morrison, September 11, 1990.

80. Author interviews with staff members, ACLU-SC, ACLU-NC, ACLU-SDIV, 1992.

81. Coliver, *Striking a Balance*. See chapters 3 and 5 above.

82. Formally, the biennial conference adopted a resolution on racism on campus that required the national Board of Directors to act, which it did on October 13, 1990: ACLU, *Report of the 1989 Biennial Conference* (New York: ACLU, 1989).

83. Lawrence, "If He Hollers Let Him Go."

84. Strossen, "Regulating Racist Speech on Campus," pp.549–61, 562.

85. ACLU, "Free Speech and Bias on College Campuses"; ACLU, Board of Directors, Minutes, October 13, 1990. See also ACLU, Special Committee on Biennial Conference Resolution on Racist Speech, memorandum, October 5, 1990; Hentoff, "ACLU Does the Right Thing."

86. See chapter 3 above.

87. Henry J. Hyde and George M. Fishman, "The Collegiate Speech Protection Act of 1991: A Response to the New Intolerance in the Academy," *Wayne Law Review* 37 (spring 1991): 1469–1524.

88. *New York Times*, March 13, 1991.

89. *Buckley v. Valeo*, 424 U.S. 1 (1976).

90. D'Souza, *Illiberal Education;* Paul Berman, ed., *Debating P.C.* (New York: Dell, 1992).

91. Facts cited in *Doe v. University of Michigan*, 721 F. Supp. 852 (E.D. Mich. 1989). Additional incidents in 1988 are cited in National Institute against Prejudice and Violence, *Campus Ethnoviolence*, pp.41–72.

92. *Doe v. University of Michigan*, 721 F. Supp. 852 (E.D. Mich. 1989).

93. Ibid., 858.

94. Ibid., 867.

95. *Ibid.*, 868. For reactions to the decision, see Symposium, "Campus Hate Speech and the Constitution in the Aftermath of Doe v. University of Michigan." See also Robin M. Hulshizer, "Securing Freedom from Harassment without Reducing Freedom of Speech: Doe v. University of Michigan, *Iowa Law Review* 76 (1991): 383–403.

96. *Texas v. Johnson*, 491 U.S. 397 (1989); *United States v. Eichman*, 496 U.S. 310, 110 (1990).

97. It is a not inconsiderable measure of the support for First Amendment values that in the wake of the first flag-burning decision Congress rejected proposals to amend the First Amendment itself.

98. Delgado, "Words That Wound."

99. *UWM Post v. Board of Regents of the University of Wisconsin,* 774 F. Supp. 1163 (E.D. Wis. 1991).

100. Ibid.

101. Ibid.

102. Ibid.

103. Ibid.; *New York Times,* September 14, 1992.

104. Anti-Defamation League, *Hate Crimes Statutes: A 1991 Status Report* (New York: ADL, 1991).

105. *R.A.V. v. St. Paul,* 120 U.S. ___L. Ed. 2d 305 (June 1992); Hentoff, *Free Speech for Me,* pp.258–65.

106. Herman Schwartz, *The Burger Years: Rights and Wrongs in the Supreme Court* (New York: Viking, 1987). David Savage, *Turning Right: The Making of the Rehnquist Supreme Court* (New York: Wiley, 1992).

107. *United States v. Eichman,* 496 U.S. 310, (1990); *Texas v. Johnson,* 491 U.S. 397 (1989).

108. *Hustler v. Falwell,* 485 U.S. 46 (1988); Rodney A. Smolla, *Jerry Falwell v. Larry Flynt: The First Amendment on Trial* (New York: St. Martin's Press, 1988).

109. *R.A.V. v. St. Paul,* 505 U.S. ___(June 22, 1992).

110. Ibid., 326.

111. Ibid., 338.

112. Ibid., 315.

Chapter Eight: Hate Speech and the American Community

1. Robert Bork, *The Tempting of America* (New York: Basic Books, 1990).

2. Justice William O. Douglas in *Terminiello v. Chicago,* 337 U.S. 1 (1949).

3. Norton, interview with author. Quoted in Samuel Walker, *In Defense of American Liberties: A History of the ACLU* (New York: Oxford University Press, 1990), p.241.

4. Richard Delgado, "Campus Anti-racism Rules: Constitutional Narratives in Collision," *Northwestern University Law Review* 85 (1991): 343.

5. Professors Harry Kalven and Lee Bollinger have both noted the rhetorical power of the early dissents by Justices Oliver Wendell Holmes and Louis Brandeis in shaping public thinking about the First Amendment. The appeal was to some-

thing deeper than the formal rational argument itself. See Lee Bollinger, *The Tolerant Society* (New York: Oxford University Press, 1986), pp.213–14.

6. Delgado, "Campus Anti-racism Rules," p.343.

7. Derrick Bell, *And We Are Not Saved: The Elusive Quest for Racial Justice* (New York: Basic Books, 1987), chap. 2, "The Benefits to Whites of Civil Rights Litigation," pp.51–74.

8. Alexander Meiklejohn, *Free Speech and Its Relation to Self Government* (New York: Harper and Row, 1948).

9. Kenneth Karst, "Equality as a Central Principle in the First Amendment," *University of Chicago Law Review* 43 (1975): 20; idem, *Belonging to America: Equal Citizenship and the Constitution* (New Haven: Yale University Press, 1989).

10. Vincent Blasi, "The Checking Value in First Amendment Theory," *American Bar Foundation Research Journal*, 1977, p.521.

11. Bollinger, *Tolerant Society*.

12. Martha Minow, *Making All the Difference: Inclusion, Exclusion, and American Law* (Ithaca: Cornell University Press, 1990).

13. Nat Hentoff, *Free Speech for Me – but Not for Thee* (New York: Harper Collins, 1992).

14. "Militants Back 'Queer,' Shoving 'Gay' the Way of 'Negro,'" *New York Times,* April 6, 1991.

15. "Professors' Race Ideas Stir Turmoil at College," *New York Times,* April 20, 1990; "Court Finds a Violation of a Professor's Rights," *New York Times,* June 9, 1992.

16. "City U. Professor Is Assailed for Remarks Attacking Jews," *New York Times,* August 7, 1991.

17. "Court Finds a Violation of a Professor's Rights." "Professor Winner in Suit on Speech," *New York Times,* May 12, 1993.

18. *West Virginia State Board of Education v. Barnette,* 319 U.S. 624 (1943).

19. *Guzofsky v. Township of Teaneck,* civil action no. 91-3979, order, September 13, 1991; brief, American Civil Liberties Union of New Jersey, *Guzofsky v. Township of Teaneck;* interview, Deborah Ellis, legal director, ACLU of New Jersey; "Teaneck Sued over March," *Bergen County Record,* September 13, 1991.

Index

AAUP. *See* American Association of University Professors

Abortion, 2, 13, 25, 110, 139, 148; offensive speech, 106, 108, 111

Abrams v. U.S., 28, 29, 48

ACLU. *See* American Civil Liberties Union

Adams, Franklin P., 85

ADL. *See* Anti-Defamation League

Advocacy: for free speech, 11, 13, 15, 149, 167; importance of, 11, 14, 78; for speech restrictions, 11, 13, 15, 126, 133, 160, 167. *See also* specific topics

Affirmative action, 131, 132, 135, 140; ACLU on, 143, 148; civil rights coalition and, 18, 192 n.13, 199 n.17

African Americans, 18, 63; demonstrations, 107; discrimination, 94–95, 112, 150; middle class, 131; strategy, 63; university enrollment, 133, 135

Alabama, 119; NAACP, 27, 116–17

Allport, Gordon W., 98

American Alliance for Rights and Responsibilities, 142

American Association of University Professors, (AAUP), 136

American Civil Liberties Union (ACLU) criticism of, 33, 40, 43, 53, 54, 120, 125; divisions within, 21, 143, 144–46; founding, 10, 18; free speech advocacy, 10, 13, 14, 15, 18, 20, 21, 53, 58, 106, 144; strategies, 42. *See also* specific topics

American Convention on Human Rights (1969), 90

American Council of Christian Churches, 85

American Jewish Committee, 18, 52, 82, 85, 99, 103

American Jewish Congress, 84, 86, 103; founding, 18; on group libel, 77, 82, 83, 99, 100; on Nazi rights, 122–23

American Legion, 22, 99

Americanization movement, 32, 33–34

Anti-Defamation League (ADL), 18, 103, 106, 125, 155

Anti-Semitism, 5; communists against, 105; group libel, 84, 99, 106; growth of, 84, 112, 154; Henry Ford, 18, 19–20, 21, 33; HUAC and, 58, 60; Jehovah's Witnesses, 65; *Near* case, 29–30; Smith (G. L. K.), 105–6; strategies against, 103,

Anti-Semitism, *continued*
105, 106, 122, 166. *See also*
Holocaust
Anti-war activism, 21, 23, 106, 108,
110–11
Argentina: hate speech law, 103
Arkansas: Jehovah's Witnesses, 75;
NAACP, 116–17
Article 19 (anticensorship group), 4
Article 19 (of Universal Declaration of
Human Rights), 5
Asian/Asian Americans: students, 133
Assembly, freedom of, 74, 92, 107;
ACLU on, 53–54, 166; KKK, 24–25;
labor, 25, 68; Nazis, 42, 50, 51,
121
Association, freedom of, 26, 104;
NAACP cases, 115, 116–17

Bad tendency test, 20, 28
Balancing test, 96, 142, 153
Baldwin, Roger, 40, 41, 42, 53, 54
*Barnette, West Virginia Board of Edu-
cation v.,* 64, 67, 72, 76
Beauharnais v. Illinois, 56, 77, 93–95,
101, 119, 121; aftermath, 124–25,
126, 138; dissenting opinions, 96–
98
Bell, Derrick, 139, 140, 161, 162,
163
Bible reading, 35, 70
Bilbo, Theodore, 112
Bill of Rights, 47, 69, 92, 162, 166;
influence of, 78, 91, 92, 102; inter-
national, 91
Birth control, 18, 25
Birth of a Nation (film), 23, 40, 85
Black, Hugo, 59, 75, 96
Blackmun, Harry A., 157
Bok, Derek, 135
Bollinger, Lee, 104, 126
Bork, Robert, 13, 102, 159
Boston: KKK in, 24, 35
Boudin, Louis, 83
Brandeis, Louis, 28, 29, 48, 75, 79,
204 n.5

Brandenburg case, 114–15, 125
Brazil: hate speech in, 4, 103
Brennen, William, 2, 119
Brown University: racism at, 129
Brown v. Board of Education: reaction
to, 26, 115–16; as speech case, 138
Brown v. Oklahoma (obscenity case),
111
Bruce, Lenny, 109–10, 112
Bryant v. Zimmerman, 25, 27, 58,
116, 118; overturned, 26
Buckley v. Valeo, 149
Burger (Warren E.) Court, 12, 156
Bush, George, 6, 131

California: ACLU in, 144–46; campus
speech codes, 144–45; KKK, 21; red
flag issue, 28–29
Campus speech codes, 6–7, 8, 14,
127–29, 132–36; ACLU on, 16, 45,
136, 141, 143, 144–47; advocacy
for, 16, 133, 134–36; attacks on individual, 145, 153; in classroom,
151, 153; Collegiate Speech Protection Act, 148–49; defeated in court,
3, 5, 7, 128–29, 134, 149, 151–54;
fighting words, 133, 137, 145,
146, 153; hostile environment, 133,
141–42, 145, 150, 152, 153; inclusion issue, 163; protected groups,
127, 133–34; variety of, 133
Canada: Charter of Rights, 5
Cantwell, Newton, 68–69, 70
Cantwell v. Connecticut, 57, 68–69,
72
Captive audience argument, 110
Carnegie Fund for the Advancement
of Teaching, 127
Catholics: on anti-Franco groups, 40;
influence, 18, 32, 36; Jehovah's
Witnesses and, 10, 44, 56, 65, 66,
68, 71, 73; KKK and, 21–22, 33;
prejudice against, 17; schools, 70
Celler, L. Emanuel, 112
Censorship, 124; ACLU and, 21, 23,
84; advocates of, 18, 99, 103; film,

23, 40, 85; literature, 21, 40, 85, 86; NAACP and, 23–24, 85; NJCRAC on, 100; sexual materials, 21, 41, 84, 93. *See also* Mails

Chafee, Zechariah, 28

Chaplinsky v. New Hampshire, 95, 97, 119, 125, 137; fighting words, 64–65, 70–71, 101, 105, 122, 124, 153

Cicero (Illinois), 108

City University of New York (CUNY), 165–66, 167

Civil Liberties Union of Massachusetts (CLUM), 82

Civil Rights Act (1964), 132; sexual harassment and, 141; Title VII, 154

Civil Rights Committee (1947), 85, 86

Civil rights groups, 8, 192 n.10; coalition, 11, 18, 103, 192 n.13, 199 n.17; HUAC and, 58

Civil rights law, 12, 86

Civil rights movement, 11, 35, 104, 108, 117, 132, 140; growth of, 11, 63, 103, 119; provocative speech and, 11, 104, 106, 112, 113, 120, 160, 161, 163; strategy, 15, 16, 24, 78, 103–4, 118, 126

Clark, William, 74

Clear and present danger test, 95, 114

CLUM. *See* Civil Liberties Union of Massachusetts

Codman, John S., 24

Cohen, Paul Robert, 110, 112

Cohen case, 111, 119, 125

Cole, William, 130

Collegiate Speech Protection Act, 148–49

Collin, Frank, 120, 121, 122, 123, 124, 125

Colorado: group libel law, 83

Comedy: offensive jokes, 133, 150; social change and, 109–10

Communists: anti-, 25, 27, 33, 49, 53, 58, 60, 96, 112, 117–18; de-

fense of, 28, 31, 40, 43, 44, 68, 115; *Dennis* case, 114; fight anti-Semitism, 105; registration, 27

Communitarianism, 142

Connecticut: group libel, 82; Jehovah's Witnesses, 68–69

Conscience, freedom of individual, 64, 76, 88, 89

Constitution (U.S.), 92, 104; is not a "suicide pact," 43, 47, 97

Constitutional law, 35; trends in, 93, 162

Content-based restrictions, 3, 26, 27, 118, 126, 128–29, 137, 138, 140; opposition to, 102, 124, 147, 152, 157, 158

Content-neutral law, 67, 68, 81, 153, 154, 158, 162, 163

Covington, Hayden, 64

Cox, Archibald, 102

Cox v. Louisiana, 107

Cross-burning, 3, 149, 154–57; Supreme Court on, 7, 9, 45, 128

Cultural pluralism, 34–35, 70

CUNY. *See* City University of New York

Curley, James, 24–25, 26, 35

Czechoslovakia, 50, 51

Dartmouth College: racism at, 130

Dearborn Independent (newspaper), 19, 20, 21

Death penalty: Supreme Court on, 13

Defamation, 81, 98, 104

De Jonge v. Oregon, 67

Delgado, Richard, 134, 137, 139, 152, 161

Demonstrate, right to, 52, 120

Demonstrations, 119, 123, 125; ban on, 50, 107, 121, 124

Dennis case, 114

Dershowitz, Alan, 202 n.75

DeSilver, Albert, 23

DeSilver, Margaret, 41

Dewey, John, 33, 85

Dickstein, Samuel, 58, 59, 60

Dies, Martin, 60
Disclosure (compulsory), 52, 85–86;
KKK, 25–27, 52, 116–17; NAACP,
27, 116–17
Disorder, threat of, 24, 67, 105,
107–8
District of Columbia: antimask law,
22
Douglas, William O., 11, 76, 97, 106,
112, 119, 160
Draft Convention on the Elimination
of All Forms of Religious Intoler-
ance (1967), 90
Due process, 11, 92
Dworkin, Andrea, 138

Eastland, James, 112
Economic rights, 92, 144
Edwards v. South Carolina, 107
Electoral process: participation in, 50
Emory University: campus code,
127
Emotional distress, 123, 125, 137,
141
Emotional element (of speech), 110–
11, 119
Enforcement: nonuse of laws, 22–23,
83, 146–47; selective, 23, 25, 26,
27, 31, 50, 52, 55
England: Race Relations Act, 103,
147. *See also* United Kingdom
English Only movement, 33, 34
Enhanced-penalty law, 9
Epstein, Benjamin, 106
Epstein, Lee, 13
Equality (equal protection), 35, 161;
affirmative action and, 132, 140,
143, 148; Fourteenth Amendment,
3, 7, 11, 12, 15, 92, 132, 138
Ernst, Morris L., 41, 43, 85–86, 183
n.94
Esquire magazine, 84
Etzioni, Amitai, 142
Exclusion, 133, 141. *See also*
Inclusion

Expression, freedom of, 1, 57, 88, 89,
99, 123, 162; commitment to, 12,
120, 123

False idea, 124
Falwell, Jerry, 156
Fascist groups, 10, 39–40, 47; com-
bating, 49–52, 58, 60, 113, 138;
threat from, 46, 53, 79
Federal Election Campaign Act, 149
Feiffer, Jules, 164
Feiner, Irving, 107
Feiner case, 107
Fighting words doctrine, 6, 64–65,
70, 105, 122, 157; in campus
codes, 133, 137, 145, 146, 153;
definition, 71; in Skokie, 101, 124
Film: censorship, 23, 40, 85
Finland: anti-Fascist measures, 50–51
First Amendment, 1–2, 4, 8, 167; ab-
solutist view, 47, 50, 58, 143;
adoption of, 12; balancing test, 96,
142, 153; clear and present danger
test, 95, 114; establishment clause,
35, 70; re Fourteenth, 3, 7, 143;
interpretation of, 8, 12, 28, 159;
scope of, 6, 31, 44, 47, 72, 95–96,
101, 114, 137
Fish, Hamilton, 54, 58
Flags: burning, 139, 152, 156; display
of, 53, 55; salute, 64, 66, 67, 72–
76, 166
Florida: antimask law, 23
Ford, Henry, 18, 19–20, 21, 33, 41
Foreign Agents Registration Act, 59
Forster, Arnold, 106
Fourteenth Amendment, 10, 31, 142,
143; education and, 128, 145; on
equal protection, 3, 7, 12, 15, 132,
138; hate speech and, 128, 138,
154; preempting state statutes, 35;
on religion, 60, 69
France: hate speech law, 103
Frankfurter, Felix, 74, 76, 77, 95–96,
119, 138

Free speech: ACLU for, 10, 13, 14, 15, 18, 20, 21, 53, 58, 106, 144; advocacy for, 11, 13, 15, 149; advocacy for restrictions, 14, 15, 16, 33, 87, 126, 160; commitment to, 1, 2, 3, 4, 12, 102, 105, 120, 129, 158, 160; First Amendment, 14, 15, 35; in other countries, 1, 4–5, 16, 62, 83, 87–90, 102–3, 159; restriction of, 43–48, 65, 79, 87, 96, 147; rise of, 12, 14–15

Free Speech League, 174 n.5

Free Speech Movement (Berkeley), 134

Friends of New Germany, 38, 39, 40, 55

"F word" issues, 108–12

Gale, Mary Ellen, 143

Genocide Convention, 90

Georgia: antimask law, 22; Jehovah's Witnesses, 67; offensive speech, 111

German-American Bund, 38, 40, 52, 60; Camp Nordland, 38, 56

Germany, 50; hate speech in, 4

Gibson v. Florida Legislative Investigation Committee, 117

Glendon, Mary Ann, 87, 91, 142

Gobitis case, 73–76; overruled, 76

Goldberger, David, 120

Gooding case, 125

Greenawalt, Kent, 111, 139

Gregory, Dick, 108

Gregory v. Chicago, 108

Group libel, 8–9, 45, 58, 77–79, 82–84, 138; *Beauharnais* case, 93–95, 96, 101, 119; decline of, 15, 77, 98–100, 104, 106, 118; enforcement, 146–47; in human rights statements, 87; Illinois, 23, 56, 77, 82, 93–95, 97, 109, 119, 124, 138; protected groups, 8–9; Skokie and, 124; term, 8

Group rights, 192 n.13; re individual rights, 11, 16, 70, 78, 104, 118

Guilt by association, 48, 50

Hacker, Andrew, 6

Hague v. CIO, 25, 68, 74

Hamlin, David, 120, 121

Handicapped persons, 9, 16

Hannegan v. Esquire, 84

Harassment policy (University of California), 144–45

Harlan, John Marshall, 110, 116, 117, 119

Harvard University: on speech codes, 135

Hate crimes: definition, 9; enhanced penalty, 9; laws, 155, 157

Hate groups: protection, 113

Hate speech, 1, 2–3, 4, 8; advocacy for restriction of, 11, 13, 15, 126, 133, 160, 167; as assault, 137–38; confronting, 45, 141, 147; context of, 81; definition, 8; prohibition of, 1, 3, 4, 5, 6, 103, 128; protection of, 3, 5, 11, 12, 18, 57, 97–98, 119

Hate speech laws, 3; arbitrariness of, 107, 108, 118, 164; nonuse of laws, 22–23, 83; in other countries, 1, 4–5, 16, 62, 78, 83, 87–90, 96, 102–3. *See also* Campus speech codes

Hays, Arthur Garfield, 40, 41, 43, 58

Hays, Will, 23

Heckler's veto, 71; definition, 105

Helms, Jesse, 131

Hemingway, Ernest, 40

Hentoff, Nat, 110, 145, 164, 198 n.4

Herndon v. Lowry, 67

Hispanic Americans: students, 133

History of Violence in America, The, 94

Hoke, Travis, 41, 42

Holmes, John Hays, 45

Holmes, Oliver Wendell, 28, 29, 30, 48, 162, 204 n.5; marketplace of ideas, 57

Holocaust: denial of, 4; impact of, 10, 63, 79, 87, 123
Homosexuals, 139, 151, 155; campus groups, 16, 134; Queer Nation, 164; protected status, 9, 36, 137
Hoover, Herbert, 38
Horton, Willie, 6, 131
Hostile audience, 71, 104, 105, 107, 108
Hostile environment: campus codes and, 128, 133, 141–42, 145, 150, 152, 153, 154, 166; in workplace, 141, 154
House Resolution 2328 (on mail censorship), 83, 84, 85, 86
House Un-American Activities Committee (HUAC), 27, 33, 52–53, 58, 60, 73, 86, 112, 183 n.91
HUAC. *See* House Un-American Activities Committee
Hughes, Charles Evans, 29
Human rights movement, 87–92, 97; international, 10, 90–93, 103, 113–14, 118, 138
Human Rights Watch, 4, 8
Hustler decision, 156
Hyde, Henry, 148, 149

Illinois, 40, 108, 120–21; group libel law, 23, 56, 77, 82, 93–95, 97, 109, 119, 124, 138; group libel law repeal, 77, 100; Jehovah's Witnesses, 64, 75. *See also* Skokie
Incitement, 62, 89, 90, 93, 95, 104, 105, 115, 153
Inclusion, 32, 36, 69, 70, 76, 162, 163
India: hate speech law, 103
Indiana: group libel, 83; KKK, 21–22
Individual rights, 48; balancing test, 96, 142, 153; emphasis on, 10, 24, 31, 47, 74, 85, 91, 92, 100, 142; limitations on, 89, 93; as recent, 12; re group rights, 11, 16, 70, 78, 104, 118

Industrial Workers of the World, 48
Institute on Religion and Public Life, 142
International Covenant of Civil and Political Rights (1966), 5, 88, 89, 102
International Convention on the Elimination of All Forms of Racial Discrimination (1966), 5, 88, 89, 90, 113
International Labor Organization, 87
International law: changes in, 87, 90
Iowa: cross-burning, 155

Jackson, Robert, 2, 64, 166; on Constitution, 43, 46–47, 97; on individual conscience, 72, 76
Jeffries, Leonard, 165–66
Jehovah's Witnesses, 56, 63–69, 163; as anti-Catholic, 10, 44, 56, 65, 66, 68, 71, 73; anti-Semitism of, 65; *Cantwell* decision, 57, 68–69; fighting words, 70–71; flag salute, 64, 66, 67, 72–76, 166; door to door solicitation, 68; tactics, 66; vigilantism against, 64, 66, 75
Jewish Community Relations Council (Philadelphia), 100
Jewish Defense League (JDL), 125, 166
Jewish Labor Council, 100
Jews, 18, 32; advocacy for, 11, 15, 18, 63. *See also* Anti-Semitism; Holocaust
Jokes, inconsiderate, 133, 150

Kahane, Meier, 125, 166, 197 n.99
Kahane Chai (Jewish group), 166
Kallen, Horace, 34–35
Kalven, Harry, 107, 111, 117, 118
Kansas: KKK, 22
Kennedy, Anthony M., 156
King, Martin Luther, Jr., 108
King, Rodney, 6, 155
Klapprott, State v., 56–57, 58, 96

Klu Klux Klan (KKK), 21–27; ACLU defends, 18, 22, 23, 24; antimask laws, 22–23, 26, 32, 45, 53; Catholicism and, 21–22, 33; *Fiery Cross* publication, 22; meetings banned, 22, 24; membership, 21; NAACP and, 23, 85; New York anti-KKK law, 19, 36, 58, 86, 116–17; parades, 18, 22–23; registration, 25–26, 27, 52, 116–17; Supreme Court on, 19, 52, 114; violence of, 22, 53
Kobylka, Joseph F., 13

Labor movement; repression of, 28, 33, 48, 53, 60; right to assembly, 25, 68
La Follette Committee, 59, 60
La Guardia, Fiorello, 40
Laughter: inappropriate, 133
Law: hierarchy of, 35
Lawrence, Charles, III, 134, 137–38, 139, 140, 143, 147, 161
Least restrictive alternative, 117
Legion of Decency, 99
Legislative investigations, 58–60, 86, 117
Lester, Anthony, 91
Levin, Michael, 165
Lewis case (offensive language), 111
Libel, 95, 104, 119, 125, 137. *See also* Group libel
Literature, 40, 86, 95–96; distribution of, 20, 30, 67, 82, 83, 85, 123, 151. *See also* Censorship
Litigation (for social change), 117
Loewenstein, Karl, 46–51, 79–80, 81
Los Angeles: violence in, 6
Louisiana: civil rights demonstration case, 107
Lovell v. Griffin, 67
Lusk Committee, 58
Lynching: law against, 86

McCormack-Dickstein Committee, 59

MacKinnon, Catherine, 138, 141, 142
Mails (use of), 23, 24, 44, 83, 84, 85, 86; ACLU on, 23, 84
Maine: Jehovah's Witnesses, 64, 75
Mann, Theodore, 123
Marshall, Thurgood, 12, 64
Massachusetts: censorship, 40; group libel, 82, 146–47; KKK, 24–25
Matsuda, Mari, 134, 139, 140, 161
Meetings (public), 22, 24–25, 40, 44, 55
Meiklejohn, Alexander, 143, 162
Merchant of Venice (Shakespeare), 99
Meritor Savings Bank decision, 141, 154
Meyers, Michael, 141
Michigan: KKK, 22; Nazis, 40. *See also* University of Michigan
"Militant democracy," 47–48, 49
Miller, Lucille, 53
Minnesota: *Near v.*, 29–30, 31, 57. *See also* St. Paul
Minorities, protection of, 11, 69, 72, 76, 152, 161, 164; emphasis on, 63, 64, 67, 87; via individual rights, 104
Mississippi: flag salute, 75
Murphy, Eddie, 109
Murphy, Frank, 76, 95, 119, 137
Murphy, Paul, 31

NAACP. *See* National Association for the Advancement of Colored People
NAACP v. Alabama, 26, 27, 116–17
NAACP v. Button, 117
National Association for the Advancement of Colored People (NAACP), 15; censorship and, 23–24, 85; coalitions, 63; founding, 18; freedom of association cases, 115, 116–17, 118; KKK and, 23, 85; registration/membership disclosure, 27, 116–17
National Association of Independent Colleges and Universities, 149

National Civil Liberties Bureau (NCLB), 23, 44, 84
National Conference of Christians and Jews, 18
National Council for Civil Liberties (NCCL) (United Kingdom), 52
National Council of Jewish Women, 85
National Institute against Prejudice and Violence: on campus racism, 130
National Jewish Community Relations Advisory Council (NJCRAC), 100, 123
National Lawyers Guild, 84, 85, 86, 192 n.10
National security, threats to, 27, 30
National Socialist Party of America, 120
Nazism, 10, 11, 38–43; ACLU, 40, 41–43, 53–54, 61, 104, 144; domestic groups, 38, 60; European, 39, 41, 42, 46, 80, 97; freedom of assembly, 42, 120, 121; free speech for, 39, 40–46, 100, 101; measures against, 49, 52–55; swastika display, 53, 122, 123, 124, 155. *See also* Skokie
NCCL. *See* National Council for Civil Liberties
NCLB. *See* National Civil Liberties Bureau
Near v. Minnesota, 29–30, 31, 57
Nebraska: English-only law, 33; Jehovah's Witnesses, 64, 75
Neier, Aryeh, 120
Neuhaus, Richard John, 142
New Hampshire: Jehovah's Witnesses, 70
New Jersey: Nazis in, 38, 39; parade permits (in Teaneck), 166–67; race hate law, 23, 44, 52, 54–58, 61, 69, 82, 96, 146
New York: anti-Franco groups in, 40; anti-Klan law, 25–26, 27, 86, 116–17; race hate law rejected, 52, 82

New York Times v. Sullivan, 118–20, 125
"Nigger" (term), 81, 164
NJCRAC. *See* National Jewish Community Relations Advisory Council
Norton, Eleanor Holmes, 160
Nye Committee, 59

O'Connor, Sandra Day, 157
Offensive speech, 108–13; First Amendment and, 18, 113, 114, 119, 158, 166. *See also* "F" word issues; Hate speech
Ohio, 21; *Brandenburg* case, 114–15; group libel law, 83; KKK, 21–22
Oklahoma: on flag salute, 75
Olmstead case, 75
Oregon: Jehovah's Witnesses, 75; KKK, 21; public school law, 33
Organizations (unpopular): 118; membership in, 113–14; registration/disclosure, 27, 52, 116–17; rights of, 125–26
Overbreadth, 151

Parades, 22–23, 39, 40, 44, 54, 71, 166
Paramilitary groups, 50, 54
PC (political correctness), 149
Peace, disturbing the. *See* Disorder, threat of
Pennsylvania: flag salute case, 74
Perlman, Nathan, 84, 86
Personal voice, perspective of, 161
Pfeffer, Leo, 123
Police: racial speech, 113
Political correctness (PC), 149
Political dissidents, 114, 116
Pornography, 47, 134, 138, 142, 143
Post office. *See* Mails
powell, john a., 143
Prayer in schools, 21, 35, 70, 102
Prejudice: nature of, 98–99; economic aspects, 131–32; education and, 130

Press, freedom of the, 42, 92; *Near* case, 29–30; restrictions on, 50, 51, 57
Privacy, right to, 14, 92, 102, 116, 130
Property rights, 92
Protest: right to, 97
Protestantism, 70
Protocols of the Elders of Zion, 1, 19
Pryor, Richard, 109
Psychic trauma, 123, 125, 141
Public opinion, 13, 80
Public Order Act (England), 103
Purdue University: racism at, 129

Quarantining strategy, 105, 122
Queer Nation, 164

Race hate laws, 58, 82. *See also* New Jersey
Race Relations Act (England), 103, 147
Racial equality, 15. *See also* Equality
Racial hate speech, 2–3, 6, 21, 87, 138
Racism, 138, 139; on campus, 129–30; comedy against, 109–10; occurrence in U.S., 17, 32–33, 94; resurgence of, 5–6, 128, 129–30, 131, 132, 135, 154, 163
Randolph, A. Philip, 63
Rankin, John, 112, 183 n.91
R. A. V. v. St. Paul, 156, 158
"Red flag" law, 28–29
Reed, Stanley, 96
Registration/membership disclosure requirement, 52; KKK, 25–26, 27, 52, 116–17; NAACP, 27, 116–17
Rehnquist, William H., 20
Rehnquist (William H.) Court, 156, 157
Religion, free exercise of, 92; ACLU and, 41; First Amendment, 10, 35, 60; Fourteenth Amendment, 60, 69; human rights movement, 87,

88, 91–92; separation of church and state, 47, 92, 103, 123. *See also* Jehovah's Witnesses
Responsive Community, The (journal), 142
Restrictive covenants, 20, 174 n.11
Revolution, advocacy of, 114
Rhode Island: censorship, 40; group libel law, 83
Rice, Elmer, 85
Riesman, David, 46, 79–81, 99, 106, 138, 140
Rights revolution, 28, 137, 142
Rockwell, George Lincoln, 104
Roosevelt, Theodore, 32–33; Court under, 15, 70
Rosenberg, Gerald, 13
Rosenfeld case (offensive language), 111
RUDs (reservations, understandings, or declarations), 89
Rushdie, Salman, 92
Rutherford, Joseph, 65, 66, 68, 74

Sahl, Mort, 109
St. Paul (Minnesota): Bias-Motivated Crime Ordinance, 155, 156–57; cross-burning, 3, 9, 128, 149, 154–58
Sanger, Margaret, 25
Scalia, Antonin, 3, 9, 128, 156–57
Schenck decision, 114
Schmidt, Benno, 135
Schneider v. Irvington, 67
Segregation, 26, 35, 86, 103, 107, 115–16, 118, 138
Sex discrimination, 138, 141, 142
Sexual harassment, 128, 141, 143, 150
Sexually explicit material, 109; censorship of, 21, 41, 84, 93
Shelton v. Tucker, 117
Shubow, Joseph S., 82
Skokie, (Illinois), 100, 106, 108, 120–25; ACLU in, 41, 45, 54, 99,

Skokie, *continued*
104, 120–21; court decision, 101, 124, 126; fighting words issue, 101, 124; threat of disorder, 123, 125, 166
Smith, Al, 18
Smith, Gerald L. K., 84, 105–6, 115
Smith College, 129
Smolla, Rodney, 3, 8, 136
Social change, 106–7, 117, 120, 160; comedy and, 109; models of, 12–13; Supreme Court and, 13
Socialist party: suppression of, 48
South Carolina: demonstration in, 107
Spanish Civil War, 40, 45
Special Committee on Un-American Activities, 59, 60
Speech: as written, oral or visual, 8
Speech, freedom of: growth of, 14–15; limitations on, 43–44, 89, 143
Spingarn, Arthur, 85
Stanford University, racism at, 129; campus code, 127, 133
State University of New York, 130
State v. Klapprott, 56–57, 58, 96
Steel, Lewis, 118
Stevens, John Paul, 157
Stone, Harlan Fiske, 75
Stone, I. F., 41
Stromberg v. California, 28–29, 31
Strossen, Nadine, 147
Subversive activities, 27, 49–50, 57. *See also* House Un-American Activities Committee
Subversive Organizations, List of, 27
Sullivan, L. B., 119
Sunstein, Cass, 143
Supreme Court: composition of, 13; national policy from, 102, 115; social change and, 13
Symbols, 3; ACLU on, 53; ban on, 3, 51, 55, 155; KKK, 150; red flag,

28–39; swastika, 53, 122, 123, 124, 155. *See also* Cross-burning
Syndicalism laws, 28–29, 33, 39, 114

Tanenhaus, Joseph, 98
Teaneck (New Jersey), 166–67
Tennessee: KKK, 22
Terminiello, Arthur, 105
Terminiello v. Chicago, 46–47, 97, 105, 106, 107, 119, 179 n.22
Texas: group libel, 83; Jehovah's Witnesses, 75; KKK, 22
Thomas, Clarence, 102
Thomas, Gwen, 141
Tolerance, 46; growth of, 31, 34, 68, 70, 76, 163
Truman, Harry, 85, 86
Turkey: hate speech, 4

Ulysses case, 85
Uniforms, 50, 51, 52, 53, 121, 124
United Kingdom, 4; free speech advocacy, 173 n.58; Public Order Act, 50, 51–52, 53, 54; Race Relations Act, 103, 147
United Nations: on human rights, 87, 88, 89; U.S. joins, 63
United States: free speech, 1, 2, 3, 4, 12, 102, 105, 120, 129, 158, 160
Universal Declaration of Human Rights (1948): 5, 62, 88
Universities: curriculum, 34, 149; faculty, 136, 165; racism on, 129–30. *See also* Campus speech codes
University of California: harassment policy, 144–46; Free Speech Movement, 134
University of Connecticut: speech code, 133
University of Massachusetts: racism at, 129
University of Michigan, 129: ACLU and, 136, 144, 147, 151; campus code, 127, 133, 137, 141, 150–51;

code defeated, 3, 7, 128, 146, 147, 149–52; racism at, 129
University of Wisconsin: ACLU and, 144, 147; campus code, 3, 7, 127, 133, 136, 137, 142; code defeated, 3, 7, 147, 152–54; racism at, 129

Vagueness issue, 25, 26, 27, 43, 44, 57, 139; campus codes, 146, 147, 151, 154
Value (of speech), 136, 143
Van Doren, Mark, 85
Victims, recognition of, 139–40
Vietnam veterans, 127, 137, 150
Vietnam War: dissent, 106, 108, 110–11
Vigilantism, 20, 36, 64, 66, 75
Viktora, Robert, 156
Virginia: censorship, 40; NAACP, 117, 193 n.17

Walker, Frank, 84
Wallace, George, 112

Warren (Earl) Court, 118; on freedom on association, 26; on free speech, 11, 107, 156, 161; on group/individual rights, 16, 47; reaction to, 31, 157
Washington (state): flag salute, 75
West Virginia, 76; group libel, 82. *See also Barnette, West Virginia Board of Education v.*
White, Byron R., 157
White Circle League of America, 95
Whitney v. California, 28, 29
Williams, Patricia, 161
Winchell, Walter, 112
Wisconsin: enhanced-penalty law, 9; KKK, 22; Nazis, 40. *See also* University of Wisconsin
Wolin, Alfred M., 166
Women: feminist movement, 110, 133–34; hate speech, 134; rights, 9, 12; on strategy, 142
Workplace: as hostile, 141, 154
Wulf, Mel, 118

Yale University: speech codes, 135